CARD CONTROL

Practical Methods and Forty Original
Card Experiments

Arthur H. Buckley

DOVER PUBLICATIONS, INC.
New York

Dedicated to my devoted wife, Helena,
my partner on and off the stage since
nineteen hundred and ten.

Bibliographical Note

This Dover edition, first published in 1993, is an unabridged republication of the work first published privately by the author in 1946 under the title *Card Control: A Post Graduate Course on Practical Methods; Supplemented by Forty Original Card Experiments*. In this edition, the photograph of the author, originally appearing on page 3, has been placed before the title page as a frontispiece.

Library of Congress Cataloging-in-Publication Data

Buckley, Arthur Herbert, 1890–
    Card control : practical methods and forty original card experiments / Arthur H. Buckley.
        p.   cm.
    Originally published: Springfield, Ill. : Williamson Printing and Pub. Co., c 1946.
    ISBN 0-486-27757-7
    1. Card tricks.   I. Title.
GV1549.B8   1993
793.8—dc20   93-31493
                                                                           CIP

Manufactured in the United States of America
Dover Publications, Inc., 31 East 2nd Street, Mineola, N.Y. 11501

PREFACE

Forty years experience conjuring with cards, diligent in the search for better and more suitable principles, ever pursuing that mythical thing, perfection — the experience gained throughout this time, I feel, qualifies me to write this text on card principles. Perhaps my compeers will forgive me if I have unwittingly erred in the assumption of being the originator of many of the methods and sleights herein described, though some have to my knowledge already appeared in print with the source of origin not always correctly defined.

This is a compendium of advanced principles, master sleights and card effects, and it is therefore assumed that my reader is already in possession of a marked degree of skill and aptitude for such things with cards; furthermore, that he is a student of other practical works on card magic by such authors as Hugard, Erdnase, Merlin, Tarbell, Downs *and many others. The sleights of this compendium are of major importance and great practical value. They are unsurpassed by hitherto known and published methods; many are difficult to accomplish and require patience and constant practice before they can be mastered or performed in a creditable manner.*

Each sleight involves a certain technique peculiarly its own, these details are carefully related, both in the text and the accompanying illustrations. The instructions, when intimately followed, will permit the sleight to be mastered and then executed indetectably and repetitiously, even though performed before the concentrated attention of one versed in this art and not entirely unfamiliar with the modus operandi or technique being employed.

It hardly seems necessary to say that a sleight is not intended to be employed for the mystification its execution affords, but rather as a subtle artifice secretly employed to bring about a magical climax.

It has been said that "practice makes perfect." This is a misnomer unless the methods practiced are basically correct and are adaptable to the end sought. Always make certain that the methods you are about to encompass are the best ones available before seriously commencing to practice, or you may find often to your sorrow that a great deal of time has been lost and many hours are necessary for the undoing.

Among my friends whose assistance and suggestions in the preparation of this book I have found most valuable are John Brown Cook, Harold Ripley, Waldo Logan, William Nicola, Richard Cardini, Bert Allerton, Russell Swan, Carmen Domico, Harlan Tarbell, Paul le Paul, George Coons, Dai Vernon, Samuel Berland, Joe Berg, Paul Stadelman, Werner C. Dornfield (Dorny), Alex Purrell and John Mulholland.

To these I extend my thanks and gratitude.

Arthur Buckley

ARTHUR BUCKLEY

If you haven's met Arthur Buckley personally, you have missed knowing one of the finest performers in the field of Magic.

Born in Brisbane, Queensland, Australia, in the year 1890, Arthur came to America in 1918. It was not until my return from Europe a year later that I met Arthur and his wife, Helena.

Most magicians start as amateurs, develop into semi-professionals and finally reach the professional stage. Not so Arthur Buckley; he started off a professional in 1908, billed as "Dante, King of Kards", this after seeing Alan Shaw, the American Coin Manipulator and Carlton, with his card magic.

After a few months of almost continuous practice, Buckley believed his act was ready for the theater. His brother, friendly with the manager of the Theatre Royal in Brisbane, Australia, arranged for his tryout. The manager, Ted Holland, after seeing the show, said, "Come back in about *seven years* and I will give you a job."

Two days later an American actor named Harry Salmon was getting a road show together and went to see Ted Holland about some acts, and whether to spite Salmon or help Buckley, we will never know, Holland gave Salmon Arthur's name. Salmon called on Buckley, who demonstrated his coin and card act in such a creditable manner that although he entirely lacked stagecraft, he was signed as a magician to a six months' contract.

The first show the house was packed, but when Buckley appeared on stage he was struck speechless. The stage manager lowered the curtain. Salmon, having Buckley under contract, had to make the best of it. Early next morning Salmon had Buckley at the theater and proceeded to teach him how to walk on the stage and how to speak his lines.

The show toured to the far north of Queensland, touching Thursday Island, Cooktown and Cairns. Under Salmon's guidance Buckley improved rapidly. In the early stages of Buckley's stage career he gained first hand knowledge from many expert gamblers.

Many of the most highly valued and closely guarded secrets of method of sleights, cuts, builds and shuffles were imparted to Buckley by these people during the leisure hours between track meetings and the shows. The very cream of all this knowledge with many important improved ideas are incorporated in the chapter of "Conjuring at the Card Table" in his book, "Card Control." His card work was highly popular with them. They would always insure him of a full house for his performances. After his magic show, which lasted two hours, they would sub-lease the theater or hall from Buckley for their card games. For this favor they would start a regular ballyhoo at the race track, between themselves, of the wonderful magician in town, etc., etc., and in the show applauded out of justification to that warranted. These experiences all took place within a year and a half from starting.

In eighteen months instead of seven years, Buckley returned to Brisbane to headline the vaudeville bill at the Theatre Royal. From that time on he played the metropolitan theaters. Then, encouraged by the newspapers in Australia, he tried his luck in America, and was placed under contract for a period of three years as a feature attraction with the Benson office and the Orpheum Circuit Club Department in Chicago. Later he played the Orpheum Circuit, and then returned to Australia under the management of the Tivoli Theatres, Ltd., and later the Williamson and the Sir Benjamin Fuller Circuits, where he and Helena, his wife, doing "mental magic", broke all records for capacity houses during their engagements; this according to newspaper reports of that period.

In 1934 he returned to America, this time as an electronic and communication engineer, which occupation he is now following in a consultant and creative capacity, associated with the George Gorton Machine Corporation of Racine, Wisconsin, the Whitney Blake Company of New Haven, Connecticut, and the Reliable Electric Company of Chicago, Illinois. He has developed numerous commercially successful patents, some of which are intricate business machines, and at the present time he is developing others. Magic with cards is his hobby.

Arthur Buckley is the logical man to write a book on "Card Control", for not only does he present his methods and original sleights, but many practical sleights which he gathered from the top magicians of the world. His inventive knowledge has enabled him to develop and present practical card sleights and magical effects to an unusual degree of perfection, many of which have stood the test of stage, club and close-up.

The book is truly a post graduate course on card handling, and is amply illustrated from photographs of the author's hands in action. This adds greatly to the clearness of the instructions.

Harlan Tarbell

CHAPTER ONE

Sleights

Table of Contents

Page

Table of Contents

CHAPTER TWO

Conjuring at the Card Table

Table of Contents   Page

CHAPTER THREE

Manipulations

                                                       Page

CHAPTER FOUR

Experiments with Cards

Table of Contents   Page

THE STRIP

This original sleight has many uses. It is what Erdnase would call culling. Suppose it is desired to take a well-shuffled pack and transfer four cards of the same denomination to the top while apparently just looking through the pack. The strip I find an excellent maneuver for just such a thing as this.

THE SLEIGHT:

The pack is held face up in the left hand with the left thumb resting on the face, first finger at one end of the pack and the other fingers up the side, similar to dealing position, only the cards are face up.

The thumb of the right hand is also on the face of the card, and in this position the left thumb slides the cards over to the right thumb and fingers, but not entirely off the pack, just as though you were looking to see if a certain card or cards are in the pack.

For our example let us strip the four Kings, and as I run the cards over I find the first King tenth card. Now I push the nine cards back on the King and insert the little finger of the left hand below the King while I square them. Then I pull the packet of ten towards the body about three-quarters of an inch in over the end of the other cards, and continue the push-off action with the left thumb until I reach another King, which I find at the twelfth place. I pick up the eleven cards and move them up as one, then slide over the King under the packet of eleven and add the King to and under this packet. The eleventh (the indifferent card) is level with the pack, and running the cards as before I find the third King at twenty-fifth position. I raise the packet of twenty-four cards to bring the third King level with the preceding Kings. I add the King to the packet of twenty-four cards and continue running the cards as before. At forty-two I find the fourth King. Raising the packet of forty-one cards to make this King level with the three preceding Kings, I square the remaining ten cards with the extended indifferent cards and then holding that packet quite firmly by pressing them into the fork of the left thumb with the left hand first finger, I withdraw the inwardly protruding packet of thirteen cards and place them on the face of the pack, but in doing so the fourth finger of the left hand is inserted to keep a break below the Kings. It remains now to undercut twice to transfer the four Kings to the top.

A BLIND RIFFLE SHUFFLE

This original sleight has stood the test of time. It has many adherents among the fraternity that it has gathered during the past thirty years. We know from experience it can be performed quite indetectably if you will only follow the details as herein described, and not be content with an inferior imitation of it.

THE SLEIGHT:

Hold the pack in the left hand, first finger bent on the back of the pack, second and third fingers gripping the pack at one end, the thumb resting on the opposite end and the fourth finger on the side edge of the pack. Riffle approximately half of the pack, letting the cards spring into the position as shown in Fig. 1.

The first finger of the right hand is on the back of the riffled cards, the second and third fingers supporting them underneath. The second and third fingers of the left hand raise the cards as in Fig. 2, and the right thumb retains them.

Each hand now holds half the pack, the bottom half in the right hand, and both packets held in the same manner. The hands with the cards are now brought into the position for riffle shuffling. The cards are riffled alternately, some cards from the right hand packet first. Their interlaced corners overlap only a quarter of an inch. This is important.

The fingers of each hand now assume the position as shown in Fig. 3. The cards in each hand are supported between the second, third and fourth fingers bent under the cards. The first finger, previously bent on the backs of the cards, is straightened, and the fourth finger is still bent along the side of the cards. The grip described is such that the cards are supported at one end free from the table, with both thumbs offering enough pressure to hold the cards from slipping.

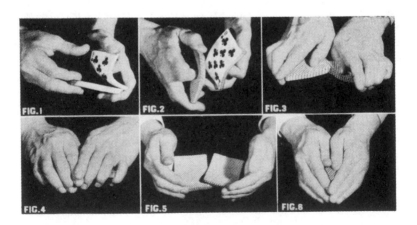

Both packets of cards are moved in an arc, inwardly pivoted under the thumbs, the left hand packet raised slightly higher than the right hand packet. As the arc is completed, the hands and cards assume the position of Fig. 4, the fingers curled under the packets are straightened, and the interwoven corners come apart as the cor-

13

ner of the right hand packet is pressed under the left hand packet. Fig. 5 depicts the cards in position as the left hand packet passes under the right hand packet. This part of the maneuver is executed under the cover afforded by both hands. The move is completed by three evenly-timed, short inward swings of the base of both palms as though the cards were being eased together as shown in Fig. 6. Fig. 5 depicts the position of the two packets. The hands are raised from the cards, showing the position of the two packets, their corners separated. This could not be discerned were the hands not opened to expose the position to the camera.

"THE FORCE THAT COULDN'T BE"

In Ted Annemann's impromptu card tricks on page 76 is a "force" by Clayton Rawson that intrigued me so much that I put a few touches to it which I now pass on to you.

The pack is fairly shuffled by the usual riffle dovetail method. The third card from the bottom of the pack is noted as the shuffle is being executed. If the thumb of the left hand is at the index corner of the packet held in that hand, it is a simple matter to see the third bottom card as it is released; then the dovetailing of the two packets commences.

As the right hand packet is pushed into the packet in the left hand, the fourth finger of the left hand falls naturally into position to keep a break above the third bottom card, the break is transferred to the thumb of the right hand, and as the pack is divided for another dovetail shuffle, the three cards below the break are reversed. See the "Reverse" described herein under that title.

The pack held face down on your left hand is offered to a person to cut. You secretly turn your left hand and the packet of cards remaining therein over to bring the card you noted uppermost. As you request someone to take the top card, you extend your hand with the card fairly quickly to cover the act of turning the cards over.

There still remains two cards on this packet to be righted. The following procedure is a highly satisfactory one.

With the left thumb I release the two reversed cards and immediately drop the packet in the right hand on the packet in the left hand, and then cut off the cards at the break made by the left thumb at the position where the two packets meet face to face; the left hand turning its packet face down as the packets are brought into position for a dovetail shuffle.

DOMICO DOUBLE LIFT

This is a sleight that has more than one way in which it can be executed indetectably. For a most enlightening description of several excellent ways of performing this sleight, I refer the reader to "Expert Card Technique" by Jean Hugard.

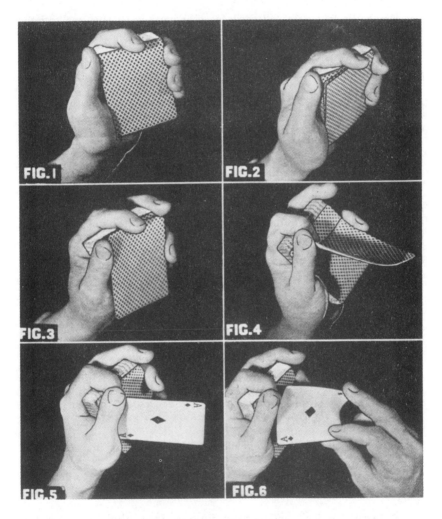

This method, however, is so different and such a perfect piece of card handling that I am proud to be able to offer it here with the permission granted by the originator, Carmen Domico of Chicago, in whose hands it is a veritable masterpiece. I shall describe the sleight as Carmen Domico taught me to perform it.

Perhaps it may seem unusually difficult, but about two hours' practice will completely change that opinion, and you will discern a perfect piece of mystification evolving at your fingertips.

THE SLEIGHT:

Hold the pack in the left hand as in Fig. 1, and release the two top cards from under the thumb.

Raise the two released cards as one card with the left thumb, squeezing them gently on the sides between the thumb and second finger, the first finger supporting the end. (Fig. 2.)

The third finger is applied to the edge of the card about the middle, and the second finger lets it go. (Fig. 3.)

The first finger now pulls the end down, cocking the opposite end up. A pivot for this action is formed between the thumb and third finger on the sides of the two cards held as a single card, all edges perfectly square with each other. (Fig. 4.)

As soon as the card is pivoted into a nearly upright position (Fig. 4), the third finger lets the two cards go. The first finger presses the two cards against the left thumb, and the cards snap into position as shown in Fig. 5. The right hand then lightly grips the two cards by their sides at the end between the second finger and thumb of the right hand (see Fig. 6), and as they are released by the first finger and thumb of the left hand, the second finger and thumb of the right hand slightly bend the cards concave, and letting go the second finger, the two cards spring around with a snap. The cards are then gripped between the thumb and first finger of the right hand. This maneuver is carried out with a well-regulated, even pace, and the cards remain squared as one throughout.

It seems incredible that two cards can thus be handled without revealing the presence of a second one; yet it is possible, even with several, and can be used successfully at a distance of a few feet.

THE EXCHANGE

For the purpose of explaining this original sleight and its associated moves, let us proceed as follows. On the table before you, within easy reach, is a packet of five red cards, face down, and palmed in your right hand, backs to palm, is a packet of five black cards.

The objective is to unsuspectingly exchange the palmed black cards for the packet of red ones on the table.

Place the pad of the second fingertip of the right hand on the table alongside the index corner of the packet of red cards on the table.

Release the first and second fingers from their hold on the palmed cards, henceforth supporting them in a bowed-out manner at the two index corners only, one corner at the fourth finger, the other corner pressed into the flesh of the thumb palm.

Place the left hand second fingertip at the side of the packet of red cards on the table to act as a stop for the move to follow.

The corner of the packet of cards in your right hand will scoop half-way under the packet of red cards on the table without altering the hold the right hand has on the packet of black cards. The packet of red cards is picked up by the right thumb at one end of the packet of red cards and the second and third fingers of the right hand at the other end of the packet of red cards.

The two packets thus held for a moment lie diagonally across each other, the palmed black one underneath. The fingers and thumb hold the packet of red ones. Only the back of the top card of the red packet is showing.

Both packets are placed into the left hand, and under the instantly afforded cover of the right hand they are squared, but in doing so the fourth fingertip of the left hand engages in and maintains a break between the two packets.

The right hand is still in position over the packets. The left thumb is at the non-index corner. The side of the right hand fourth finger is pressing at the side near the index corner of the top packet and causes the packet of five red cards to arc to the left, fulcrumed at the left thumb. They swing indetectably up into the right palm. As the cards are palmed, the first finger and thumb of the right hand move along the end edges of the packet in the left hand. The left hand carries this packet forward, and the left thumb pushes off the cards from the top, one by one, and they are caused to fall, faces down, in a row on the table.

The right hand at the same time is lowered on the pack of cards and places the palmed packet of red cards on the pack as it carries out the act of moving the pack away or placing it into its case.

The whole procedure is in effect that you have simply picked up a packet of five cards from the table with your right hand, placed them on your left hand, and by a simple, one-hand deal dropped them off the packet, one at a time, so they lie spread in a row before a spectator.

To a close observer you also removed the pack of cards and afterwards placed it in its case. The proper execution of the top palm is very important in the correct performance of this sleight.

GREEK SHIFT

This is a beautiful and indetectable sleight taught to me by a restaurant owner in Los Angeles in 1923, and unknown to magicians. It is a sleight used by Greek gamblers to insure a desired color being made trump. At least that is how I was then informed. The technique of the move is not easily grasped, but when mastered it is invaluable. I will describe it as it was taught to me, and then give you my own variation.

17

THE SLIGHT:

The selected card which the performer wants to later force is secretly manipulated to the bottom of the pack, and in the handling is not exposed to view.

The pack is then placed in the left hand exactly as shown in Fig. 1. Particularly note that the index corner of the pack rests at the fork of the third and fourth fingers of the left hand. The left thumb is then placed on the back of the pack.

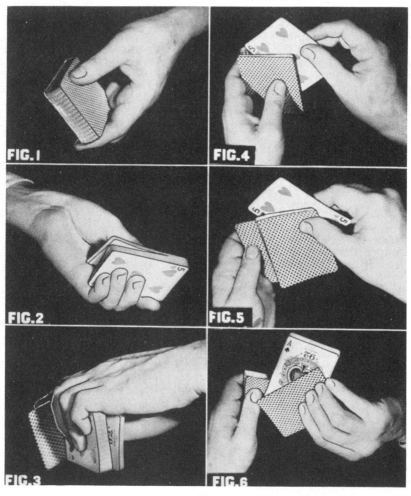

With the right hand take away about a dozen of the bottom cards of the pack, and drop them onto the packet in the left hand, keeping the two packets separate with a very wide break. See Fig. 2.

The left hand, holding the cards in this manner, is turned over, bringing the side of the pack onto the table. The break is now partly closed by pressure of the left thumb, and completely hidden. Fig. 3 shows the break exposed especially for the camera.

The right hand openly draws off the face card and uses it to square up the end of the pack. This action is shown in Fig. 3.

This card is then put into the pack, either by you or a spectator, but it must enter into the pack about the middle for the sleight to succeed. See Fig. 4 showing the card taken from the bottom inserted face up about the middle of the pack. The desired card is about twelve cards from the top of the pack, directly above the palm flesh break.

The left thumb releases its pressure on the back of the pack, and the left hand given an almost imperceptible little toss, thus causing the twelve or so cards above the flesh break to assume the position shown in Fig. 5. At the same time, blending with the move of the left hand, the right hand seizes the twelve top cards and the inserted face-up card, and withdraws them. The illusion is that the cards were cut at the inserted card. The packet, with the inserted card held so innocently between the thumb and second finger of the right hand, is turned over as in Fig. 6, with the selected card at the bottom of the packet. What more perfect piece of chicanery could you desire for revealing a spectator's card?

GREEK SHIFT — BUCKLEY'S METHOD

The preliminary moves consist of having a card peeked at (see my method) and performing same up to the move where the fourth fingertip of the left hand is holding the break.

The right hand now takes the pack and maintains the break while the pack is shifted to the left hand into the position of the Greek shift flesh grip. From here on the moves may be terminated as just described, or as I sometimes do. I insert the bottom card that was used for the squaring maneuver all the way into the pack, then cut at the break and riffle shuffle, keeping the card on the bottom, and end the illusion as fancy dictates. This is really an excellent piece of manipulation, and until now I have kept it exclusively.

HINDU SHIFT

This is a most useful sleight. It is a method I originated for secretly transferring a card from the top of the pack to the bottom of the pack while carrying out the accepted procedures of the "Hindu Shuffle". The indetectable simplicity of this sleight is an excellent recommendation for its practical useage in a great many card effects.

THE SLEIGHT:

With the selected card on the top of the pack, the pack of cards is held face down in your left hand, left thumb on the side and near the non-index corner, second and third fingers close together at the opposite side of the pack and near the index corner, first finger of the left hand at the end near the corner.

The right hand first and second fingers and thumb grip about half the cards of the pack and carry them from the bottom as in cutting. It then places them on the selected card, but just as the packets are placed together, the fourth finger of the left hand secretly drops on the back of the selected card.

The under packet is again drawn away with the right hand in the manner just described, but by applying a light downward pressure with the ball of the left fourth finger, the selected card is retained as the packet is drawn away in the right hand and drawn off in small packets onto the cards in the left hand. The second finger and thumb of the left hand accomplish this drawing off of the packets from the right hand packet to the left hand packet.

This sleight is particularly handy if you have several cards withdrawn and returned separately to the top of the pack, executing the above moves after each card is placed on top of the pack. In this manner all the selected cards are brought together at the bottom to await your pleasure.

VERNON MULTIPLE SHIFT

Here is one of the outstanding sleights of all time, truly beautiful and perfectly deceptive. Its simplicity and perfection are worthy of that master, Dai Vernon.

THE SLEIGHT:

The pack is held in the left hand, and four aces are held in the right hand, as shown in Fig. 1.

The aces are inserted into the pack, one at a time, as follows: Several cards are released from the corner of the pack by the left thumb, and the first ace is inserted into the break between the released cards and the pack. Several more cards are similarly released, and the second ace is inserted. This procedure is repeated until the four aces are occupying the position shown in Fig. 2. About one inch of each ace is protruding from the other cards.

The right hand grips the pack on the sides near the bottom corners between the second finger and thumb. The first finger is about one-third up from the bottom edge and in the middle. The second finger is at the index corner, and the third finger is under the bottom edge giving the pack substantial support for the move to follow.

The left hand seizes the aces, first finger on top, thumb at index corner, second finger at the opposite corner, third finger along the side of the aces and fourth finger along its adjacent side of the pack. This position is depicted in Fig. 3.

Push the aces down into the pack. If the pressure is correct on the sides of the pack held by the right hand and the pressure is also correctly applied by the thumb and second finger of the left hand while pushing the aces into the pack, then the pack when the aces are pushed down will assume the position shown in Fig. 4.

The left thumb and second finger now apply holding pressure to the aces and the cards in front of them. (See Fig. 5.) The right hand, without altering its position at all, easily withdraws the cards interwoven with the lower extremities of the aces, and when clear of cards in the left hand packet, places them on the front of the pack. (See Fig. 6.) The aces are together on the back of the pack.

The moves as described may be carried out with the pack face down to bring the aces to the bottom of the pack.

The moves, when made properly, give the illusion that the aces are deliberately pushed into the pack and the pack cut. No more perfect piece of deception could be devised.

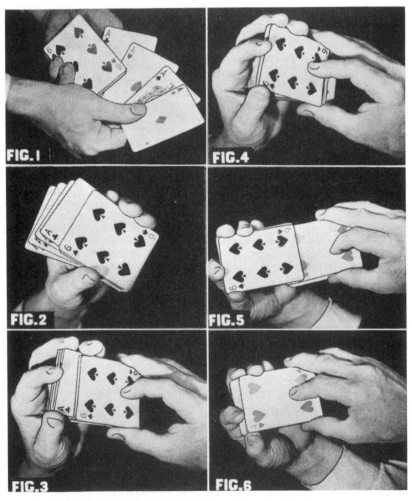

MULTIPLE SHIFT — BUCKLEY'S METHOD

This sleight is not so smoothly operating as the Dai Vernon multiple shift. Nevertheless, it is far too important to be overlooked, and it has one major difference in purpose; it brings the cards to the top of the pack when the cards are held face down. Sometimes that is desirable. It can be performed quite indetectably by use of the mechanics herein described.

THE SLEIGHT:

The four aces having been inserted part way into the pack as described in the Vernon multiple shift, but this time faces down. The left hand with the cards assumes the position in Fig. 1, thumb diagonally across the side, first finger bent on face card, second finger at index corner of pack, third and fourth fingers helping support the pack which is held at a forty-five degree angle with the floor, facing the left palm. The position is important. The picture was taken at the angle most revealing.

The right hand assumes the position as shown in Fig. 1, right thumb at the index corner of the pack, first, second, third and fourth fingers of the right hand resting on the protruding edges of the four aces.

The aces are pressed diagonally into the pack by pressing with the first finger of the right hand in counter clockwise arc moving around the corner of the pack and then along the edge to the position shown in Fig. 2. Note carefully this position—pressure by the right hand holds the pack between the thumb and second finger. The fourth finger of the left hand is on the side corner of the four aces and presses them even, along their sides with the pack proper. The aces protrude about an inch from the end of the pack, but are completely concealed by the position of the right hand. The effect is that the aces were pushed into the pack; actually they were pushed in and partly through, causing their ends to protrude from the inside end of the pack. (See Fig. 3.)

The right hand with its thumb remaining on the side position, moves in an arc until the third and fourth fingers lie along the protruding edge of the aces. (See Fig. 4.) Simultaneously with the making of this move with the right hand, the first finger of the left hand engages a packet of about fifteen cards from the rest of the pack. They are immediately forced down to the protruding level with the aces as shown in Fig. 5, and are firmly held now by the thumb and third and fourth fingers of the left hand.

The right thumb moves up to grip the remainder of the cards, and the right hand withdraws the aces and the protruding packet. (See Fig. 6.) It pulls them clear of the left hand packet and drops them on the top of the packet in the left hand. The series of moves is carried out without any change of pace, and blend into a perfect sleight that gives the appearance that the aces were simply pushed home into the pack and the pack cut.

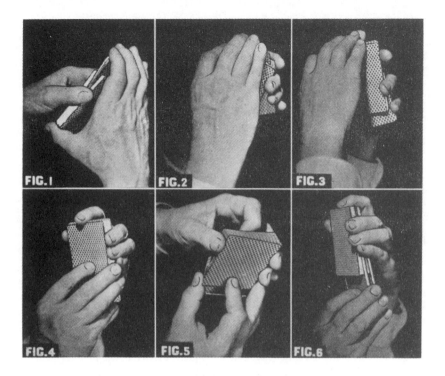

FIG.1   FIG.2   FIG.3
FIG.4   FIG.5   FIG.6

BUCKLEY'S SLAP SHIFT

This is a sleight I used in an effect I originated and performed on the stage for many years. I called the effect "The Triple Climax", and a description of it can be found in "Thirty Card Effects" by Arthur Buckley, published by Fitzke. This unusual sleight instantly and secretly shifts a selected card from the bottom to the top of those cards the spectator deals face down on your outstretched left hand. I consider it among the real top notchers of card sleights, and definitely indetectable, as repeated performances have proved.

A selected card is secretly positioned on the top of the shuffled pack. The pack is given into the hands of a male spectator standing at your left side with the request that he count the cards face down on your outstretched left hand, one at a time. After three cards are dealt he is told by you to stop dealing the cards at any time he wishes to do so, and not to allow himself to be influenced in this matter.

THE SLEIGHT:

As the first card from the top is dealt into your left hand (that's the selected card), you partly close and again open the fingers of your left hand on the card, and on each card dealt by the spectator.

As each card is dealt, the right hand slaps down on the card firmly, but not viciously, covering the cards. Each time this covering move is made, the cards slide over the edge of the first card, and the inside edge of the selected card is uncovered. (See Fig. 1.) It is then very lightly gripped by the base of the right thumb and first joint of the first finger. (See Fig. 2.)

You call, "One! Two! Three!", etc., very deliberately as the cards are dealt, pausing no longer than is necessary with the hands together, the dealt cards between them, sufficient to give the dealer time to say, "Stop," if he is going to do so. If "Stop" is called, you lift the bottom card six inches above the packet dealt. Fig. 3 is a camera view from the rear showing hand with card slightly tilted, and it is thus placed on the top of the other cards already dealt. The photos are intended to show how card is brought up from the bottom of the packet in the left hand and unsuspectingly placed on top of them. You have the spectator name his card, and then let him lift it off the packet.

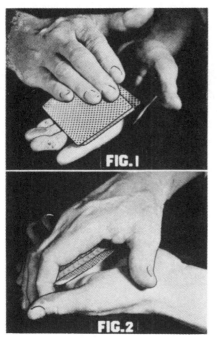

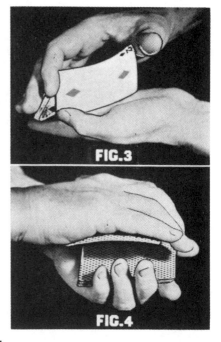

BUCKLEY'S SINGLE CARD SHIFT

A USEFUL SINGLE CARD SHIFT

This is a sleight figured out by me along with my card effect called "The Triple Climax" and first incorporated into my card act in 1912. It is very useful when a card peeked at is to be smartly and secretly shifted to the bottom of the pack without disturbing the position of the other cards. It is not a difficult sleight to learn and has many useful applications, though it is doubtful if it can be executed indetectably under all circumstances as angles and timely execution play an important part throughout. I use it frequently when performing close-up card effects.

THE SLEIGHT:

The spectator standing at your left side is asked to lift up the cards at the corner and note the name of the card he sees. Say, "Lift the cards like this," and illustrate the act, only don't let the card be exposed when doing it, or he may remember the card he then sees instead of the one he sees later.

The spectator carrying out your instructions lifts the corner, but unlike the usual peek where the thumb is pressed on the back of the pack, the cards now open bookwise, and as spectator releases the cards the thumb presses on the back, closing the opening. At this moment pressure by the little finger causes the fleshy part of the ball of this fourth finger to be caught into the opening and secretly maintains the location of the card.

When you get accustomed to this method you will appreciate its advantages over the method of using the first finger, which, by comparison, is obvious. The right hand takes the pack from the left hand holding it between the fingers at one end and the thumb at the other, and in this manner keeps open the break below the peeked at card.

As the pack is taken by the right hand, turn to someone at your right side and say, "Would you mind looking at a card? Just raise the corner like this." Now, here lies the essence of the timing, because while you say just that or something equivalent to it you deliberately execute the shift as follows:

The pack is placed into the left hand again, only this time the right hand retains its position, opens the cards bookwise at the break (see Fig. 1), slides the top packet about half an inch to the right, presses this top packet lightly onto the fingertips of the left hand (see Fig. 2) and pushes the top packet back into the left hand square with the other cards. Only the peeked-at card, the King of Spades, will be protruding from the side, owing to the friction of the left second and third fingertips. The left fingers are then straightened and thus force the peeked-at card farther out and up into a position between the third and fourth fingers of the right hand, where it is gripped at the index corner.

The right hand, without releasing the pack, arcs slightly over, withdrawing the King of Spades from the pack. The balls of the fingers of the left hand draw it into place on the bottom. (See Fig. 4.) All this blends into a single, unhurried action and is completed by the right hand illustrating to the person on your right how to look at a card. Performed this way it is indetectable.

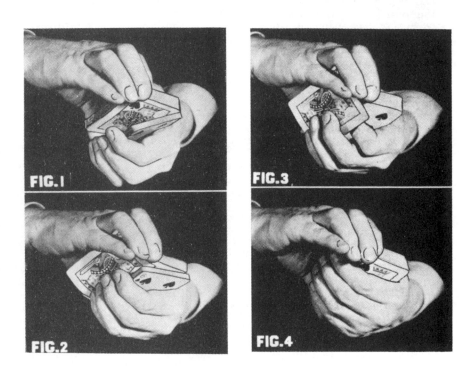

SHIFTING A CARD FROM THE BOTTOM OF THE PACK

This is a sleight that is very useful in effects where two selected cards are made to appear successively on the bottom of the pack.

THE SLEIGHT:

The pack rests face down on the left hand, one side pressed into the fork of the left thumb by the fingers curled up the other side.

The second joint of the first finger of the right hand is at the index corner of the pack, and the first joint of the right thumb is at the opposite end corner. The left hand relaxes its hold on the pack as the ends of the pack are firmly held by the right hand.

The left hand fingertips slide the bottom card between the right palm and the left fingers until the index corner of the bottom card reaches the third and fourth fingers of the right hand. The index corner of the card is then gripped between the sides of the third and fourth fingers.

The thumb and second finger then slightly raise in bookwise fashion about half the cards. The left hand fingers then draw the card back into this opening in the pack.

These moves are the same as in the preceding card shift, only they are made in reverse motion.

IMPROVED DOVETAIL STOCK SHUFFLE
TO KEEP THE TOP STOCK

A stock of five cards is on the top of the pack which you are holding in your left hand. You cut off half the pack, taking the top half with your right hand. Proceed with the dovetail riffle shuffle as follows:

Release several of the bottom cards in the right hand packet. Then commence the dovetail, but riffle the top stock, that is, the top five cards of the right hand packet, together into the left hand packet, letting ten or a dozen cards in the left hand packet fall on the right hand packet. Squeeze the packets together with the fingers of the left hand, the right hand fingers at one end and the right thumb at the other end of the pack providing a covering action. Under this cover the little finger enters above the stock cards, double cuts, and the stock of five cards is then on the top of the pack again.

The whole procedure is carried out in the hands without the aid of a table, and is truly indetectable and may be used repetitiously.

TO KEEP THE BOTTOM STOCK

This procedure differs from the method of keeping the top stock, and is performed as follows:

The left hand holds the pack face down, and the thumb at the index corner releases by the riffle about half of the pack.

The right hand takes these cards and riffles them into the left hand packet. The left hand releases several cards from the bottom of its packet first. Then the stock of five cards at the bottom of the right hand packet is released together into this break, and the remainder of the cards in both packets are riffle shuffled.

The left hand squeezes the packet together, the right hand providing a covering action. The fourth finger of the left hand keeps a break below the stock of cards as the two interlaced packets are squeezed together. The double cut is not immediately practical here because of the very few cards below the break made by the fourth finger, so the following method is employed.

The near end of the pack is gripped on the sides between the second finger and thumb of the right hand, which action permits the break to be maintained by the side pressure of the thumb and finger of the right hand. The thumb and second finger of the left hand grip the pack at the sides of the opposite end, and in this manner the left hand draws off the top of the pack about a dozen cards at a time into the left hand, until about fifteen cards remain in the packet in the right hand. These are dropped onto the packet in the left hand, but as this is being done, the fourth finger of the left hand enters the break in this packet of fifteen cards. Half the packet below the break is then cut to the top, and then the remainder of the cards below the break are cut to the top. The stock cards are now on the bottom again.

BUCKLEY'S METHOD OF SECRETLY PLACING A BRIDGE

This old, old friend, long ago fallen into disuse by most of the magi fraternity, is, however, a top notch sleight. You will find several effects in one chapter of this book in which it is indispensable.

THE SLEIGHT:

The cards are casually sprung from the right hand to the left hand, waterfall flourish. A distance of about three inches is best. This bends the cards slightly concave. Now riffle the cards (not noisily), increasing the pressure slightly as you pull them back as you would if you were trying to take the concavity away that they have just acquired. By these two simple and unsuspicious acts the cards on the top of the pack are slightly convexed, and those on the bottom are slightly concaved. Cut the pack and observe the bridge. You can almost drive a car through it.

Repeat the process many times until you can just see it, or better still not see it but cut at it when you use the Charlier pass.

Personally I prefer varying the procedure by the use of the overhand shuffle for the lower half of the pack. Try it. The bridge is there for the top cards of the pack. Other times I use the so-called Hindu shuffle instead of a simple cut, and, best of all, I like to follow up after the bridge is made at center by using the Erdnase triple cut ("Expert at the Card Table"), and saying, "That's a gambler's cut, and, of course, it's cheating. I'll cut fair, like this," and you cut at the bridge. Until you try this simple dodge on your associate card experts you will not fully appreciate its effectiveness.

BUCKLEY'S "OUT OF THIS WORLD"
FALSE SHUFFLE AND CUT

This is a shuffle that I created especially for card effects such as "Out of This World" by Paul Curry. The sleight is performed entirely without the need of a table, and all the red cards and the black cards are kept separate. The top cards remain undisturbed. Only those of the bottom half are disturbed.

Commence by having the twenty-six red cards on top of the twenty-six black ones. Wait, let me give you my method of getting them into position. Hand the pack to someone to shuffle, and have a card selected. Crimp it as it is returned. Have the pack again shuffled, and say as you take the pack, "I shall now proceed to find your card by a process of mathematics. With the cards held up to your view so no one else sees exactly what you are doing, separate the reds from the blacks, obtain the crimped card, take it from the pack behind another card, show the face card and say, "Is this the card?" The answer is "No." You say, "Of course not," and carelessly throw the card face down, but in reality throw the selected card. (See throw-down change for method.)

Then continue the process of sorting reds and blacks. When finished, say, "That's unusual for me. I'm afraid I cannot find it. What was the card, please? Oh, that's this one. Didn't you remember it?" The last statement is made as you turn over the face-down card on the table.

Having secretly accumulated all the red cards separately, you are ready to false shuffle.

THE SLEIGHT:

Hold the pack in the hands as depicted in Fig. 1, first finger bent supporting cards at back of pack, third and fourth fingers gripping pack by pressure against root of fourth finger.

The left thumb applies bending back pressure on the cards, letting them spring from under this applied pressure. In this manner about twenty cards (not more) are released. (See Fig. 1.)

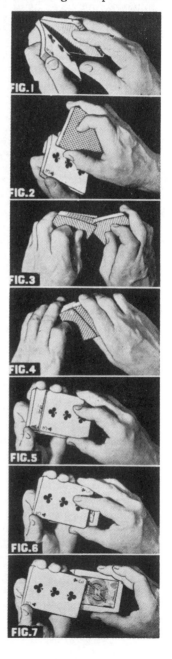

FIG. 1
FIG. 2
FIG. 3
FIG. 4
FIG. 5
FIG. 6
FIG. 7

29

The right hand takes these twenty sprung cards between the first finger and the second finger.

From this position they are tipped up by the tips of the fingers of the left hand to the position shown in Fig. 2 where the thumb of the right hand supports them. The right hand now has approximately twenty black cards, and the left hand thirty-two cards, twenty-six red and six black. The Three of Clubs is depicted as the bottom card of the left hand packet, the Ace of Spades as the bottom card of the right hand packet. Each hand holds its cards in the same manner.

Without changing the hold of either hand, the cards are brought into position for riffling, and the packets are riffle shuffled together. (See Fig. 3.)

The left hand riffles four or five cards (not more), and then the right hand riffles cards, alternating with the left hand. This interweaves the black cards from face of cards up, black into black and then black into red, with some red cards at the top and some black on the bottom of the pack.

The cards are then straightened, the right hand packet protruding from the end of the packet in the left hand. (See Fig. 4.)

The right hand supports the pack for a moment, and the right hand shifts its position, holding the pack at the sides near the bottom corners between the second and third fingers on one side and the thumb on the other. (See Fig. 5.) The left hand grips the protruding black cards at the top side corners between the second finger and thumb as in Fig. 5.

The left hand now presses down as if to force the protruding cards into the cards supported by the right hand. Actually, this pressure and grip allow the several bottom black cards in the right hand, with the Three of Clubs, to come level with the black ones in the left hand held packet and the Ace of Spades. (See Fig. 6.) The left hand seizes the cards, which are pushed up, firmly with its already held packet. Without hurry or hesitation the right hand then withdraws the cards it is left holding (see Fig. 7), and places them on the face of the packet held in the left hand. But secretly the little finger of the left hand is bent in time to hold a secret break between the two packets.

The right hand takes a position on the ends of the pack, thumb at one end and second, third and fourth fingers at the other, first finger on the face of the pack.

The right hand maintains its position as the left hand carries away about half the cards below the break made by the fourth finger of the left hand and places them fairly on the face-up card, then returns and takes the remainder of the cards below the break and places them on the face-up card. Examination will reveal that the red cards on the top of the pack are undisturbed, while the black cards have sustained a simple cut. I would like to add that this cutting process, which I developed, is so simple in itself that it seems almost absurd to say I created the idea, yet it is really so important that I use it in almost every trick I do.

SIGHTING OR GLIMPSING THE TOP CARD SECRETLY

This is a very desirable sleight that can be performed by a number of different methods, some of which have advantages and are more suitable than others, according to the working and technique employed. I shall describe several methods which have great merit to recommend them.

FIRST METHOD:

Place the pack face down either on the table or in your left hand, and with your right hand lift off the pack about twenty cards. The thumb is at one corner along the side, and the first finger is at the index corner. The second and third fingers are close to the first finger. The fourth finger, which is the finger that does the work, is on the back of the top card.

Press on the back of the card with the fourth finger while you apparently look at the face card. You are thus permitted to secretly see the index of the top card. Fig. 1 clearly depicts how the index is seen when performing the sleight.

FIG. 1

SIGHTING THE TOP CARD, SECOND METHOD

Place the pack of cards in your right hand, face down, as if you were going to deal from that hand.

Place the first finger of your left hand on the index corner, your fourth finger of the left hand on the back of the top card at the non-index corner, the left thumb at the non-index corner of the opposite end of the pack.

With the left hand placed thus, lift off about twenty cards from the top of the pack.

Now hold the packet in your left hand at right angles to the packet in your right hand.

Pressing the top card at the corner with your fourth finger of the left hand, cause it to arch and clearly expose to your view the index under the first finger of your left hand, which provides an ideal cover for the movement of the card from the eyes of those who are really watching for such intimate details.

This method can also be used to glimpse the second, third or fourth card down from the top. Try it.

Fig. 1 illustrates the manner in which the left hand holds the pack at the ends while the fourth finger executes the sleight.

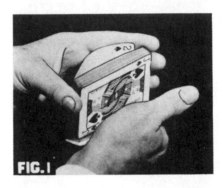

SIGHTING THE TOP CARD, THIRD METHOD

This is an excellent method used, and no doubt invented, by some clever manipulator of the gambling fraternity. It has come to be known to a few of the better informed magicians in the past few years.

Fig. 1 tells the story very completely. The pack of cards is held in the left hand, ready for dealing, and at the moment the right hand distracts the attention by placing a card on the table, the left thumb presses the top card of the pack, causing it to bow up between the thumb and first finger until you can just see the index of the card.

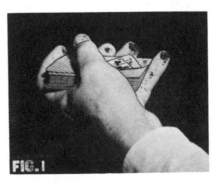

FOURTH METHOD:

This is another method, no doubt, invented by some gambler. The picture tells the complete story.

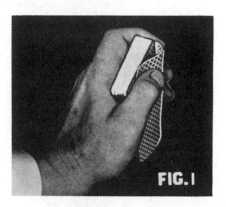

FIG. I

IMPROVED PEEK

The peek is used preparatory to a sleight.

The sleight which follows is usually the retention of the location at which the card was peeked (looked at by a spectator while the pack was held in a more or less closed position by the performer), for the delayed or immediate secret sighting of the peeked-at card, or the secret cutting of the peeked-at card to the top or bottom of the pack. In order to avoid descriptive repetition, the description of the peek will be treated separately, and if you will try it as described you may find these added subtleties of value.

THE SLEIGHT:

Hold the cards in the left hand, the first finger reclining over the top, the second finger about half an inch down from the index corner on the side, the fourth finger at the bottom corner pressing lightly on the cards and the left thumb pressing lightly on the top inside edges, spreading the edges slightly. All these simple things are indeed important.

A spectator is asked to lift the cards any place, preferably about the middle, with his left hand, and thus look at the index of the one card he exposes.

Illustrate by lifting the corners of the cards just as they are expected to do this.

The cards open bookwise—this is important.

The spectator lifts the corner, and because there is little or no resisting pressure, the cards easily separate bookwise and return to their position again, aided by the left thumb, which moves over the back of the packet as the spectator opens the pack to look at a card.

SIGHTING AFTER THE PEEK

Let us proceed through the moves as described for the peek.

The position of the first and second fingers of the left hand permits a break to be made by a spectator only at the index corner. (See Fig. 1). The position of the thumb of your left hand insures the pack opening bookwise. The pack is square on all sides except the end which is shielded by your body.

The next move of this sequence follows without hurry. Open the palm flat, not the fingers. Apply pressure on the side of the upper packet with the second and third fingers. (See Fig. 2.) This pressure causes a small step at the card below the fourth finger, bringing the Six of Hearts into your line of sight as the hand and the pack are rotated. (See Fig. 3.)

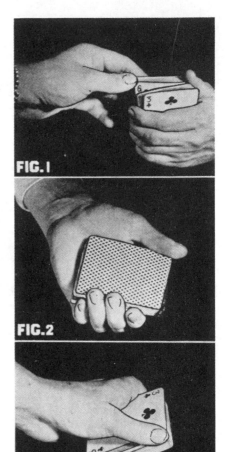

FIG. 1

FIG. 2

FIG. 3

OTHER LOCATIONS AFTER THE PEEK

Here is something different that may surprise you when you try it out. Perhaps it has been done before, but if so, I have not heard or seen it. Until now I have guarded it closely from my conjuring associates. Just a simple rubber band, not too tight fitting, is slipped around the middle of the pack. You will find it helps rather than hinders. All the locations previously described associated with the peek are quite practical with the rubber band in place—the step, the pass, the glide, the sight and what have you? As I said, it helps rather than hinders. Try it, but be sure you can do these things expertly without the rubber band before you try to do them with it.

THE TURNOVER SIGHT LOCATION

Performer receives a pack of thoroughtly mixed cards from a spectator whom he has requested to shuffle, and receiving the cards performer riffles one end of the pack slowly and invites the spectator to say stop! The performer cuts the pack at the place stop is called, and shows the bottom card of the cut off packet to the spectator, and requests the card be remembered. This packet is laid on the table, the spectator's card on the bottom of this packet. The performer says, "perhaps I did see the bottom card of this other packet, so will you shuffle it please and place some of the shuffled cards on top of the packet and also some on the bottom, so I will not be able to tell your card by knowing the card next to your card; that would be cheating. Cut the cards, please, and spread them face up on the table; place your finger, just the tip, on my right hand. I can feel the vibrations as I pass my hand over the cards. They are more pronounced when I come to your card." Performer picks out the spectator's card in this manner.

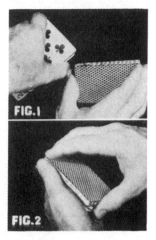

FIG.1

FIG.2

THE WORKING:

At the point explained, where you receive the pack after the spectator has shuffled, you do not know the position of any card.

When you riffle and stop and cut off the packet of cards at the place stopped, you do this with your right hand as in Fig. 2, and as you hold up this packet for the spectator to see, the card you were requested to stop at, you turn over your left hand holding the bottom packet and execute the "Glide" as in Fig. 1 and sight not the bottom card but the top one, the two of spades as seen in Fig. 1.

Then for a moment only you bring the top packet in the right hand on to the two of spades, and lift it off along with the top packet. In doing this the top packet is never square with the bottom packet, and no one will dream you stole the two of spades.

Lay the top packet on the table, have someone shuffle the bottom packet, cut it in two, lay some on top and the rest on the bottom, and have the pack cut.

35

STEPPING AFTER THE PEEK

This is a delayed action and a beautiful sleight in certain effects where the delay can be intelligently made use of. The delay in execution enhances the difficulty of penetration, but the delay must be logical.

The moves up to a point are the same as those described in the execution of the sleight, "Sighting After a Peek," so let us assume the position of the break made by the flesh of the ball of the fourth finger. The step is made by the straightening of the palm and pressure of the second and third fingers. The right hand takes the pack as this move is completed, gripping it at the ends between the fingers and the thumb. The left hand releases the pack altogether, but just before doing so, the left thumb presses the top cards slightly over to submerge the break and make it less conspicuous. The pack is not entirely square. The right hand, now holding the pack, places it on a drinking glass on the table, face down. There it remains until the time arrives to learn the name of the peeked-at card or to cut it to the top or bottom of the pack. To do this the pack is taken up in the right hand in exactly the same manner in which it was laid down. I have herein previously described these moves of double cutting.

The name of the card is learned either by looking at the face of the pack and noting the index of the stepped card, or by cutting by the Charlier or the Buckley double cut method of bringing it to the bottom.

My favorite method of executing the step after the peek is to move the right hand forward ever so little while it holds the break in the aforesaid manner by the tip of the fourth finger of the left hand. This action causes a step about one-sixteenth of an inch at the end of the pack, and the pack of cards is placed on a glass without any risk of losing the step. The pack, when taken up, is freely handled without danger of squaring the ends if the fingers are confined to squaring the sides only. You may by firmly holding the sides of the pack with the fingers of your left hand, simulate a squaring action of the cards by drawing the pack back and forth several times between the fingers and the thumb of the right hand placed at opposite ends of the pack.

When the time arrives to cut the peeked-at card to the bottom, the right thumb presses the ends of the pack, and the fourth finger of the left hand engages the step again and holds the break thus made. By the double cut the peeked-at card arrives at the bottom of the pack.

THE SLIDE

This is a favorite sleight of long standing. It can be executed quite indetectably in slow motion, and therefore has numerous practical application in the working of close-up card effects.

THE SLEIGHT:

After having made a double lift as herein explained, or by your own pet indetectable method, take the two cards as one between the thumb and second finger of the right hand.

Then insert them into the middle of the pack face down, as shown in Fig. 1. The left hand fourth finger presses down on about twenty-six cards, leaving a break or opening near the middle to receive the two cards as one. About one inch of the two cards protrudes.

The second finger of the right hand on the edge of the underneath card, the Two of Spades, slides the card towards the pack. The first finger of the left hand takes up a position on the end of the Six of Clubs, and the Two of Spades is pressed into the pack. This takes only a second without haste. (See Fig. 2.) The whole act is concealed by the Six of Clubs left protruding, which is pulled about three-quarters out of the pack. (See Fig. 3.)

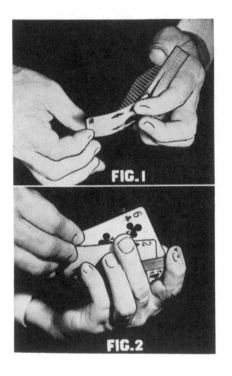

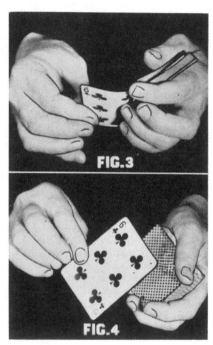

At the right moment this card is withdrawn, either by the spectator whose card it is or by the performer, as the effect of the change may call for. (See Fig. 4.)

Personally, I have a preference for withdrawing the underneath card sideways into the pack instead of endwise. It seems more natural to have the tips of the second and third fingers of the left hand press the underneath card of the two cards into the pack sideways under the cover of the topmost of the two cards, rather than have the first finger of the left hand press it home into the pack endwise, the usual method of performing this sleight.

THE INVISIBLE LOCATION
(One Hand)

This is another one of those indetectable and original subtleties that should find great popularity among those who prefer good things that are easy to do. It will hoodwink the experts as easily as the neophite unfamiliar with the modus operandi.

THE EFFECT:

Any card that has been previously withdrawn from the pack by a spectator is afterwards pushed into the pack, which is lying face downward on your left hand in a similar position to that in which you hold a pack of cards for dealing. The exact position is unimportant. The pack is then meticulously squared, though you are complete master of the situation because you have, even under these aforesaid circumstances, retained the exact location of the selected card.

You may now "double cut," bringing the selected card to the top, "double lift," show this card, and place it back on the pack. Then have spectator place his finger on the top card, ask him to name his card, and have him lift it off the top where a moment ago he was convinced it was not there.

METHOD:

The return of the card into the pack is most fair, and herein lies the true beauty of this slight. With the pack resting on your left hand, face down, insert, or allow the spectator to insert, the card of his own selection. Do not allow the card to be pushed right into the pack. Pressure on the back of the pack with the left thumb readily controls this from happening, and the card is inserted to your liking. The card should be left protruding from the end about an inch, so that you may hold up the pack held in your left hand for one and all to see the protruding selected card.

After this the pack of cards is held face down in the left hand on a plane parallel with the floor, and the protruding card is pushed straight home into the pack, not by your right hand, but with the first finger of the left hand, which extends out under the card to the protruding edge.

There is one little secret, and here it is—while the card is being deliberately and slowly pressed into the pack in the aforesaid manner, the thumb and fingers of the left hand press slightly against the sides of the pack. Fair enough so far, but only when about one-eighth of an inch of this card remains to be pressed home, the side pressure on the pack is relaxed entirely, and the result is the selected card finishes its journey carrying the cards above it along on its back, so that there is a step about an eighth of an inch on the inside end of the pack of cards right above the selected card.

The left thumb presses on the back of the pack and the right hand, fingers at one end, thumb at the "step," squares the ends of the pack. In doing so, the "step" is changed to a "break" by the upward pressure of the right thumb.

Of course you may use both hands if you want to do so when pressing home the selected card. The one-hand method takes a little more practice, but it seems to be more effective.

BUCKLEY'S REVERSE

This sleight is quite indetectable when performed as herein described. It is of my origination, although my friend, Tarbell, by an oversight failed to credit me for it. There are, however, some most important details omitted in the Tarbell description of this sleight which, when included, help to make the execution of the sleight completely indetectable.

THE SLEIGHT:

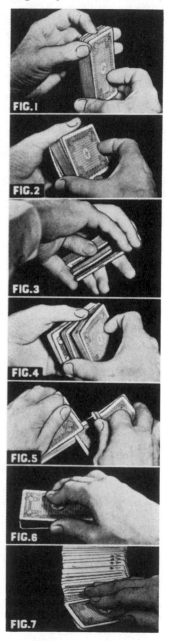

FIG. 1

FIG. 2

FIG. 3

FIG. 4

FIG. 5

FIG. 6

FIG. 7

Having completed the Vernon multiple card shift, bringing the four aces together on the bottom of the pack (note this important wrinkle), do not remove the first finger of the left hand from the end of the aces when the Vernon sleight is completed, but hold a small break between the aces now on the bottom of the pack and the rest of the cards. (See Fig. 1.)

The right hand then takes the cards, second and third fingers at one end, thumb at the other end. The break is shifted from the first finger of the left hand to the second finger of the right hand, and then to the fourth finger of the left hand, and then to the thumb of the right hand. (See Fig. 2.) The left hand now changes its position after transferring the break from the fourth finger of the left hand to the right thumb, which is at the inside and near the corner. (See Fig. 3.) The pack is now in position for executing the "Reverse" of the four bottom cards.

The left hand is brought up alongside the right hand so that the side of the pack rests on third joints of fingers. The left thumb reaches through the arch formed under the right hand above the pack, and slides about twenty of the top cards of the pack across the backs of the other cards until the edges just meet (not off the pack, remember). (See Fig. 4.)

In this position the two packets are brought together momentarily, and the fourth finger of the left hand slides into the opening above the aces and transfers the aces to the left hand

39

packet from the right hand packet in reverse position. Wait! There are yet moves of considerable importance to follow before the sleight is completed. Note carefully the position of the hands and the manner in which each hand holds its packet. The only major change in the next move is made by the right hand as the packets are brought into position for shuffling (riffle shuffle). The third and fourth fingers of the right hand bend under the end of the right hand packet to grip it more firmly. The index corners of the cards are shuffled together (see Fig. 5) without taking on a fresh hold before the riffle shuffle. The right hand finally pushes the right hand packet into the left hand packet. The left hand holds its pack firmly during this action.

The pack is either cut or the aces brought to the middle of the pack by a Hindu shuffle; i.e., taking all the cards in the right hand and pulling off small packets from the top, with the second finger and thumb of the left hand, in the left hand.

The pack is then placed on the table at right arm's length and spread, showing the aces reversed. (See Figs. 6 and 7.)

SIGHTING WHILE CUTTING THE PACK

This original sleight can be executed indetectably. Its usefulness lies in secretly learning the name of the bottom card of the pack as the pack is cut and then completed. This is important in some instances where a key locator card is used, and it has uses at the card table. To my knowledge nothing like it has ever been printed.

THE SLEIGHT:

The pack of cards is on the table at which you are seated, and is evenly squared up, ready for you to cut. Place your right thumb on one side of the pack near the middle, your second finger at the middle of the other side, your first finger in the center of the back of the top card. Your third finger is to do the secret work, and it rests close to the second finger, but more than two-thirds of the ball of this finger is below the place at which the cards are to be cut.

Raise the top half of the pack three inches above the other cards, and at the same time press the bottom card with the inside edge of the ball of the third finger, causing the bottom card to convex about three-quarters of an inch radius. (See Fig. 1 showing the index of the bottom card as seen by you.) Place these cards on the table and complete the cut. The move should be made at an even, unhurried pace. Never tilt the cards. If you are seated at the table and the cards are cut on your right, it won't be necessary to tilt them. Try slightly bending the cards before you commence. Another thing—use a regular full size pack. It is then easier to do this sleight than it is with narrow cards. Fig. 2 shows how the cards are held in the hand, exposing the move, by turning the hand over.

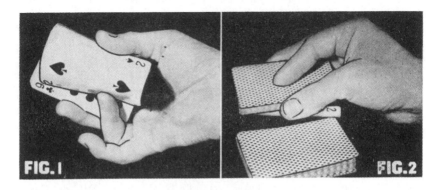

THE GLIDE

This is a perfect sleight that can be repeated ad infinitum without fear of detection. It has many applications and should be deftly acquired by all card conjurers. I shall explain two methods, though actually they are the same in both instances, only with the pack held differently.

THE SLEIGHT:

Hold the cards in the left hand—faces away from the palm, thumb at index corner, first finger at the adjacent corner, and the second, third and fourth fingers close together.

Bend the second, third and fourth fingers over the sides and under on the face of the bottom card.

Move the pack with the thumb and first finger and hold the face card, the Four of Hearts, still with the second, third and fourth fingers. The distance moved should be about half an inch. (See Fig. 1.) Try the foregoing moves with the pack held face down about three inches off the table, and draw off the second bottom card.

I could fill a volume with card tricks embodying the use of the "glide".

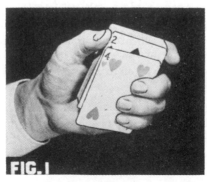

FIG. I

Second Method: Hold the cards in the right hand, this time with the thumb at the index corner and the first finger at the corner lengthwise from the index corner at the other end of the pack. The second, third and fourth fingers are along the end of the pack and can easily be bent around the face of the card, the Queen of Spades. The first finger and thumb move the pack forward. The second and third fingers bent on the Queen of Spades hold it stationary, and the cards move away from the end that is not held. The result is as depicted in Fig. 2, but of course the pack is held at a proper angle to prevent this maneuver from being seen.

There are numerous applications for this sleight. An excellent one is described by me in Sam Berland's book, "Blue Ribbon Card Tricks", page seven, entitled "Surprise Card Through the Case".

A third application, and a somewhat different one, is the four ace effect to which I claim credit, published in Dorny's "Trix and Chatter" (1919).

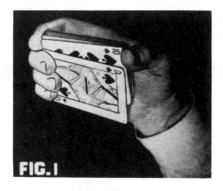

FIG. I

THE GLIDE LOCATION

With the pack of cards held in dealing position in the left hand, "thumb riffle" the cards, requesting someone to say "Stop." With the right hand cut off the cards at the break stopped at, allowing the top card of the packet in the left hand to be looked at by the spectator.

As the packet cut by you is replaced, secretly perform the "glide" (see Fig. 2), and this card will be left protruding to the side of the pack, protected by the right hand. Undercut twice with the left hand to this card, and the spectator's card is on top of the pack.

BUCKLEY'S METHOD OF SIGHTING
WHILE FANNING THE CARDS

In my manuscript of "Thirty Card Tricks" I describe an effect that calls for a dexterous handling of this sleight because it must be performed repetitiously. There is no danger of detection if the sleight is properly executed.

A packet of six cards, the faces of which are unknown to you, are face down on the table. What you do secretly know is that the second top card is a card which has been selected, and you desire to secretly learn the name of this card.

THE SLEIGHT:

The cards are picked up with the right hand and placed, face to palm, held spread out, in the left hand, as shown in Fig. 1, holding them at a 30° angle with the floor.

The cards held in the hands in this position are raised to face the spectator. You ask him if he sees his card. As the cards are being raised, the left thumb tilts up the index corner of the second top card sufficiently to glimpse it. A split second does it, and you secretly look at the index of the spectator's card under the cover afforded by the other cards, as shown in Fig. 2.

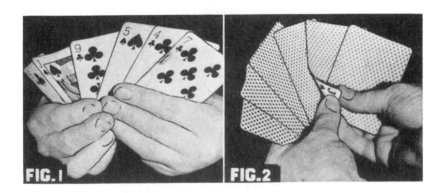

GLIMPSING THE BOTTOM CARD

Every now and then a sleight of outstanding importance to card conjuring is perfected in all its details so that its everlasting association with expert card handling is assured. I do not know who originated this, but I learned it from a gambler over thirty-seven years ago, and have used it consistently when performing with cards. Certainly it has often been described before, and I have little to add to those previous descriptions, but I feel these pages would be lacking if I failed to include so great a friend.

THE SLEIGHT:

The pack is held in the left hand, parallel with the floor, at waist height six inches in front of the body.

The first joints of the second, third and fourth fingers of the left hand curl up the side of the pack, with the thumb very lightly on the back of the top card.

The forward end of the pack is level with the first finger of the left hand, the tip of which rests on the index of the bottom card.

The right hand then holds the pack with the second and third fingers at one end and thumb at the other end.

The pack rests very lightly in the left hand as the right hand holds the pack stationary. The left hand is drawn in towards the body, the first finger of the left hand pressing up on the index corner of the face of the bottom card, causing it to double under into the cupped palm. This action clearly exposes the index corner of the card to your view. (See Fig. 1). Oh, it's very simple, but for that reason, do it well. Here are a few pointers. When you make the move, don't look down at the card for at least five seconds afterwards, and when you turn your gaze away again, don't slide the bottom card into place for at least another five seconds. The glimpse at the card takes only a fleeting glance, but speed may create suspicion. Take your time.

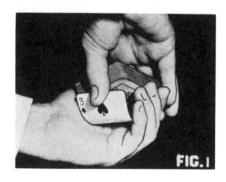

BUCKLEY'S DIAGONAL LOCATION

This is another of those simple little devices that add so much appeal to expert card control. A card is inserted into the middle of the pack which is then squared and cut in the most undeceiving manner, and the card, without any suspicious movements, returns to the top to await the double lift or do your timely bidding!

THE SLEIGHT:

The pack is held in the left hand. The left thumb supports one side of the pack. The first joints of the second, third and fourth fingers support the other side. The first finger is bent underneath. The partly inserted card protrudes about an inch before the fingers of the right hand push it into the pack. The first finger does most of the pressing, and makes the card assume a slightly diagonal position, causing the corner near the fourth finger of the left hand to protrude about an eighth of an inch. See position in Fig. 2 showing right hand shielding the move while making it, and see position of card exposed in Fig. 3.

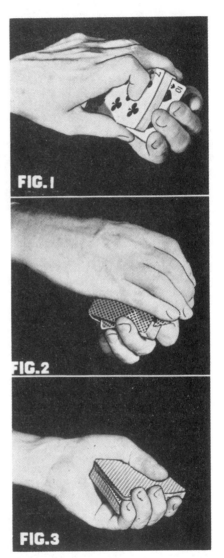

At this position the fourth finger of the left hand is placed on the protruding corner and thus causes an indetectable break above the inserted card. The pack is immediately cut, using Buckley's double-cut, to bring the card to the top of the pack.

Obviously if you do the self-same moves, but insert the fourth finger of the left hand under the corner of the inserted card instead of on top of it, the card will then be cut to the bottom of the pack, where it may be glimpsed.

THE BREAK SHUFFLE

THE SLIGHT:

Hold the pack in the left hand, ready for the common overhand shuffle.

Carry away the lower three-fourths of the pack between the second finger and thumb of the right hand.

Lower this right hand packet over the left hand packet, and grip both packets between the thumb and second finger of the right hand. In doing this, you will cause a natural division between the two packets to form; in fact, if you don't let go the right hand packet in taking the left hand packet, you can't prevent it. Therein lies the secret; but wait.

The right hand now starts up with all the cards, but the left thumb applies pressure to the top edge and causes about six or more cards to slide off into the left hand. Small packets are thus drawn from the right hand packet into the left hand until the break is reached, and then the remaining cards are dropped onto the packet in the left hand. This maneuver leaves the top part of the pack undisturbed, but that is only a minor point.

Try it again, and this time do as follows:

Note the bottom card of the pack—Five of Hearts. Undercut three-fourths of the pack as before, taking the two packets into the right hand and drawing the cards off in small packets into the left. When only eight or a dozen cards are left above the break, drop all the cards onto the cards now in the left hand. As you do so, the tip of the fourth finger of the left hand is inserted below the Five of Hearts to hold the break. Now execute Buckley's double cut to take the Five of Hearts to the bottom of the pack.

Exert a light pressure on the top and bottom cards, and continue the overhand shuffle. The Five of Hearts remains secretly on the bottom.

One more important detail. Have a card peeked at by the method herein described, and with the fourth finger retaining the break as shown with the cards in the left hand, the right hand covers the pack, fingers at one end, thumb at the other, and then arcs around the fingers of the left hand into the described position.

The left hand then assumes its position for drawing off the first small packet of cards, drawing the cards off in packets or singly until only a few remain above the break. These are dropped on the others in a packet, the fourth fingertip of the left hand maintaining the break. The Buckley double cut is made to bring the Five of Hearts to the bottom.

During this whole procedure do not look at the hands. This is one of the essentials of the real secret.

BUCKLEY'S METHOD FOR DEALING SECONDS

After having carefully studied the various methods published for performing the sleight called "dealing seconds," and having watched a host of experts among the conjuring fraternity attempt it, I make this statement without prejudice. I have yet to see more than two magicians, "Carlyle" and "Domico," perform this sleight indetectably, or in a manner that would pass unobserved, that is, without undue movement of the hands to confuse or cover some defect therein.

Furthermore, I sincerely doubt if there has ever before been published a description of dealing seconds that, if truthfully and implicitly followed in the most expert manner, could ever be performed indetectably; but of course that is only my opinion.

This description of the sleight is original with me, and is the result of tedious and careful study of each and every detail involved. If it were practical to do so, I would exact a promise from you not to teach this method to anyone not in possession of this book, because in passing its teachings on to you in these pages I believe that you are receiving a method of performing this sleight which is one of the finest pieces of card artistry in the whole range of card conjuring. It is a weapon so excellent that you will rate as a master among the less initiated, even though you may possess the ability to do little else.

However, it behooves me to warn you that this is no easy road to Utopia. The method is difficult to learn, very difficult in fact as sleights go, but if you will practice the sleight as explained, watching each detail, you will, after sixty hours of practice in half-hour sessions or thereabouts, graduate into a class you have only dreamed about.

The sleight itself is not really the most difficult thing to learn with cards, nor is it the most important. The success of its practical execution, that is, indetectability, resides in the preliminaries of its actual execution. Therefore I find it essential to teach you a manner of holding the pack while dealing the cards which is natural enough not to excite comment or suspicion from the most fastidious of card players. It is really a little unusual, but is very necessary. Secondly, you are to be taught how to deal cards from the top of the pack, and to do this properly, several hours should be ungrudgingly devoted to the procedure in order to obtain the desired flexing of the thumb muscles.

You are to be taught how to extract the cards from the top in an exceedingly rapid manner, and this while your hands move in the easiest and most normal manner, and how to engage yourself in matters unrelated to the execution of the deal.

Lesson One—Holding the pack for the deal.

Referring to Fig. 1, you will observe the left hand holding the pack in position for dealing.

The first finger is relaxed, lying along the end of the pack, and has its tip almost to the corner and partly above the level of the pack.

The second finger is curled up at the side and near the corner of the pack, and is completely relaxed in that position shown.

The third finger is hugging close to the second finger, and the tip is a little above the level of the pack.

The fourth finger is hugging close to the third finger, but has its first joint line pressing lightly on the side edge of the bottom of the pack.

The thumb rests diagonally across the pack, lying straight, and reaching nearly to the corner of the pack, leaving only approximately a quarter or three-eighths of an inch of the corner showing, and very lightly resting on the top card.

Lesson Two—Left thumb action.

With the pack of cards held in the position just described and depicted in Fig. 1 plate, move your left thumb a quarter of an inch down towards the side of the pack, very lightly touching but not moving the top card. Now raise the thumb off the card and swing it back to its original position. Repeat this action until you are quite accustomed to it.

Lesson Three—Right and left thumb action, dealing from the top.

Place your right hand in this position: The tip of the right hand first finger is under the second finger of the left hand. The tip of the second finger of the right hand is on the knuckle of the third finger of the left hand. The third finger of the right hand touches the fourth finger of the left hand. The ball of the right thumb is poised above the nail of the left thumb. (See Fig. 1.)

The right thumb descends on the card, and simultaneously the left thumb moves into its second position as it was trained to do. The position of the two thumbs is shown in Fig. 2. The left thumb is raised imperceptibly off the card.

The next action is to slide the top card partly off the pack with the right thumb and without moving any part of the hand except the thumbs.

The move is made very rapidly, and terminates in the position shown in Fig. 3.

The right thumb is lightly pressed down on the top card, and smartly draws it over the left fingertips, to be squeezed between the right thumb and first finger of the right hand. The left thumb moved up to position one again. This is to be done as soon as the right thumb is clear, permitting the left thumb to do so.

The right hand moves away several inches at an even and well-regulated normal dealing pace, and drops the card by simply opening the fingers and thumb, returning to the aforesaid position for another card.

Deal all the cards many times in this manner until it is like second nature for you to do so. Don't hurry any of the moves except the right and left thumb action, the speed of which passes unseen because of the relatively slow hand action which follows in separating the two hands as the card is drawn off. It is absolutely necessary that you train yourself to deal the cards off the top of the pack in this manner if you would perform the "second deal"

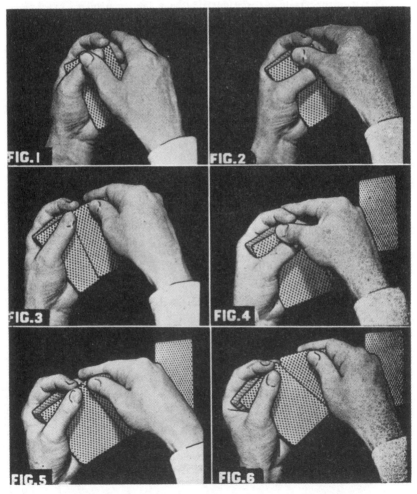

(to be explained) indetectably. The whole procedure should be smooth and easy—no jerkiness or change of pace. The deal is completely antithetical to the "strike" wherein the card to be dealt, either top or second as the case may be, is struck with the right thumb and carried away off the pack by the sheer speed of the movement of the right hand departing with the card.

In this method you get the speed and also the strike action of the thumb, but only the thumb moves the card. The hand motion is, as I have already said, relatively slow, and the quick thumb action and the slow hand action have no distinctive separation. They both are made to blend into one continuously smooth, natural action of dealing.

Dealing the Second Card:

If you understand clearly what I have been trying to teach you about dealing the cards from the top of the pack, then the dealing of the second top card will be greatly simplified.

In dealing the top card the right thumb did all the work; the left thumb simply got out of the way of the right thumb. Now it has a job to do.

As the right thumb is brought to the pack to take off the top card, the left thumb presses on the top card with just sufficient pressure to move the card with it as it moves down, and only far enough to expose the white border of the second top card, no further. This is very difficult to do, so at the beginning you may expose a half an inch of the second card, and by practice reduce the amount to the white border only.

The right thumb is placed very lightly on the exposed corner of the second card—very lightly, I said! That is really important.

The right thumb draws the second top card half way out of the pack, while the right hand otherwise has not moved. (See Fig. 5.) At the same time the left thumb moves the top card back and square with the pack.

The right hand moves away from the left hand. The latter moves only the very least amount, while the right hand draws the card away (Fig. 6) and drops it where you will—face up, face down, in front of yourself, or any place on the table—it makes no difference to the indetectability of the sleight.

If I have seemed to overstress certain actions of this sleight, it is because of my desire to really teach you the true principles involved in its execution. With these properly and clearly understood, practice is the only thing that can convey to you the true beauty of this piece of card *magic!*

One thing more—as you practice doing this sleight, read a book aloud. This insures two important factors—dividing your attention and stopping you from looking at your hands while dealing.

THE DOMICO LOCATION

This piece of manipulation is a masterpiece in Domico's hands, and I am indeed fortunate in having his permission to publish it for the first time.

The pack is held in the left hand and run from left to right while the spectator makes a choice of any one card in the pack. Then the pack is squared in your left hand, and your thumb riffles the cards until it pleases the spectator to return the selected card at an opening caused by the thumb riffle. A card is returned to the pack at any place the spectator indicates during the riffle, your right hand pushes the card into the pack in the fairest possible manner, or so it seems. However, in doing so, the card is forced against your left thumb nail, which secretly nicks the side edge, as it is pushed past the left thumb. This causes a white line about a sixteenth of an inch long on the side of the spectator's card which can be easily detected by your looking for it, but would pass the keenest observer not in the know.

The spectator shuffles and returns the pack to you. Locate by cutting it to the top and then request the spectator to name a number, second deals to the number named, turning up the card.

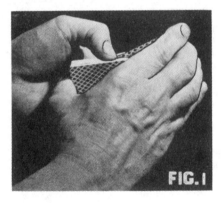

FIG. 1

CARDINI'S LOCATION

Every card conjurer can spring the cards from hand to hand, so I will assume this flourish to be already well understood.

This beautiful piece of "Cardini" deception is to have a selected card unsuspectingly returned from ten to fifteen cards from the bottom of the pack. The fourth finger of the left hand is partly inserted to maintain a break below the selected card. But, lo! Although it seems impossible, the location is maintained as the cards are sprung from hand to hand under these circumstances.

The spring commences while the two hands are together, and the break is passed before the hands separate, still continuing the springing. A master stroke of deception! It is these little things that are really important to the expert.

51

THE COUNT

It is quite important that in performing the simple rudimentary feats with cards, such as counting, shuffling, cutting and turning over a card or cards, that the performer does such things in a manner that discloses a complete mastery of the act. I have heard it argued that the more clumsily you do these things, the less the audience will associate the climax of your trick with dexterity. That is true, but don't be foolish enough to think they will believe you a "Mandrake". No, they will probably dismiss the effect as being a simple enough feat, like a puzzle, for anyone to master if the secret working were known. More than likely that is true, because an expert is seldom, if ever, deficient in the artistry of such matters.

My way of presenting an effect has always been to analyze it very carefully, studying every detail critically, testing each sleight from the beginning to the end as it applied to the working for the desired climax, testing it before a mirror, and later, when proficient in its execution, before the paying customers. I mention these matters to you because they are important. This count was original with me sometime in 1909 when I first learned to perform the "twelve cards to the pocket," an effect I used successfully to open my card act for many years. It is one of the prize gems of card conjuring. There are, perhaps, another twenty deserving to be listed in the same category.

THE SLEIGHT:

Place twelve cards in the right hand in the position shown in Fig. 1. The hand is

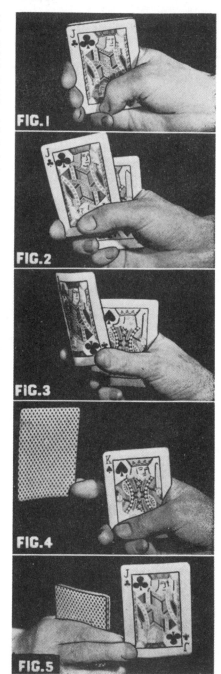

FIG. 1

FIG. 2

FIG. 3

FIG. 4

FIG. 5

held about level with your chin and from twelve to fifteen inches in front of you. The packet of twelve cards is facing you. The bottom end at one corner rests on the fourth finger. The first, second and third fingers are on the side and thus press the cards into the fork of the thumb. The tip of the thumb rests on the bottom end of the card, about half way between the two corners. This is the first position for the count. (See Fig. 1.)

The second position (Fig. 2.) is arrived at by pushing up the Jack of Clubs with the thumb until the ball of the first finger, not seen in the figure, and the ball of thumb hold the card at the bottom midway between the corners. The second finger stretches out and presses the corner and bends it around the tip of the first finger (Fig. 3.) The first and second fingers stretch out with the card thus gripped at the corner. The card, released by the thumb, swings around and makes a sudden appearance at the fingertips of the first and second fingers (Fig. 4). It is important that the card be kept square with the pack or the sleight loses a great deal of its artistry.

The card is removed by the left hand, and the sleight is repeated with the remaining eleven cards, one at a time.

THE FALSE COUNT FOR MORE

This is another sleight that I originated to meet the requirements of the "twelve cards to pocket effect" wherein six cards are counted as seven, and later three cards are counted as five.

THE SLEIGHT:

A packet of six cards is placed in the left hand, face down. The four fingers on one side press the other side into the left thumb fork. The thumb can push the top card well out over the tips of the fingers, and can readily draw it back again square with the other cards.

The first card is pushed out in this manner, and the right hand is brought up to receive it in the following manner. The thumb of the right hand reaches over the back of the extended top card of the packet till it touches the far corner of this card. (See Fig. 1.) That puts the index corner into the fork of the right thumb, and in this manner this card is drawn off the packet into the right hand. Then another card is pushed off the top of the packet in the left hand exactly as before, and the right hand holding the first card approaches to take the second one. The position assumed when the two hands come together is as follows. The four fingers of the right hand with the card pass under the back of the left hand. The thumb reaches the far corner of the extended top card of the packet in the left hand and simulates the act of taking the card, but the left thumb draws it back, and the move is falsified. (See Fig. 2.)

The illusion is indistinguishable to the eye from the actual taking of the card, but wait! The illusion can be further heightened or completely destroyed because in taking a card in this manner there is a sound peculiar to the move. Therefore it becomes an essential part of the illusion to make the noise of the false move and the real move exactly alike. This is accomplished by the amount of pressure of the right thumb squeezing down on the cards as the hands are drawn apart. Close your eyes and listen. It won't take you long to make the move indetectably.

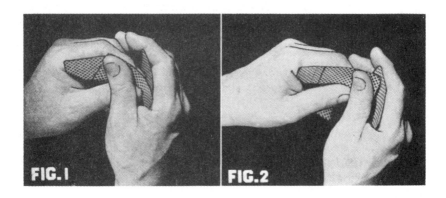

FIG. I   FIG. 2

THE FALSE COUNT FOR LESS

In such effects as the "Repeat Card Trick" it behooves the conjurer to count cards held in the hand as a fewer number than he is actually holding. Excellent means for accomplishing this have been developed by John Booth, Carlyle, and others. I have no disagreement with these methods, but you may like to try another and see which suits you best.

THE SLEIGHT:

Hold fifteen cards in the left hand, backs up, thumb along the side of the packet pointing to the floor at an angle, first finger at the corner, second, third and fourth fingers along the other side. If you press on the index of the card at the corner with the first finger, you should, if your position is correct, be able to bend this card back. (See Fig. 1.) Take off with the right hand, one at a time, four cards, the left thumb pushing each card over the fingertips, then pinching the cards between the thumb and the first finger of the right hand at the index corner. One card at a time is removed. The first finger of the left hand keeps the underneath card pressed back from the corner as shown in Fig. 2. The fifth time the thumb and first finger take all the cards except the one card the first finger of the left hand held back. This card is then flicked with the third finger of

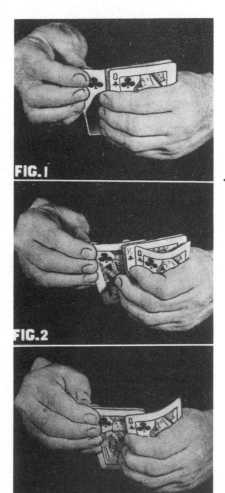

the left hand while held by the thumb and the first finger of the left hand, and is then laid on the face of the cards in the right hand. These are placed openly in a tumbler, and the procedure repeated until only six cards remain.

THE SIDE STEAL PALM

At this late date it seems to me desirable to say a few words about this basic sleight. I am informed by Mr. Hilliard's "Greater Magic", page 31, that this sleight is a conception of the master manipulator, T. Nelson Downs. I have seen it effectively used by Nate Leipzig, Max Malini, and more recently by Dr. Daley, and much less effectively by a host of others. It is for this reason that I am prompted to make these remarks which, to my way of thinking, can make or completely ruin the deceptiveness of the sleight. Like many other descriptions of sleights, the author either did not know the true intricacies or carelessly omitted including them, and it is just such things that distinguish a Daley, a Vernon and a Cardini from the common exponent of card butchery.

THE SLEIGHT:

A card which the performer desires to secretly palm into the right hand from the pack of cards held in the left hand lies waiting at a position above a "break", a "jog", a "step", a "crimp" or a flesh grip, or perhaps it is on the pack next to your left palm. The essential thing is that you want to secretly get the card into your right palm, so for the purpose of an example let this card be above the break held by the little finger in the middle of the pack. The pack is transferred to the right hand, and the break with it. The right hand, fingers at one end, thumb at the other end, holds the pack. The right thumb maintains the break by simple pressure on the divided end of the pack, while the fingers and thumb of the left hand slide up and down the sides of the pack to insure the cards being definitely squared.

The left hand now grips the pack, fingers at one side, thumb at the other, and thus maintains the break while the fingers and thumb slide back and forth along the ends of the pack to insure the ends being square, and silently disillusion any ideas to the contrary that all is not fair and honest. This is all preliminary to, and has nothing to do with, the actual sleight. My reason for including it is to emphasize the importance of the details to follow.

The pack is pressed firmly into the fork of the left thumb by the second and third fingers of the left hand. The little fingertip maintains the break below the card to be palmed.

The right hand takes up its station for the sleight, resting the middle joint of the first finger of the right hand on the back of the pack at the index corner, and the first joint of the thumb at the corner of the other end of the pack. The third finger of the left hand is bent into the break under the card, and by an upward and outward pressure the card is forced out an inch under the cover of the right hand, which remains quite still. As the left hand moves away with the pack, the fingers of the left hand straighten out, pressing the card up flat into the right palm. At this point in the maneuver the right side edge of the pack of cards remains concealed by the side of the first finger of the right hand, and now comes the one important detail that justifies this description.

Before the right hand moves away from the left hand, the tips of the fingers of the left hand must be curled up around the edge of the pack, and all action or movement of same must have ceased, or the illusion is destroyed and a capital sleight rendered in a class of mediocrity.

Another detail that may not be fitting to all types of hands, but which I find essential in my own case, is to slide the card a little towards the fingers after it is under the palm. The fingers of the left hand do this indetectably so that no perceptible movement of gripping the palmed card is observable.

THE SIDE STEAL PALM — BUCKLEY'S METHOD

This sleight, the basic conception of T. Nelson Downs, is sufficiently modified to warrant a description not previously given. The method which I am about to disclose is original with me, and I have no knowledge of anyone using it up to the present time.

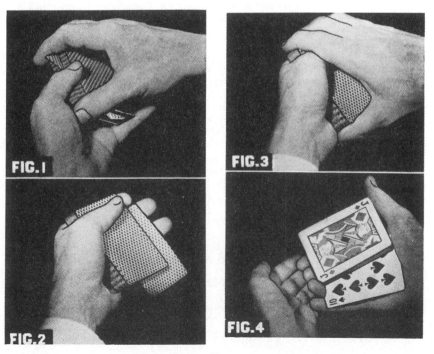

It is not just another way of performing the sleight, for it offers simplified advantages which the basic method of T. N. Downs under similar circumstances does not embrace. Like other valuable sleights it requires practice, but above all else a clear understanding of the correlated action involved during its execution.

THE SLEIGHT:

A selected card protruding from the pack which is held, face to palm in the left hand, supported by the fingers on one side of the pack and the thumb on the other side.

Cover the pack with the right hand, your right thumb at the index corner, your first finger at the non-index corner of the protruding card, and the second, third and fourth fingers of the right hand on the end of the protruding card.

The selected card is pushed into the pack diagonally so that this card protrudes, its index corner lying alongside the right thumb, which continues to support the pack at its inner end index corner. (See Fig. 1.)

The third and fourth fingers of the left hand are now on the protruding side of the selected card.

Then while the right thumb and fingers support the pack at both ends, the selected card is pivoted on the right thumb and is caused to protrude from the pack about half an inch, both at its side and end. (See Fig 2. The right hand is removed for purpose of illustrating.)

The fourth finger of the right hand is now on the end of the protruding card near its index corner. (See Fig. 3.)

The pack is pushed firmly into the fork of the left thumb and thus held firmly by the left thumb only. Fig. 4 is the same as Fig. 3, with hands separated for illustrating the position of the cards.

The right hand now shifts to align the protruding card into palming position. The card is withdrawn as the right hand simulates a squaring action of the pack and slides back over the pack with the card now palmed, the fingers at one end, the thumb at the other.

ORIGINAL METHODS OF PALMING CARDS
FROM THE BOTTOM OF THE PACK

"The Expert at the Card Table" was written by S. W. Erdnase. This name spelled backwards is E. S. Andrews—probably Erdnase is the correct name. It would be of considerable interest to know something about this man who, nearly half a century ago, advanced the art of card magic to such an extent that no publication on cards has outmoded his famous book on sleights embracing shifts, cuts, palms, changes, passes, blind shuffles, top and bottom dealings, etc.

On page 86 Erdnase explains a bottom palm which everyone interested in this procedure should learn to do. And again on page 154, "Sixth Method," Erdnase explains the most perfect piece of card palming it is possible to imagine. This is for stealing a single card from the deck to the palm in slow motion, and with the pack in plain sight during the complete action. Study it carefully or you may miss the true beauty of this sleight.

I do not hope to surpass these methods. What follows is simply another, rather than a better way.

THE SLEIGHT:

Hold the pack face down by the ends and at the corners between the second finger and thumb of the left hand. The second finger rests alongside the first finger and separates the pack from the cards you desire to palm. The right hand is brought under the pack, palm up, thumb across back, finger up one side, the other side in fork of right thumb. In this manner the pack is moved up and down the fork of the right thumb a couple of times to simulate a squaring action of the cards.

The right hand then takes up this position. The index corner of the bottom packet is pressed against the palm about one inch from the wrist and a half inch in from the side of the hand. (See Fig. 1.)

The second finger releases its hold, and the top packet is held as before by the first finger and thumb, while the bottom packet is suspended between the left thumb and the right palm.

The right hand is drawn back, and the bottom packet pivots around the left thumb, coming squarely and noiselessly into the right palm. (See Fig. 2.)

The left thumb changes its position to the middle of the end of the top packet, and shifts the packet into a concealing position in the right hand. (See Fig. 3.)

PALMING FROM THE BOTTOM
AFTER A RIFFLE SHUFFLE

THE SLEIGHT:

For example, assume the four cards on the bottom of the pack are queens, Queen of Clubs on the bottom.

The bottom half of the pack of cards is taken in the right hand, and the top half in the left hand, the two packets riffle shuffled together with the precaution that the four queens on the bottom of the right hand packet are released first, then a few cards from the left hand pack fall on them, and the rest of the cards in both packets are riffled indiscriminately. The right hand packet is then pushed into the left hand packet endwise until only a half inch of the end of the cards remains protruding. (See Fig. 1.)

The right hand is now placed under the pack and palms the four queens. This is simple because the position the queens occupy prevents you from taking more than the four queens, as a trial will readily prove. (See Fig. 2.)

The right hand, with the queens now palmed, rotates around the end of the pack and grips the pack in the same manner as the left hand has been holding it. The left hand passes under the pack and assumes the position from the left end which the right just occupied from the right end of the pack when the right hand palmed the queens.

With the left hand in position under the pack, the fingers and fork of the left thumb press the protruding cards square at both ends, and the right hand places the pack on the table.

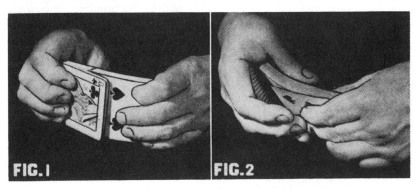

FIG. 1   FIG. 2

60

THE PERFECT CARD PALM

This simple original sleight is capable of being executed in a manner that is entirely indetectable.

THE SLEIGHT:

Hold the pack in the left hand in position for dealing. Bring the right hand over the pack. (See Fig. 1.)

Particularly note the position of the thumb of the left hand lying across the back of the top card of the pack, the position of the first finger along the top edge and the second, third and fourth fingers along the sides. The fourth finger presses the cards against the base of the thumb. If the pack is held as explained and shown in Fig. 1, you can readily move the thumb into the position shown in Fig. 2 without disturbing your former grip on the cards.

At this position a firm downward pressure is made on the side of the cards by the ball of the left thumb, and the top card or cards are allowed to open. The thumb now swings under the top card into position in the right palm, as shown in Fig. 3.

The fingers of the right hand move along the top edge, and the thumb of the right hand moves along the opposite edge, simulating the act of squaring the pack. (See Fig. 4.) This action is done twice. At the end of the second time the pack is held be-

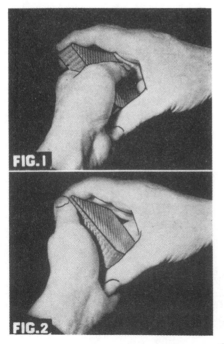

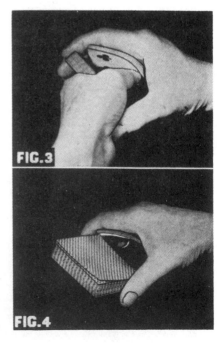

tween the thumb and first and second fingers of the right hand, and then the left hand shifts position, and the thumb, first and second fingers move twice up and down the sides of the pack, simulating the squaring up action. The right hand moves away from the left hand with the pack and places it on the table. The card is palmed.

It is no more difficult to repeat the foregoing to palm off two or more cards. The thumb of the left hand releases the desired number. Each move described is carefully planned, and until you know of a very good reason for changing these mechanics, don't. The pace should be natural and even all through.

THE REPLACEMENT

To replace a card on the top of the pack in a truly indetectable manner is a simple matter if the moves essential to such a procedure are known and carefully rehearsed, but very few card performers know these simple rudiments.

THE SLEIGHT:

You have palmed one or a packet of cards from the pack in the manner just described and desire to restore them to the top of the pack.

You will find that a light pressure of the palm at the base of the right thumb on the corner of the packet of cards palmed will cause them to bend in an arch away from your palm. The size of the arch depends on the amount of pressure. (See Fig. 1.) It is an easy matter with the cards arched in this manner to let the thumb of the left hand pass through the arch between the cards and the palm of the right hand. This is done as the right hand is brought over the packet in the left hand for the purpose of squaring the pack (see Fig. 2), cutting, or transferring it from the left to the right hand. Remember, though this is a very simple procedure, it is almost unknown, and is of considerable importance to good card magic.

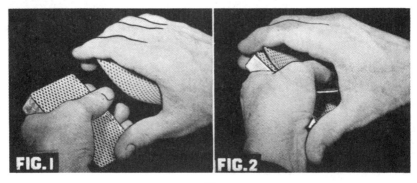

BUCKLEY'S MULTIPLE CARD PALM STEAL

This is a beautiful card steal, and all the moves blend into a rhythmic whole. It is not easy to do well, calling for considerable practice. When mastered it can be performed repeatedly in an indetectable manner.

THE SLEIGHT:

The cards that are to be palmed are first inserted into different parts of the pack fanned out in the left hand. The cards to be palmed are left protruding from the fan as they are inserted, one by one, from the right hand. The right hand closes the fanned cards together and turns the pack face down in the left hand.

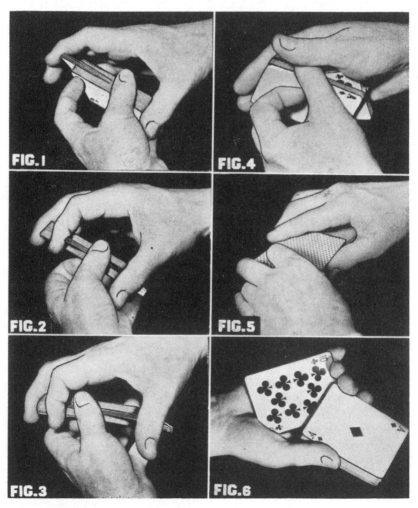

The protruding cards are then pressed into the pack diagonally (Fig. 1), and assume the position in Fig. 2, the corners protruding at the sides and ends of the pack. The fourth finger of the left hand then shifts its position and presses on the sides of the protruding cards, pushing them up into an opposite diagonal protruding position. This position is shown in Fig. 3. The corners that a moment ago protruded at the sides now protrude at the end, while those corners that protruded at the ends now protrude at the inside.

The index corners of the protruding cards are then pressed by the fourth finger of the right hand into the fleshy part of the palm of the right thumb, and the remainder of the cards are held by the left hand (see Fig. 4), which reveals the cards in position for the palming sleight to be executed.

The right hand draws the cards it is now holding almost, but not quite, out of the pack. See Fig. 5, and note position of the thumb and the second finger of the right hand. The second finger and thumb of the right hand now press on the sides of fifteen to twenty cards of the bottom of the pack and carry them from underneath to the top of the pack in a natural cutting of the pack action. (See Fig. 6.) The right hand then moves away with the required cards secretly palmed.

Don't "butcher" this sleight by not cutting the cards.

OVERHAND SHUFFLE AND MULTIPLE SHIFT

Turn to the Buckley's Multiple Card Palm Steal—now perform the palm steal as directed up to the move where the right hand is placed on the corners of the cards to be palmed. Then, instead of palming, place the pack back towards the left palm, in the crook of the fingers of the left hand, for an overhand shuffle. The right hand palm is facing the bottom of the pack, the first finger of the right hand on the top side, the other finger of the right hand at one end of the pack, and the thumb the other. The cards to be shifted lay diagonally in the pack, the first finger of the right hand moves along the side and presses the cards to be shifted further out of the pack, and as the right hand lifts the pack to commence the shuffle, the third and fourth fingers of the left hand encircle the protruding cards and retains them in the left hand as the pack is moved away to commence the shuffle.

The cards in the right hand are shuffled on the cards in the left hand. The cards first to fall are jogged in so the wanted cards may be cut or shuffled to the top.

BUCKLEY'S DOUBLE PEEK LOCATION
SHUFFLE AND PALM

Ever so often an outstanding piece of card artistry is developed by a devotee of card manipulation, and it is with a certain feeling of pride that I publish this short series of moves that blend so perfectly to deliver two cards peeked at successively in widely separated points of the pack to your palm in perfect secrecy. The effects that may be written about from that point of accomplishment are almost limitless. I shall remain content to describe only one, for the real secret is in the art of getting the two cards together and into the palm.

THE SLEIGHT:

Hold the pack, faces to palm, in your left hand, the fingers curled up at the side and pressing the opposite side into the fork of the left thumb.

The left thumb is at the side and near the non-index corner.

With the second finger of your right hand on the index corner of the pack, and your right thumb on the back of the top card near this index corner, pull the corner of the pack back and release the cards singly; in other words, riffle the corner of the pack.

Repeat this riffle and stop at about the thirteenth card (a quarter of the pack). The exact card or exact number is not important, so long as the first card stopped at is about thirteen plus or minus three.

A spectator is asked to remember the card as you hold up the pack before him and widen the break at the index corner for him to see the card.

You then close this break, but maintain a small break with the flesh of the pad of your fourth finger.

Riffle the end of the pack with the fingers of your right hand, right thumb giving support to this act at the opposite end of the pack.

Lift up packet above fourth finger break a little and insert fourth finger well into break, and spring the pack from right to left hand, keeping break with left hand fourth finger during this entire springing operation. (This method of retaining the location is the "Cardini Sleight," explained elsewhere herein.)

After springing the cards thus, take the pack between the thumb at one end and the fingers at the other end, and remove left hand, all the while maintaining the break by the simple procedure of pressing on the two ends of the pack.

Place the pack in your left hand as you come face to face with spectator number two, and transfer the break to the fourth finger pad of your left hand.

With your right hand riffle the corners of the pack as you did before for spectator number one, and ask spectator number two to remember one of the cards. With your right thumb, riffle the corners of the cards about thirteen from the top and widen the break so the corner of the card is plainly visible to him.

Close the break, but as you do so catch a portion of the flesh of the palm at the base of the thumb at the inside index corner of the pack below the spectator's card just looked at.

This is easy if you have your left thumb at the non-index corner of the pack when the card is being peeked at by the spectator, and you open the break by raising the top packet momentarily about three-quarters of an inch from the lower packet.

You now have two breaks—one with your fourth finger pad below number one spectator's card, and one with your left thumb palm flesh grip below number two spectator's card.

Hold the pack in your left hand firmly, and riffle the end of the pack with your right fingers. You may do this quite freely without losing your locations, but anyone not conversant with this fact will have surrendered himself to the idea that the cards are definitely no longer under your control. You augment this by taking the pack from your left hand into your right hand, maintaining the two breaks by the end pressure on the pack with the right thumb and fingers.

Now with your left hand take away from the pack the cards below the first spectator's card, and place them on the top of the pack.

This is just a simple cut, and it brings the first spectator's card to the bottom of the pack. The second spectator's card is now about the middle of the pack, and you are keeping the break with pressure on the ends of the pack with right thumb and fingers.

Insert the fourth finger of the left hand into the break as you lay the pack in the left hand to change the hold on the pack with your right hand in order to enable you to riffle shuffle the cards to bring the two peeked-at cards together at the bottom of the pack.

This is best accomplished by the right hand taking off the top packet (above fourth finger of the left hand), right thumb at inside index corner and second and third fingers at adjacent non-index corner of the packet.

The two packets are riffled together, the right thumb releasing the bottom card of its packet first, and then the left hand releasing one or several cards. The order in which the cards are riffled is inconsequential. However, the two packets are pushed together endwise, for reasons that shall be made clear.

The riffle shuffle is repeated. The top half of the pack is taken in the left hand, the bottom half in the right hand, and the corners riffled together in the following manner.

The two bottom cards of the right hand packet are the two peeked-at cards, so they are released first by the right thumb riffle as the packets are brought together for the shuffle, and then cards from the left hand packet are riffled onto them. The remainder of the shuffle is inconsequential.

The packets are pushed together endwise as before, but when there is about an inch of the packets protruding one from the other, the action is stopped, and the left hand takes the pack of cards, thumb at one side and fingers at the other side, and lays the pack lengthwise on the palm of the right hand. This action brings the two cards on the bottom of the pack into perfect register for palming the cards in the right hand, and only the two cards wanted, because of the manner in which they lay.

The palming of the two cards takes only an instant. The right hand, with the two cards thus palmed, swings over the back of the pack, and the side of the first finger of the right hand presses on the end of the protruding packet of cards, forcing them home square with the pack.

The left hand carries the pack to the table and gives it a fair cut as the right hand with the two palmed cards enters the inside coat pocket to take out an envelope.

The cards are secretly dropped into the envelope which is then sealed and instantly brought forth to be opened and the selected cards discovered.

BUCKLEY'S TOP PALM SLIDE OFF

This is another of those unique pieces of artistry in card manipulation. Like many other methods herein described, it is only for the fellow that wants to do things correctly.

THE SLEIGHT:

Hold the pack of cards in your left hand, faces towards the palm, left thumb lying across the middle of the top card, first finger at the index corner of the pack. The second, third and fourth fingers are at the side of the pack with the tips of the fingers a little above the level of the top card.

The right hand now covers the pack, thumb at middle of end of pack, first finger at non-index corner of other end of pack, second and third fingers adjacent to first finger, and fourth fingertip on the extreme corner of the top card of the pack.

With a light downward pressure, the top card is moved outward and a little over the end of the corner of the pack, and then turned diagonally, pivoted at the fork of the left thumb, to assume a position running exactly parallel with the right hand covering the card.

At the time of the pivoting action of the card, a light downward pressure of this right hand fourth finger causes the inside end of the top card to tilt upwards. This upward action is checked by the left thumb lying across the pack and a little above it.

The right hand now moves slowly towards the right, the right thumb sliding along the inside and to the corner of the pack, and the fingers of the right hand sliding along the other end until the first finger of the right hand reaches the corner of the pack. In this manner the card is moved with and under cover of the right hand, and also under the left thumb, which at no time during the moves described changes its position across the pack.

The top card clears the left thumb tip as the right first finger and thumb reach the corners of the pack, and the top card springs into the right palm.

The right hand is not immediately withdrawn with the card palmed, but slides back along the ends as if squaring the pack. This time the card palmed is carried over the left thumb and not under it as before. The left thumb aids in positioning the palmed card in the right hand.

A few simple trials will prove how really effective this method is in practice, and also prove to your own satisfaction the small amount of skill required to perform it indetectably.

BERG'S TOP PALM

The pack is held face down in your left hand in dealing position.

Now move your left thumb to the non-index corner of the side of the top card of the pack, where it remains during the sleight.

The fourth finger of the right hand is rested on the back of the top card at the index corner.

The first finger of the right hand is on the non-index corner near the left thumb.

The right hand is over the top of the pack, but does not completely hide the pack from view, leaving at the inside corner a quarter of the back card in view.

A light pressure on the top card under the fourth finger of the right hand pivots the top card at the corner against the left thumb and causes it to turn diagonally up into the right palm quite indetectably.

The right hand moves back and forth along the ends, simulating a squaring action of the pack in order to heighten the illusion of complete fairness.

THE ALLERTON TOP PALM

This is a method originated and used with complete success by Bert Allerton, the society entertainer, and a master of close-up skullduggery.

THE SLEIGHT:

The pack is held in the left hand, face down on the palm, as just described in the Berg Top Palm. The left thumb is at the non-index corner.

In this position the left thumb can count any desired number of cards by simply applying downward pressure on the corner of the pack, and letting the cards spring away from the thumb, one at a time. This counting is done very quickly as the right hand approaches the pack to take up its position of squaring the ends, or simulating such an action. At the moment the right hand covers the pack, the left thumb passes between the pack and the counted-off cards, pressing them into the right palm.

ONE HAND TOP PALM — JUDSON COLE

This is a masterpiece in manipulative magic with cards. It has been published before, and my reason for including it here is that I believe it was originated by Judson Cole, some twenty years or more ago. The reason for its apparent obscurity for so many years is undoubtedly due to the extreme difficulty to do the sleight well and without undue hesitation.

It should, however, be mastered by all top ranking card manipulators, for it has no equal to my knowledge. It fulfills all the requirements of perfect magic.

You cut the pack and palm the card, not only indetectably, but without a trace of a movement of the fingers in doing so, and all this with one hand.

THE SLEIGHT:

The pack is squared up, and is lying on the table ready to be cut. The right hand is placed in the following position to cut off half the pack.

The right thumb is placed near the index corner of the inside end of the pack, and the first finger at the non-index corner of the opposite end of the pack.

The second finger near the first finger aids in holding the pack, but the third finger is a passenger, and remains idle alongside the second finger.

The fourth finger rests on the back of the top card about a quarter of an inch from the corner.

As the top twenty or so cards are lifted off the pack between the thumb and first and second fingers of the right hand, the fourth finger presses on the back of the top card and causes it to move in a pivotal action against the second finger until it clears the thumb, and then it springs up into the palm. It sounds easy, but it's a real corker to acquire the knack. I wish I could describe it better. It seems to me as I do it while writing this that it is a matter of the right amount of pressure at the various places that can only be acquired by practice. However, it is really worth it. The real accomplishment is in completing the palm in the time it takes to normally cut the pack.

PALM OFF THE SECOND TOP CARD WHILE TOP CARD IS VISIBLY DRAWN ONTO THE PACK

This is a very deceptive and practical sleight that has many applications for a skillful operator or one partial to double lifts.

THE SLEIGHT:

Having secretly lifted two cards as one from the top of the pack (see "Double Lift"), the two cards are placed face up on the top of the pack, half the two cards protruding over the side of the pack and held between the second and third fingers of the left hand, second and third fingers on the back, and the left thumb on the face.

The two cards are turned face down by catching them at both ends between the fingers and thumb of the right hand, but otherwise retain their position protruding over the pack.

When they are turned face down, the left thumb draws the visible card onto the pack, while the left fingers press upon the under card, pushing it into the right palm. The presence of this card is unsuspected if the moves are carried out correctly.

The right hand with the card palmed should square the pack, cut it or place it on the table. It is nearly always best to perform some commonplace act after the card is palmed rather than abruptly move the hand away with the card palmed, although there may be some exceptions. I cannot recall any at the moment.

TO PALM FROM OFF THE TOP OF THE PACK AN EXACT NUMBER OF CARDS UP TO TEN

This is a perfect piece of deception, and leaves nothing to be desired. In some respects it is like the Berg method described herein for palming a single card.

THE SLEIGHT:

Hold the pack face down in your left hand, first finger at the end about three-eighths of an inch from the index corner, the second finger up the side also about three-eighths of an inch from the index corner, the third and fourth fingers up the side, the thumb on the side at the non-index corner.

The position described is for executing the left "thumb count" or corner "riffle."

By pressing down on the side edges of the cards near the non-index corner with the left thumb and bending over on the pack the second, third and fourth fingertips, the cards are easily allowed to spring away from the left thumb silently, with just sufficient movement to enable you to release the required number of cards, six for example.

The thumb then presses against the side of the packet of six cards which it has just released, and causes them to move against the second finger over the edge about an eighth of an inch.

Looking down on the pack, the cards show no sign of disarrangement because the left thumb conceals the step made by moving this packet of six cards.

The right hand is now brought over the pack, the right thumb at one end and the first, second and third fingers at the other end. The inside of the fourth finger at the first joint is placed against the side corner near the index, and by pressure with the fourth finger on the side of the packet of six cards, the cards are caused to pivot against the left thumb over the first finger of the left hand. Then by a light down pressure of the fourth finger of the right hand, they are caused to pivot on the tip of the first finger of the left hand and flip up into the right hand palm.

The fingers and the thumb then execute a sliding motion along the ends of the pack as if squaring the cards.

Your time will be well spent in mastering this sleight.

You may try holding the first finger of the left hand along the side of the pack and pivot the packet up into the palm over the index corner of the pack, instead of over the first finger as described above.

TOP PALM
ONE OR SEVERAL CARDS

This is another of those little method originalities that may have an appeal to my readers.

THE SLEIGHT:

The pack is held face down in your left hand, left thumb in position at the non-index corner for a thumb count, first finger at the end of the pack, second, third and fourth fingers of the left hand up the side of the pack.

Thumb count the number of cards you desire to palm off the pack. Lift and press this packet of cards to be palmed between the left thumb and second finger so that it may thus be moved up and over the pack.

The third and fourth fingers of the left hand press the pack against the left thumb palm.

The packet of cards to be palmed is held between the left thumb and second finger level and squared with the rest of the pack until the right hand is brought nearly over the pack. At no time does the right hand completely cover the pack.

The left thumb and second finger carry the packet to meet the right palm as it takes a position, right thumb at one end and right fingers at the other end.

The pack is thus transferred to the right hand from the left hand, and the packet of cards is palmed.

I repeat, the sleight can be performed without undue haste quite indetectably and it has several practical advantages over other top palms. However, it requires correct timing, sureness and an easy manner. These are acquired from practice and practical usage.

The above actions reversed may be used advantageously for replacing cards from the palm onto the pack.

THE FAN LOCATION

THE EFFECT:

With the pack held in the left hand, face down, the left thumb on the back of the index inside corner, the right hand pressure fans the cards in a half circle, and a spectator is asked to touch one card.

The card touched is withdrawn partly from the pack, spectator notes the card, and you return the card to the middle of the pack, pushing it home level with the other cards.

You close up the fan, square the edges and cut the pack.

The spectator's card is on the bottom of the pack.

THE SLEIGHT:

This is a beautiful piece of deception almost unknown in principle among more than a few experts. I have made use of it for many years, but have refrained from being over-zealous showing it.

The principle lies in a simple maneuver, which is as follows:

When you place the card in the center of the fanned-out pack, the end of the card is square on the semi-circle of fanned cards. It is pushed all the way home into the pack all right, and therefore looks quite fair and regular, for the position described.

You close the fanned pack, into which the selected card is in the middle, by placing your second and third fingers of your right hand on the right side edge of the pack and pushing the cards together into the fork of the left thumb.

Then take the pack in the right hand between the thumb and middle fingers, thumb on top, and turn the pack over endwise. This action brings the cards face up in the left hand.

Firmly tap the outer end of the pack with the fingers of the left hand to square ends, but don't touch the inside ends of the cards in the pack.

If you have followed these instructions, the selected card will be projecting inwards from the pack by three-sixteenths of an inch, and by a "double cut," as explained under that title, the card can be secretly brought to the top of the pack.

If you wish to learn the name of the card, you may do so secretly in the very simplest manner. When the card is the top card of the pack, next to your hand, pack face up in your left hand, the index end of the top card is exposed to your view by the left thumb pushing all the cards but the one next to the left palm, and thus exposing the index of the selected card momentarily.

THE FAN LOCATION AMPLIFIED

I have already described this sleight for bringing the card to the top of the pack. The difference between the method of bringing the card to the bottom from that of bringing the card to the top resides in action of closing the fan. If the card is to be cut to the bottom, then after returning the selected card all the way into the fan of cards, you rely solely on the fact that its end edge is not lying on the same circular line with the end edges of the other cards, resulting in a slight protrusion of one end when the fan is closed.

If you close the fan from the left side, the ends are reversed by this action, and cutting to the protruding card by the double cut method, that is, by pressing down on the protruding edge with the right thumb as it pushes it home into the pack, you make the break above the card and permit it to be immediately double cut to the top.

If you desire to cut it to the bottom, the thumb lifts the protruding end slightly as it presses home the card into the pack, and thus forms the break below the card which permits it to be immediately double cut to the bottom of the pack.

A NOVEL PALM

This is a simple sleight that has several good features to recommend it, besides being original and never before (to my knowledge) published.

Palming a Card From the Bottom of the Pack With the Left Hand After Shuffling, and Returning the Card Reversed to the Bottom of the Pack.

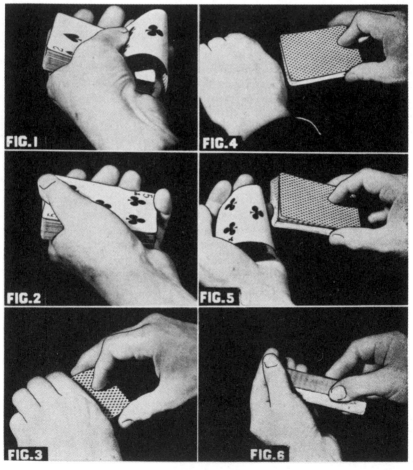

THE SLEIGHT:

After an overhand shuffle, hold the pack in your left hand, first, second and third fingers on one side of the pack, fourth finger at the end of the pack sticking straight up, and thumb on the back of the top card near its top end. (See Fig. 1.)

The left thumb presses on the face of the bottom card and slides it against the fourth finger, causing the card to bend. (See Fig 2.) The left hand at the same time turns back of hand uppermost, bringing the pack face down.

The right hand seizes the end of the pack protruding from the left hand (Fig. 3), and carries the pack away, lays it on the table and cuts it.

The left hand remains still, holding the card concealed (Fig. 4), while the right hand carries out the cutting operation.

The right hand takes up the pack and returns it to the left hand in position for dealing. As the right hand approaches the left hand, the left hand is brought face up, and the pack is laid on the concealed card.

A trial will disclose the fact that the moves can be made indetectably. However, it does take some practice to synchronize the moves in a continuous, well-timed function.

CHANGING A CARD IN THE ACT OF TURNING THE CARD OVER

This is a very deceptive move as you will shortly discover after a trial.

Place two cards together on the table. Bend them so they stay as one. Moisten them ever so little if you find it necessary to do so. The two cards are lying face up as one, the right hand has the pack held between the third and fourth fingers and the fork of the thumb. The left thumb tip is placed in the middle, about one inch from the end of the card, and the second and third fingers slide under the two cards at the far side. In this manner the two cards are turned face down.

The left thumb draws the bottom card of the two onto the bottom of the pack, and the second and third fingers press on the back of the card to hold the other card on the table.

Of course, you may commence with the cards face down and change the card in the act of turning it face up. In the latter instance the pack of cards should be held facing the palm so the card will be the same way as the other cards of the pack when the move is completed.

THE THROW CHANGE

This sleight has stood the test of time.

I have used it since 1910 in an effect called "The Card Under the Foot," published in "Thirty Card Effects." It is too good to pass up. I do not know of its publication elsewhere.

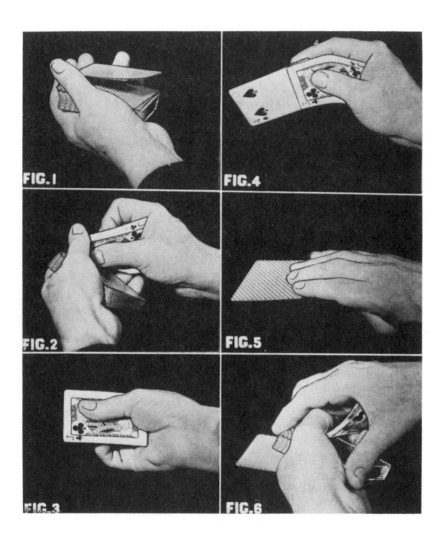

FIG. I

FIG. 4

FIG. 2

FIG. 5

FIG. 3

FIG. 6

THE SLEIGHT:

The pack of cards is held in the left hand, and two cards are lifted as one off the top of the pack. (See Fig. 1.)

The two cards are held in the right hand and shown as one to the spectator (See Fig. 2), who rightly denies it is his card; whereupon the performer seemingly throws the card on the floor face down. Actually the right thumb draws the face card into the palm, and the fingers push the other card forward and let it slide to the floor. The hand is only six inches off the floor when the move is executed.

The card palmed in the right hand is conveyed to the top of the pack.

The moves should be made deliberately and unhurriedly. This sleight can be used to form the basis for many good card effects.

HINDU SHUFFLE AND CUT LOCATION

This is an original sleight which is useful, very pretty and is extremely simple to perform.

THE EFFECT:

Performer, holding the pack of cards in his left hand, withdraws about twenty-six cards from the bottom of the pack endwise with his right hand, and proceeds to draw off small packets consisting of six or seven cards from the right hand packet onto the left hand packet.

When all the cards are in the left hand, the right hand then takes the pack and with a short toss causes the pack to separate, and about half the cards from the top of the pack pass into the left hand. The cards remaining in the right hand are placed on the cards in the left hand. The top card is taken and placed on the table.

The moves described are repeated, and another card is dealt off the top of the pack. On turning over the cards dealt, they are seen to be the chosen ones. This is an excellent sleight for finding four aces preceding any ace trick.

THE SECRET WORKING:

The four aces are secretly brought to the top of the pack by methods herein explained.

Executing the moves as explained in the described effect, place your fourth finger of the left hand down on the aces as the lower half of the pack is Hindu shuffled onto them.

Take the pack in your right hand, fingers at one end and thumb at the other at the outside corners. A light pressure on the ends of the pack retains the secret break above the aces. Toss the cards above the aces off into the left hand, and place the cards remaining in your right hand on those in the left hand. The aces are then on the top. Take only one off and repeat the shuffle and cuts as described. The moves should all be performed at a brisk, even pace.

BUCKLEY'S METHOD OF DOUBLE CUTTING CARDS
TO THE TOP OF THE PACK

This sleight is one of the most useful sleights in card conjuring, and unless one is fully aware of what is happening it is impossible to follow, though ridiculously simple to perform. It should be practiced thoroughly before being used in public.

THE SLEIGHT:

Place the pack in your left hand face up and cut off about half the pack with the right hand. Note the card cut to (say it is the three of clubs), and that is the card it is desired to bring to the bottom of the pack. Remember, the pack is held face up.

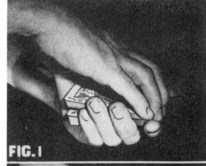

FIG. I

When the cards lifted off above three of clubs are replaced, the tip of the fourth finger of the left hand is inserted above the three of clubs to retain a break. (See Fig. 1.)

The thumb of the right hand retains this break while the left hand is shifted to form a second break about halfway between the three of clubs and the top of the pack. (See Fig. 2.) The illustration depicts this latter break to be at the nine of spades.

FIG.2

The right hand transfers the packet with the nine of spades at the bottom of it to the bottom of the pack. The act is a simple cut.

FIG.3

The right hand returns to its former position, obtains the packet with the three of clubs and transfers this packet to the bottom, and that's all there is to it.

Of course, you may hold the pack face down while performing this sleight, depending on the requirements of the effect.

Perhaps I should elaborate on the above to better convey the beauty of this simple sleight. Say the bottom card is the ten of clubs. The pack is face down on the table. Pick up the pack, perform a riffle shuffle, keeping the ten on the bottom, and square the pack on the table. Cut off about twenty-six cards with your right hand and place them on your left hand. Place the remainder of the pack on top of the packet in your left hand, inserting the little fingertip as you do so. Square the pack.

Then using the double cut as just described and illustrated in Figs. 1, 2 and 3, double cut and the ten of clubs will be on the bottom, and no onlooker unfamiliar with the description will have the least suspicion of the ruse employed.

THE TRANSFER OF A CARD

by John Brown Cook, that brilliant "Close Up" card and coin manipulator

This is an extremely novel sleight that lends itself to the secret transfer of a card placed into the pack to the top position. It is accomplished as follows.

Performer shows a card, the Ace of Spades. Holding the Ace in the right hand and the pack in the left, he riffles about ten or a dozen of the top cards of the pack with his left thumb and inserts the Ace into the break in the pack below the riffled cards, leaving about one inch of the Ace protruding.

The right hand is then placed over the pack, the fingers on the protruding end of the Ace of Spades and the thumb on the index corner of the opposite end of the pack.

The first finger of the right hand presses the Ace into the pack, causing it to pass in diagonally. The fourth finger of the left hand presses the Ace, causing it to align on the sides with the other cards, but protrude from the inside end of the pack, extending therefrom about an inch. The position of the right hand completely hides this from view of the spectators.

The right hand is brought down the pack lengthwise to a position about one inch from the end farthest from the body, and the tips of the fingers of the right hand, pressing lightly on the card, slide it openly over the end of the pack towards the body, until it is level with the protruding end of the Ace of Spades.

The right thumb then presses up on the face of the Ace, and the top card and the Ace are withdrawn as one card.

As the two cards leave the end of the pack, they are rotated endwise and turned over, bringing the Ace of Spades face up on top of the pack. The thumb and fingers of the left hand maintain a break between the two cards and the top of the pack to facilitate their being turned over again. This time they are turned face down by the finger and thumb at opposite ends.

The top card is drawn off by the right thumb, and, without exposing the card, it is placed into the pack, aided by a thumb riffle as made the first time; and the Ace of Spades is again shown to be on top of the pack.

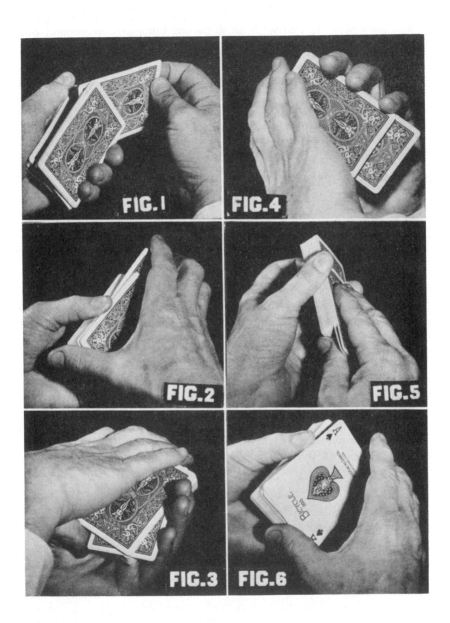

THE PASS

A pass, in the true acceptance of the term, in conjuring parlance, is the act of interchanging the upper and the lower sections of the pack secretly and without apparent unnatural movement of the hands or cards. If you read anything differently into the act, it no longer continues to be a "pass". When these conditions are relaxed, most magicians can execute a so-called "pass" in an acceptable manner. Some methods rotate the pack and expose the bottom card. Such a pass is only conditionally practical, no matter how secretly it may be performed.

For those who do not wish to replace the "pass" by more recently developed sleight that attain not the same but similar sought after results, then I recommend to your attention the following:

PASS AND DOUBLE LIFT

Hold the pack in your left hand, face down, left thumb across the pack, the first joint of the left second finger one inch from the adjacent corner, the left first finger bent under the pack against the bottom card, the left fourth finger maintaining a break at the place the pass is to be executed.

The right hand holds the pack—the mid-section of the right thumb at the inside non-index corner end. The second joint of the right first finger at the adjacent end index corner. The first and second finger of the left hand carry the under packet across under the top packet, without tilting it, to the right hand, second, third and fourth fingers, which curl over the end of the lower packet and grip it. The left hand may now be removed as both packets are held in the right hand. The left thumb pushes over the top card about half an inch toward the right hand, and the right hand turns inward through an arc of 30 degrees without changing its grip, causing the under packet to be brought up under the protruding top card. At this moment the fingers of the left hand extend under the right hand around the side edges of the shifted packet, and press it home under the protection of the top card.

You may either lift off the top card and place it in the pack, or double lift. It's as near perfect as any I have seen, and was imparted to me as a table shift, in 1909. I have slightly modified the basic principle.

When you can do this "pass", try this "shift" instead of the "pass". Hold the pack on the right hand as just explained, and with the fingers of the left hand push out a card from the center of the pack, under the right palm, but instead of trying to palm it, crook the second, third and fourth fingers of the right hand under it and remove the left hand. Isn't that something! It beats the side palm all to pieces.

A FALSE SHUFFLE PAR EXCELLENCE

This original shuffle keeps the red cards and the black cards separated from each other. It can be performed before anyone and will defy detection, that's how good it is. Try it for yourself.

THE METHOD:

With the red cards above the black cards, or vice versa, hold the pack in your left hand, the first finger bent on the back of the pack, the second, third and fourth fingers on the low side, and the thumb at the index corner of the high side.

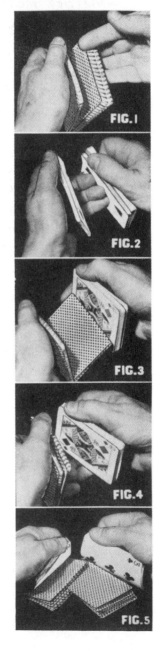

FIG. I

FIG. 2

FIG. 3

FIG. 4

FIG. 5

Riffle three-fourths of the pack with the left thumb. The second, third and fourth fingers of the right hand support the riffled cards. (See Fig. 1.)

The second and third fingers of the left hand raise the packet of cards to the right thumb. (See Fig. 2.) Note the position of the right thumb holding two-thirds of the cards of this packet, with a small division indicating the other third held against the right thumb by the left fingers.

The right hand is raised, and the thirteen or so cards that are not retained by the right thumb are rotated back to the left thumb, which retains them. (See Figs. 3 and 4), and note in Fig. 4 a slight opening separating the packet of red cards from the packet of black cards held in the left hand.

The hands are brought a suitable distance from each other and the cards riffle shuffled, as in Fig. 5.

A condition that must be observed while carrying out the riffle shuffle is as follows: Exhaust the under packet of the two packets in the left hand while riffling into them less than half the cards in the right hand.

Riffle more than half the cards in the right hand before commencing to riffle the top packet, the red cards, in the left hand. That's simple enough to remember and do. Try it.

All the moves should be performed at a brisk, even pace, without haste or undue hurry, and the result is amazing and will pass indefinitely as a fair riffle shuffle, unless you are foolish enough to say, "Tell me, what do you think of this false shuffle?"

ANOTHER METHOD OF REVERSING A CARD

The effect described depends on a very subtle method of reversing cards that several spectators peek at in the pack. Without any further handling of the pack the cards are spread face down across the table. The several cards peeked at by the spectators are seen reversed, as depicted in Fig. 5.

The sleight itself has numerous possibilities, and was first called to my attention by Egon Pischke, a member of the Society of American Magicians showing considerable promise at card handling. However, I do not know whom to credit with the origination of this sleight. The first part of the move is similar to my method of shifting a card to the bottom, but the turnover is distinctly different.

The method of executing the sleight is as follows:

The performer, with the pack held in his left hand, opens the pack at the corners about sixteen cards from the bottom with his right hand, inviting a spectator to note the card shown. The corners are released, and a break held by the left fourth finger.

The right hand momentarily withdrawn from the pack to indicate by said action that no breaks are held. (Don't say anything about breaks.) Performer approaches another spectator several feet from the first, and, bringing his right hand to the pack, executes the turnover of the first card.

See the illustrations. Fig. 1 depicts the first peeked-at card, the Jack of spades, about sixteen from the bottom, being pushed out of the pack by the fingers of the left hand under the cover of the right hand. The card is pushed thus and engaged at the corner between the third and fourth fingers, and a slight movement of the hands brings the Jack of spades clear of the pack as in Fig. 2.

The fingers of the right hand raise the top packet of cards as the Jack of spades is dropped into the crook of the fingers of the left hand, as shown in Fig. 3, and the fingers of the left hand press on the face of the card, causing it to be pressed into the pack reversed, as in Fig. 4. All this takes but a second, as you address spectator number two, instructing him or her to note a card also.

For the best effect the position of the cards noted should be approximately evenly spaced when the cards are spread, as in Fig. 5.

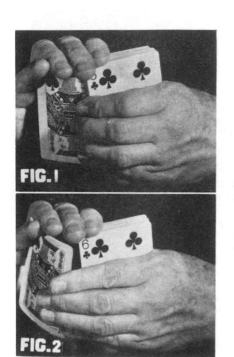

FIG. I

FIG.2

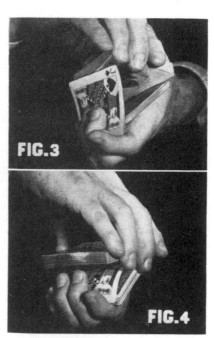

FIG.3

FIG.4

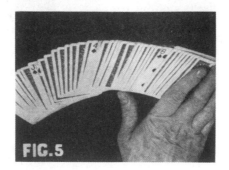

FIG.5

85

THE EXTRAORDINARY QUEENS

THE EFFECT:

The performer, after shuffling the pack of cards, extends his left hand, holding the pack, and invites a spectator to peek at a card near the middle of the pack. Performer squares up the pack, and without shuffling or cutting, turns the top card of the pack over, face up, on the pack, remarking, "Ah, a queen. An extraordinary card is a black queen. They always go in pairs." Then he turns over the next card, using the first queen to do so. The two cards are turned face down and held together in the right hand between the thumb at one end, and the second and third finger at the other.

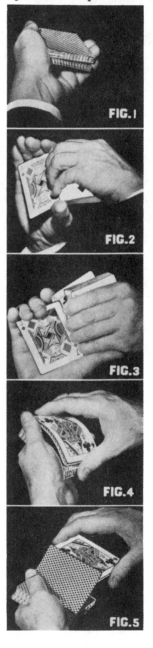

FIG. 1

FIG. 2

FIG. 3

FIG. 4

FIG. 5

The left thumb riffles about a dozen cards, the right hand inserts the two cards into the break, and the two cards are pushed diagonally through the pack and drawn out the other side between the fingers and thumb, which hold them together face down. The spectator is asked to name the chosen card. When it is announced, the two face down cards are spread apart, and the chosen card is seen face about between them.

ARRANGEMENT:

Two black queens on top of the pack.

SLEIGHTS:

False shuffle to retain the two top cards on top of the pack.

The peek.

The fourth finger flesh break to retain the position of the peeked-at card.

The side slip to remove the peeked-at card from the center of the pack to the right palm, and from the palm slip it under the top card of the pack.

A double lift.

THE WORKING:

After the card is peeked at by a spectator, the performer retains its position by secretly inserting his fourth finger tip under the card. See Fig. 1.

The right hand squares the pack while the fingers of the left hand execute the side slip, secretly pushing the peeked-at card into the right palm without removing the fingers and thumb of the right hand from the ends of the pack. (See Fig. 2.) The top queen is pushed over the side of the pack about a quarter of an inch by the left thumb, and the palmed card in the right hand is slipped under it (See Fig. 3) and the pack squared.

The top queen is turned face up. As this is being done, the spectator's card is pushed over slightly, and the tip of the little finger of the left hand is placed under it. (See Fig. 4.)

The queen now face ·up is laid squarely upon the spectator's card, and the two cards lifted off the pack as one card.

The next queen is flipped over with the queen held face up with the spectator's card hidden beneath it. (See Figs. 5, and 6.)

The three cards are now held together, turned over, inserted in the pack, pushed in diagonally, (See Figs. 7 and 8) drawn out the other side, (See Fig. 9) and spread apart, revealing the spectator's card face up between the queens. (See Fig. 10.)

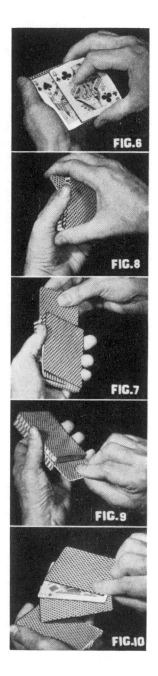

87

A DIFFERENT TOP CHANGE
Mass Hypnotism

THE EFFECT:

The top card of the pack of cards, face to palm in the left hand, is pushed over the pack by the left thumb as the pack is raised up before a spectator.

The card noted by the spectator is drawn back onto the pack, and in the fairest manner the noted card is pushed off the top of the pack and falls face down on the table or floor. The described moves are repeated several times, each time before a different spectator. The spectators are requested on the count of three to name the card in front of them and turn it over. The spectators all call the same card, but on turning over the card before them they are seen to be different cards than the card named. The performer says, "That, ladies and gentlemen, is mass hypnotism."

The effect is entirely dependent on a one hand top change as follows:

The top card of the pack, say the Jack of spades, is pushed across the pack by the left thumb, and is supported on its underside by the second and third fingertips, and on its bottom end by the fourth finger, against which the card rests while the pack is held at a slight angle. (See Fig. 1.)

The left thumb draws back the second top card, the two of spades, as in Fig. 2, until it clears the inside edge of the top card, the Jack of spades, as in Fig. 3.

The Jack of spades is drawn back on the pack passing under the two of spades as in Fig. 3.

The two of spades is then pushed off the top of the pack by the left thumb and allowed to fall face down on the table. The same moves are repeated as often as the performer thinks advisable, but no spectator should be allowed to see the card twice, so perform the sleight at well-distributed points among your audience. I have given the foregoing routine merely to show the possibilities of the sleight.

AN AMAZING LOCATION

A pack of cards is shuffled, and without looking at any of the cards, the performer springs the pack from the right hand to the left several times, and a spectator is requested to tell you to stop, which you do as requested. You extend the packet of cards already sprung into the left hand, asking that the spectator look at the card at which he stopped you. The balance of the cards are replaced on the noted card, and the pack is riffle shuffled several times and cut. The cards are spread face up on the table.

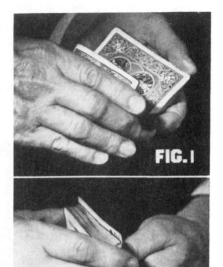

FIG. I

FIG. 2

The performer asks the spectator to place the tips of his fingers on the back of his performer's hand. He passes his hand over the cards and finds the chosen card.

The whole effect is based upon the riffle location, a little known sleight. Spring the cards from the right hand to the left hand and observe how easy it is to retain in your right hand the last card, that is, the top card of the pack. Simply request a spectator to say "Stop!" while you riffle, and you stop with only the top card in your right hand. Ridiculously simple as it is, it will not be apparent to anyone. Try it. (See Fig. 1.)

The second top card is the chosen card. Don't look at the top card or any of the cards. Simply replace the card in your right hand on the noted card as if you were replacing a packet of cards, and spring the pack once again just to emphasize all is fair. Then proceed to riffle shuffle, but retain the two cards on top. Execute an overhand shuffle and sight the chosen one. (See Fig. 2.)

Shuffle fairly and spread the pack face up. Ask the spectator to tell you if he sees his card, and proceed to locate the card by telling him it will be quite impossible for him to avoid giving you an indication which is the card while you pass your hand over the cards if he will only rest his fingertips on the back of your hand. Of course if you prefer it you may know the second top card before you start and then let the spectator shuffle as you know the card before it is chosen.

ONE HAND CRIMP

Your Card?

The Effect:

The performer has someone shuffle the pack of cards so that it is not possible to know the location of a single card in the pack.

After receiving the shuffled pack from the spectator, the performer holds the pack face down in his right hand, and with the first finger and thumb draws off small packets of cards into his left hand, simulating the "Hindu Shuffle".

When approximately the center of the pack is reached, the performer holds up the packet in his left hand, and with his left thumb pushes the top card of the left hand packet over the edge of the packet so the name of the card may be observed by the spectator, whom he requests to remember the card.

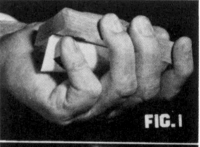

FIG. 1

Performer drops the right hand packet on top of the spectator's card, squares the pack, riffle shuffles, cuts the pack about the middle, replaces the cut and squares the pack.

Performer, holding the cards face down in his left hand, then turns over the top card and remarks, "That is not your card." Removing the card, he turns over the pack and replaces this card face up on the now face up pack, turns the pack face down and asks the spectator to name the chosen card. The pack is spread, and the spectator's card is seen in the middle of the pack face up in the face down pack.

FIG. 2

The Sleights:

Convexing a card; the double lift.

The Working:

Commence by having a spectator remove a pack of cards from its case and thoroughly shuffle the pack, remarking, "Do it well and don't let me see any cards because I am going to try my best to mystify you."

On receiving the pack of cards, the performer places the pack face down on his left hand and lowers his hand with the pack to

90

his side while talking. He executes the "crimp" by bending the bottom card back with the little finger. (See Fig. 1.) Fig. 2 is an audience view of Fig. 1. If you do this with the other fingers, the move may be detected, so practice the move with the little finger only.

Execute the Hindu shuffle until you reach the middle of the pack, and have the top card of the left hand packet noted by a spectator. Drop the right hand packet on the noted card, square the pack and riffle the pack. Cut the crimped card to the bottom. The spectator's card is then on top. Riffle shuffle, keeping the spectator's card on top, and finish the effect in your own pet way. Personally I prefer to ask the spectator to call "Stop!" while I deal and produce his card at the position stopped. That, however, requires second dealing.

Edward Marlow, one of the most brilliant card manipulators of this century, offers a use for this method of "crimping" in his book "Let's See The Deck".

The Count

(Second Method)

This is in all probability the simplest and most deceptive means of falsely counting a number of cards as a lesser number.

Hold the packet of cards to be counted in your left hand, face down, first finger at one end, second, third and fourth fingers up the side, and the thumb at the non-index corner of the top card. The thumb slides the top card across the pack into the right hand, and the right hand receives it on the fingers with the right thumb. The left thumb returns to the edge of the packet at the same position it pushed off the first card. (This is important.) The second card is pushed over the packet into the right hand as before.

Now for the false move. The left thumb again returns to the non-index corner and this time pushes off all the cards as one card, except the bottom card of the packet, and the right hand receives them as it did the first two. The last card is snapped around to emphasize that it is but one.

Try it. You will be amazed. Some practice may be necessary before the sleight can be executed smoothly.

The Palm Unsurpassed

(Original)

This is probably the best method yet devised of palming off the pack either one, two or three cards. Try it, and prove or disprove it for yourself.

The pack is held face down in your left hand, the four fingers up one side, your thumb across the top card. The right hand is over the pack, fingers at one end, thumb at the other.

The right hand, in the position described, slides the pack forward in the left hand. The left hand, in the position described, retains the bottom card, that is, it prevents the bottom card from moving, and the pack, minus the bottom card, is moved forward until the back end of the pack is a little more than half way across the back of the bottom card, thus bringing the tip of the right thumb, supporting the end of the pack, into the middle of the back of the bottom card of the pack. The left thumb and fingers retain the pack, and the right thumb moves down to the end of the bottom card and bends the exposed end of the back of the card up around the end of the pack, and the left thumb clips it onto the back of the pack. The right hand moves the pack out a little. This position is shown in Fig. 1.

The left hand now supports the pack and the bottom card wrapped around its end, the first, second and third fingers on the bottom, the thumb on the top. The right hand may be removed for a moment to perform some natural action, to return a moment later and relieve the left hand of the pack in the most open manner while the left hand retains the bottom card, holding the hand in a position to palm a card seems impossible. See Fig. 2. The hand may be placed without haste in the pocket and the card removed. I suggest if the card is palmed in the left hand, the hand be inserted in the right breast pocket.

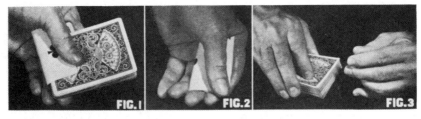

The moves are the same for two or three cards. Of course, you must straighten the card or cards before bringing them from your pocket. An excellent strategym is to transfer the pack from the left to the right hand with the card bent around the pack as described, and palm the card in the right hand as the pack is again returned to the left hand.

Those who learn to master this sleight will find it worth more than the price paid for this book.

Bottom Palm of a Single Card

(Original)

Hold the pack in the right hand, face down, the first, second and third fingers together at one end of the pack, the thumb at the other end of the pack, about the middle. The fourth finger is at the side of the pack near the corner and close to the third finger so there is no space between the fingers. It is very necessary to hold the pack fairly close to the right palm, well down into the fork of the right thumb.

The fingers of the left hand, in the act of taking the pack from the right hand, pass under the pack, the thumb above the pack. The first finger pushes the bottom card, causing the bottom card to pivot against the fourth finger of the right hand and swing out under the right hand palm, where the card is easily engaged at its index corners, only one end, between the third and fourth fingers, and the other index corner at the base of the right thumb. The left hand removes the pack. The right hand retains the card palmed. No other movements are necessary, nor should they be made.

The Top Palm

(Improved Method)

Hold the cards face down in your left hand, index corner pressed into the fork of your left thumb under pressure applied to the opposite side corner by the first and second fingers curled up the side of the pack near the bottom end. Just the tips of the first and second fingers protrude above the pack. The left thumb is drawn back across the pack so that it lies straight up the side edge of the top card, see fig. 1. The left thumb presses lightly on the back of the top card and is moved down, describing an arc. This action of the left thumb carries the top card down in an arc, pivotal point at the index corner at the fork of the thumb, see fig. 2. The top side of this card is then level with the bottom edge of the pack, the pack being held by the first finger on the side pressing the pack into the fork of the thumb, see fig. 3.

At this position the second and third fingers press the end of the card into the fork of the thumb. The right hand takes the pack from the left hand and leaves the card palmed in the left hand.

If you will practice this as instructed before a mirror, you will see the angles at which the pack must be held. The sleight is indetectable when properly performed.

THE GLIDE SHIFT

The "glide shift" is performed as follows: See the illustrations. Hold the pack of cards in your left hand. Cut off about half the pack with your right hand as shown in Fig. 1, and hold the right hand packet up so the bottom card of the right hand packet may be seen, and if desired, marked by the spectator while you hold this packet of cards as depicted.

The next picture is taken from an angle to expose the sleight to the reader's view; note the second, third and fourth fingers executing the glide with the bottom card, the ace of spades, of the right hand packet, and also observe the left hand holding its packet at the corner with the thumb ready to receive the ace of spades. In the last figure is the replacement of the right hand packet on the left hand packet, and the spectator's card, the ace of spades, goes secretly to the bottom of the pack. Try this indetectable move in front of a mirror.

Card Control

CHAPTER TWO

Conjuring at the Card Table

CONJURING *AT THE* CARD TABLE

There are very few people in the world who have the ability, the nerve and the desire to cheat successfully in card games for large stakes, especially where the rules of shuffling, dealing and discarding are rigidly adhered to.

The player who carelessly disregards these aforesaid requirements is inviting trouble. It takes no marked degree of skill to manipulate the cards with reasonable surety of doing so indetectably when the rules of make up, shuffling and discarding are relaxed. The conjurer demonstrating how gamblers cheat is fortunate in this respect. He can make his own rules because no one is betting, and the results are therefore often both spectacular and entertaining.

Under this heading shall be disclosed a number of cuts, shuffles, methods of dealing and securing a winning hand. A conjurer adept at this work and possessed of an entertaining manner can secure a very profitable livelihood by dispensing his wares for entertainment.

For years I performed this class of entertainment for the press for the publicity received in the newspapers thus deriving my profit indirectly for the time and labor spent and the pleasure it afforded in acquiring this knowledge and skill.

One essential is a pleasing disarming manner. This can be acquired by most of us individuals not fortunate enough to be thus endowed at birth.

An indetectable false riffle shuffle is a terrific advantage. The one described in the first chapter will meet most of the essential requirements. The Erdnase Triple Cut is also an invaluable asset. Bottom and second dealing are very desirable but not essential and few card conjurers can do these sleights well enough to deceive anyone but themselves but they are veritable masterpieces of this art when performed well.

A few simple builds and run-ups and lots and lots of naturalness, ease of manner and ingenuity are essential. A cold deck at the climax is a weapon not to be lightly discarded.

More than a hundred names I associate as active with playing cards today in the U.S.A. and possibly one hundred others whom I should also mention (forgive me for my memory):

Cardini, Blackstone, Rosini, Vernon, Scarne, McDougall, Carlyle, Thompson, Daley, Henri, Le Paul, Cottone, Mora, Dorny, Brane, Mulholland, Miller, Christensen, Meyer, Kardo, Sall, Haskell, Proseth, Judah, Ellias, Steel, Johnson, Walsh, Stadleman,

Marlo, Curry, Coons, Cook, Berg, Jones, Bennett, Collins, Tarbell, Allerton, Zingone, Karson, Abbott, Fox, Hugard, Grote, Haber, Cohn, Sherman, Hudson, Blackridge, Games, Brandwien, Bloom, Bulson, Fleming, Sznek, Gordon, Lotts, McKay, Kanter, Sterling, Hummer, Nimbrough, Manning, May, Jackson, Proskauer, James, Clever, Bates, Baker, Gardner, Dalban, Churchill, Christ, Wise, Lyons, Paulson, Bowyer, Rawson, Scarles, May, Dodson, Berland, Burman, Holden, Torsberg, Alberto, Boston, Farrell, Martin, Mandrake, Christofer, Flosso, Morris, Swan, Hall, Kosky, Cole, McCaffery, Zens, Smith, Schuellen, Hopkins, Channin, Osborne, Woods, Wagner, Edwards, Eckam, Marks, Wise Lyons, Reese, Rybolt, Cramer, May, Pischke, Seigal. These men are all capable of entertaining with a pack of cards, some more proficiently than others, but all very capably.

FALSE TABLE RIFFLE SHUFFLE

This should resemble to a very marked degree the true riffle shuffle so let me explain that procedure first.

The Riffle Shuffle and Cut:

The cards are placed in the middle of the table at comfortable arm's length in front of you.

Both hands seize the pack, the second fingers on one side, both thumbs on the other and the first fingers in the center.

The right hand draws away with about thirty of the bottom cards and assumes the position for the riffle shuffle.

The right hand thumb riffles about five or six cards first, and then both thumbs riffle the cards so the cards weave alternately together, a few cards from the right hand packet falling on top of the left hand packet. The packets are straightened and assume the position as shown in Fig. 1.

The third finger of the right hand and the third finger of the left hand are at the corners of the pack. The thumbs are on the side of the packets near the body. The second and third fingers of each hand are touching the ends of the cards. The two packets in this manner are pushed together entirely by the pressure of the two third fingers, one finger at the end of each packet.

As soon as this maneuver is completed, the hands draw the pack towards you, moving same at least six inches inwards. At the end of this short journey the right hand draws off the bottom half of the pack, raising the right hand with this packet of cards about three inches, and slaps them squarely on the top.

This is the riffle shuffle and you should practice these moves carefully till you can do them in a creditable manner, because until you are proficient you are not prepared to incorporate the false maneuvers which are designed so carefully to secretly blend into them.

THE BLIND RIFFLE: Do exactly as explained for the riffle shuffle. You will note a tendency for the cards to move diagonally when the third fingers press the two packets together, which in the real shuffle you prevented. Let the cards of the two packets move slightly diagonal with each other, and force them together with a steady, even pressure of the third fingers through and beyond each other about half an inch. See Fig. 3, and note the position of the third finger of each hand as the packets pass through each other and change hands. Fig. 4 shows the proper position before the cut is made.

The cut is executed as in the real shuffle. The right hand packet is drawn out of the left hand packet by the third finger and thumb and placed onto the left hand packet. Drawing the pack towards the body just before this move is made helps to deceive a close observer.

It is a move greatly admired by card players because it complies with what is expected more than other types of shuffles.

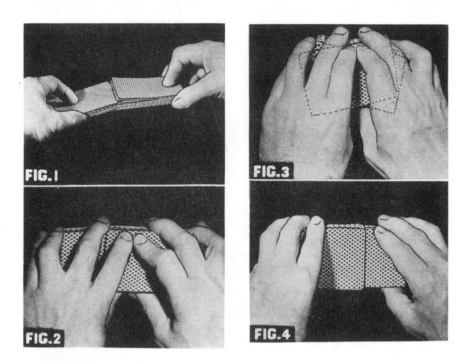

FALSE TABLE RIFFLE SHUFFLE AND CUT

An original master stroke for the execution of same—this is another of those expert subtleties.

Before commencing the preceding "false table riffle shuffle," prepare the pack to receive a bridge. To do this simply spring the cards from right to left hand a couple of times—about a two inch distance will suffice. Do it nonchalantly without any apparent purpose.

Now instead of taking the thirty or so cards from the bottom of the pack with you right hand as heretofore described, take about thirty of the top cards in your right hand. That is the only difference from the description previously given.

Be careful when you are riffling not to bend the cards too much or you may eliminate the bend already set for the bridge, which will be about twenty cards down when the pack is squared up after the false riffle shuffle is completed.

Push the pack to the center of the table and cut at the bridge, and fool the fellow that is not acquainted with this wrinkle.

THE SHIFT AND SHUFFLE

Here is a unique combination of a shift and shuffle. The Ace, King, Queen, Jack and Ten of Hearts are shown and pushed, one at a time, into the end of the pack held face down in the left hand. The pack, with the five cards still protruding, is taken into the right hand, thumb at index corner, second finger at opposite corner. The left thumb and second finger hold the five cards at the protruding corners, first finger at the end. (See Fig. 1.)

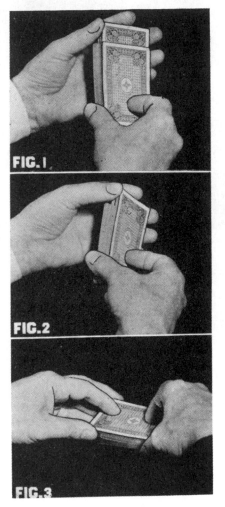

The five cards are pushed apparently into the pack. Actually they are pushed level at the end with the cards above the topmost of the five stock cards while the cards below the lowermost of the five stock cards are moved down by the action of apparently pressing the five stock cards into the pack. (See Fig. 2.) This move so far is the same as the Vernon Shift, but the cards should be held backs up as depicted.

Now make the following moves without letting go of the pack. Swing the left hand over the ends as though the first finger and thumb of the left hand were a pivot. (See Figs. 2 and 3 for these positions.)

The right hand now draws out the cards at the end, leaving the left hand holding the five stock cards on the bottom of its retained packet, and without changing the position of the fingers of either hand the two packets are riffle shuffled, care being taken to let the five stock cards fall first before the dovetailing of the cards is commenced. If this sleight is executed with ease and skill it is in a class by itself for a most perfect piece of deception.

Now here is a fine addition to the foregoing moves. With the two packets, one in each hand, ready for the riffle shuffle, riffle from the right hand packet about a dozen cards onto the table. Then riffle the stock cards, and a few extra for safety, onto the ones riffled from the right hand packet, and continue riffling both packets.

Now if you hold the right hand packet and the left hand packet at the end between the second finger and thumb and press them one into the other, but as you do so raise them about an inch off the table, you will find that the indifferent cards of the right hand packet, below the Aces on the bottom of the left hand packet, tilt to the table naturally because they lack support, and when the pushing of the packets together is complete, it is a simple, natural "cutting" action for the right hand to draw away the indifferent cards below the stock and place them on the top of the pack. This is a beautiful piece of business.

FALSE SHUFFLE

THE PUSH THROUGH SIMPLIFIED

Commence by taking not quite half the cards with the right hand from the top of the pack held face down in the left hand. Riffle the two packets together, first releasing about six or seven cards from the left hand packet. The last card of the right hand packet falls onto the top card of the left hand packet.

Push the two packets almost together, and when they are about one inch off square at the ends, slide the top card across square with the left hand packet, and pull out the right hand packet from the left hand packet and place it on top of the left hand packet.

The result is a beautiful false shuffle, with one card shifted from the top to the twenty-first position, or thereabouts.

CUT, RIFFLE SHUFFLE AND RETAIN THE TOP STOCK

Hold the pack face down in the left hand, thumb on the side at one corner, and the second and third fingers at the opposite sides near the index corner. With the thumb and second finger at opposite ends of the pack, grip about half the pack and pull it out from under and place it over the top packet, but hold it separated by the first finger, which grips it against the left thumb.

Pull out half of the lower part of this top packet and place it on top. Then draw out the under packet and fairly riffle shuffle the two packets, riffling the top portion (the stock) of the right hand packet onto the top.

BOTTOM STOCK BLIND RIFFLE

This is a sleight which I devised to deceive those acquainted with the Bottom Stock Riffle explained by Erdnase in "Expert at the Card Table." Let us prepare by having the bottom stock consist of Ace, King, Queen, Jack and Ten of Hearts. We desire to riffle the pack in a manner that those who are acquainted with the present position of these cards will be deceived by the modus operandi employed.

THE SLEIGHT:

Shuffle the same as explained in the beginning for the real riffle, with this important but slight difference. The left hand releases the first ten or so cards, commencing with the riffle shuffle. The right hand then releases at least all of the stock cards. The rest are then interwoven, and the two packets are fairly pushed together. The right hand raises its packet at the end slightly as it is pushed in, and in this manner the ten or so cards below the stock cards are separated from the stock cards. The right thumb and second finger grasp them, and drawing them out, complete the cut. I have seen some top notchers fooled by that one.

My method is to follow it up with a side squaring riffle which prepares the pack for an endwise bridge. Then fairly cut the pack once, and the bridge is in.

Now cut the pack by the Erdnase triple false cut, and say, "That is how the gamblers who cheat cut cards." Push the pack into the middle of the table and say, "I always insist on a fair cut." As you say this, cut at the bridge, complete the cut, and if you are equal to it, deal several hands and deal the stock cards from the bottom.

I will describe my method of dealing from the bottom, but I realize it is almost impossible to learn this sleight from a printed description as there is a certain touch and pressure that is only acquired from experience.

RETAINING THE STOCK

This is a method, most difficult to detect, of shuffling and retaining a stock of several cards. I may go so far as to say it is another of those original little things with cards that distinguishes between mediocrity and perfection.

THE EFFECT:

The pack of cards is riffle shuffled and cut, and again cut, riffle shuffled and cut in such an apparently fair and effective manner that to know the location of any card seems next to impossible. But in spite of this procedure the four aces remain the top four cards of the pack.

THE METHOD:

Four aces are on the top of the pack (or whatever cards you desire). The pack rests on the table, face down, side of the pack facing you, second and third fingers of each hand at the far side of the pack, thumbs at the near side, first fingers on the back of the top ace.

The right thumb secretly bends up the index corner of the top ace. This is accomplished as you riffle by bending all the cards up slightly by the thumbs and riffling them once or twice. Cut from the bottom of the pack with the right hand about twelve cards, and drop them fairly on the top of the pack.

Then cut off from the top of the pack with the right hand about twenty-six cards, and proceed to riffle the two packets together.

Inspection of the right hand packet before the riffle shuffle will disclose that the four aces reside in this packet with about twelve cards above the aces and ten cards below them.

Therefore, if the riffling is done as follows, the aces will not be separated. Release from each packet as evenly as you can, without the procedure being in the least laborious, card for card for about eight cards from each packet. Then release about seven or more cards together from the right hand pack. These include the aces. Continue the dove-tailing with the remainder of the two packets. The cards are carefully squared, and the cut brings the four aces to the top of the pack again. The cut is simplified because of the crimped ace.

If you want the aces all on the bottom, crimp all four at the beginning instead of only the top ace. Or if the effect you aim to produce requires two aces at the top and two at the bottom, then crimp the corners up of the two top aces. The sleight requires considerable practice to do smoothly and well.

THE SWITCH AT DRAW POKER

This is a sleight used at a gambling table where the company is a little careless. The magician can make good use of it when demonstrating how they win.

THE SLEIGHT:

Having secured secretly five cards of suitable value on the bottom of the pack, slightly squeeze them on their sides so that the faces are convex.

Deal several hands of cards at draw poker, including five cards to yourself. Place the pack down and take up your hand and inspect it, then place it down in front of you, all five cards squared together, and take up the pack to deal the cards required for the "buy." At the completion of the deal for the "buy," take the pack in the right hand, second finger at the index corner, thumb at the other end of the pack. (See Fig. 1.)

As the left hand reaches the packet of five cards on the table in front of you, intending to pick them up, the right hand brings the pack over them. The second finger and thumb of the left hand seize the five bottom cards of the pack (See Fig. 2) and moves to your left with them. Simultaneously the pack is dropped on the five cards on the table, and you slide the pack to the middle of the table. (See Fig. 3.)

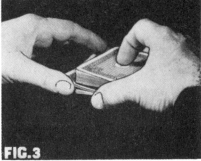

The switch is aided by the convex cards which make it less difficult to take five cards off the bottom. If you watch the move closely and are aware of what is going to happen, you can detect it. Otherwise you would never know the switch was made when expertly performed. Try it as directed.

DEALING FROM THE BOTTOM

An experienced gambler once said, "You can close your eyes and hear the cards dealt from the bottom of the pack." That is not always true, but it is an excellent point to watch and try to guard against. Did you hear the story about the "sucker" who suddenly said to the dealer, "Say, you're dealing off the bottom!" and the dealer replied, "So what! It's my deal, isn't it?"

THE SLEIGHT:

Hold the cards in the left hand. The first finger of the left hand is at the top end of the pack, the second, third and fourth fingers straight up the sides of the pack, and the thumb resting across the back, as the right hand thumb approaches to apparently draw off the top card. (See Fig. 1.)

The cards are very lightly held as the right hand approaches to take a card. The left hand swings in a short arc of several inches from the wrist, and the left thumb at the same time pushes the top card of the pack over from the other cards slightly.

The second finger of the right hand slips under the pack between the first and second fingers of the left hand, and presses up and outwards on the bottom cards. (See Fig. 2.) The pressure exerted is all-important to the success of the move.

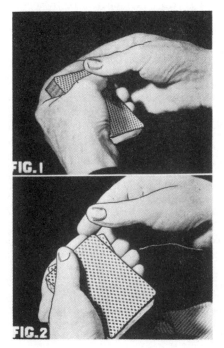

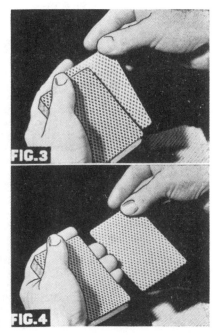

The card is drawn out as shown in Fig. 3, the first and second fingers of the left hand straightening to give passage to the card. At that moment, the left thumb exerts increasing downward pressure on the back of the pack and returns the top card to square up with the other cards. Thus the card coming off the bottom is already free of this pressure on the inside corner of the pack, and the course of the bottom card is now changed and comes away over the tops of the second, third and fourth fingers of the left hand. See position of card leaving pack in Figs. 3 and 4.

The left wrist swings with the pack to the left again as the card comes free, and the first finger of the left hand moves back into place on the end of the pack actually before the card from the bottom is away.

In fact, the whole procedure blends into a split second, and yet does not appear to be an unnecessarily hurried action, but there is a slight swishing sound present as the card is drawn off the bottom. This can be made less apparent if the cards are loosely held and the sound of the top card when dealt is exaggerated.

When you master the sleight you may deal all the cards off the bottom for the other players and take only your own stock hand from the top. This ruse deceives the listeners, but is very difficult indeed. I like to do "out of this world," dealing one color from top and the other from the bottom in packets composed of the number of cards named that I should deal, always dealing an equal number into one packet from the top as I dealt in the other packet from the bottom. Try it for practice.

THE CUT AND USE OF THE BRIDGE

If you have ever watched a school of players at a game where the stakes were important, you probably observed that when the dealer shuffled the cards and placed them to the player on his right to be cut, the player cut the cards by lifting off approximately half of the cards, placed them on the table, placed the remaining half squarely on top and pushed them over to the dealer. That procedure, while not entirely excluding all chicanery that may be practiced, certainly narrows down the field. A really smart crook would probably do nothing else than try to see which player developed the habit of cutting at the same place (this is more common in practice than you may imagine), and having found his mark, do his best to sit in the game in the required relationship and see that he always placed the pack in exactly the same spot to be cut.

Be that as it may, you require something much more certain for a demonstration, and you don't give two hoots about being detected by Mr. Eagle Eye, so long as you entertain. You may bridge the cards about the middle. The size of the bridge I will leave up to your imagination, but it is sufficient in most cases if it cannot even be seen. Try it. In the foregoing pages I have explained how to put the bridge in the pack. Such display of card handling would be looked on askance in "fast" card company, but you make your own rules for demonstration work at the card table. Therefore the following methods are excellent material for such a show of dexterity. Do them well and you will receive well-deserved credit for the exhibition.

RESTORING THE CUT

When the cards are cut into two packets and thus left to you to restore, there are several very excellent and difficult-to-detect methods of restoring the two packets to their original positions. They should be performed deliberately, but in accordance with the rules set down herein for their proper execution.

None of these cuts evolved from the minds of magicians. They are or were the closely guarded secrets of a section of the gambling fraternity who were always on the watch for the unwary player. I received most of these sleights directly from such men more than thirty-five years ago, and I have no doubt they were in use many years previous to this. In some instances I have added touches to enhance their deceptive value.

The first method is called the "draw shift."

THE SLEIGHT:

You set the cards over to be cut, as far from you as the arm will allow without looking awkward. This is so that the top of the pack will be placed nearer to you than the bottom half.

Pick up the bottom half with the thumb and second finger of the right hand by the sides. (Don't use the left hand at all during any of these moves.) With the cards thus

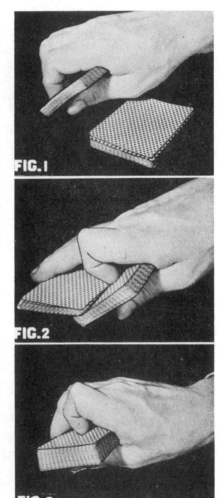

FIG. I

FIG. 2

FIG. 3

107

held, slip the thumb under this packet and press the packet into the fork of the thumb and first finger. (See Fig. 1.) Now place the second, third and fourth fingers on the table at the place where you pick up this packet, and don't lift these fingers off the table until the move is complete.

Pass the hand with the cards in it over the packet on the table. This is done in a non-stop running move, and when the position is attained as shown in Fig. 2, the fingers gather the packet on the table onto the top of the packet in the hand. All the time the cards are being drawn towards you in an evenly paced sweeping motion. (See Fig. 3.)

Second Method — The Drop: The pack is cut. You pick up the packet that was at the bottom before the cut and hold it at the ends between the thumb and the first finger of the right hand. (See Fig. 1.)

Place it fairly and squarely on the top packet, but don't let it go. With your thumb still holding the cards and the free third finger, pick up nearly all the cards, and move towards the left hand with this double packet. At a distance of several inches separating the two hands, let go the top packet held by the thumb and first finger, and retain your hold on the packet held by the thumb and third finger. (See Fig. 2.) This action, if the speed of motion is correct, will cause the packet that the first finger released to be projected into the waiting left hand. Without hesitating, the packet retained by the third finger and thumb is dropped on the cards left on the table. (See Fig. 3.) This packet is then gathered up and placed on the packet in the left hand. The cards are now in the same order as before the cut.

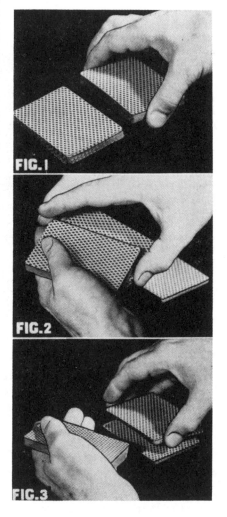

FIG. 1

FIG. 2

FIG. 3

Third Method: This method is as near to being an indetectable shift as it is probably possible to make one.

The cards are cut into two packets. The bottom half is picked up and held in the right hand by the thumb at one end and the first finger at the other. Now note in Fig. 1 just how the packet is held, or you will have undue difficulty later. See how the corner of the cards rests on the half of the ball of the thumb, and how the first finger holds the other corner by the extreme edge.

FIG. 1

FIG. 2

FIG. 3

Now pass over the packet on the table with the packet held in the hand approaching from the right side of the packet on the table, stopping when the second finger of the right hand reaches the left side distant corner. Then pick up this packet as shown in Fig. 2, and on the way over to the left hand, which waits to receive the cards, you draw up the under packet into the curled-up second, third and fourth fingers of the right hand, as shown in Fig. 3. The hand is moving towards the left during this procedure. On arrival at the left hand, the bottom packet is dropped into the left hand, and the other packet is squared on top of it. The sleight requires proper timing and an even pace of execution.

Bottom Stock Shift: This method is for the retention of the bottom stock only, and is a useful adjunct to bottom dealing. The cards are concaved very slightly before putting them down to be cut. Take from the top of the pack a packet of about twenty-six cards and place it in the left hand. Do this with the right hand as shown in Fig. 1. Then pick up the bottom packet in the right hand as shown in Fig. 2. The thumb is at one side and the second finger at the other side. The third finger is partly under this packet, while the fourth finger is under it. The first finger is on the top card. In this position the thumb easily releases about half the cards it is holding, and the little finger prevents them from falling. This forms a good sized opening. The move is made as the packet is brought towards the left hand, and thus the stock cards are secretly returned to the bottom as the packet in the left hand enters the opening in the packet in the right hand (see Fig. 3), and the cards are squared up by the left hand.

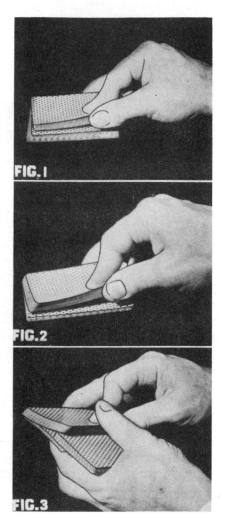

FIG. 1

FIG. 2

FIG. 3

RESTORING THE CUT
(My Pet Method)

My pet method of restoring the cut is as follows:

Five cards bottom stock; shuffle by riffle to retain bottom stock (method described herein), cutting the card below the stock to the top. Now firmly press the pack down with the first finger of both hands, second and third fingers on the side, and thumbs on the other side. The thumbs rapidly bend up and release in a riffling motion about half the cards.

The maneuver described has prepared the cards for receiving a bridge. Push the pack across the table to be cut. Say, "Complete the cut, please." The bridge is at the ends of the pack and is barely perceptible to the eye, but easily cut at.

Place the pack in your left hand, ready for the shift to follow. With the right hand cut at the bridge and lift the top packet up about three inches above the packet in the left hand. Drop the packet in the right hand back onto the packet in the left hand, but in this act secretly insert the fourth finger of the left hand to keep a break. The second finger of the left hand bends over the back of the top card. The thumb and second finger of the right hand hold the bottom pack at the corners, pull it up above the top packet and drop it on top. The stock cards are now on the bottom again.

These moves are to be made nonchalantly while not looking at the hand or cards. It is as near to being indetectable as a pass can be from all angles. Try it, and don't be discouraged—it takes a little practice to do well.

A CUTE FALSE CUT

Place the pack in your left hand ready for dealing, and then as an afterthought cut the pack by taking half the cards away with the right hand and placing this packet on the table. Then the right hand takes the remainder of the cards from the left hand and places them on the packet on the table.

The subtlety lies in secretly taking the bottom half first. Try it.

RUNNING UP TWO HANDS

Unduly long shuffles of the overhand count are to be avoided. They are tiresome, even when executed well. There are easier methods that are more effective. The best of these for entertaining purposes is the bottom stock milk build.

THE SLEIGHT:

Secretly place K, Q, J, 10 and 9 of hearts on the bottom of the pack and secretly place the four aces on the top of the pack. Riffle shuffle so as not to disturb the top or bottom cards, false cut and deal four hands of poker, cards face down. Say, "That's the other fellow's deal," and pick up the hands of cards, one by one, glancing quickly at them, and say, "It is always necessary to know where you want to deal are in the pack." This is purely a bluff. Actually you deal the four hands to make the aces the bottom card of each hand, and when you pick the hands up and place them on the pack, they lie fifth, tenth, fifteenth and twentieth from the top. If you wish you could deal five hands and the aces would of course fall to you, but here is a better ruse. Shuffle the pack, now using the milk build, that is, you shuffle off one card from the top of the pack into the left hand, and at the same time pull one card from the bottom, that is, one of the heart stock and an ace. Now shuffle off one at a time four cards from the top of the pack, and then together again the ace from the top and another heart from the bottom, four more cards single and then another ace from the top and a heart from the bottom together. Then four more singly from the top and the fourth ace and the fourth heart from the bottom together, and then four more from the top and an indifferent card from the top and the fifth heart from the bottom together. Then four cards from the top. False shuffle, false cut and deal six hands face down. The fifth hand holds the aces. You have the straight flush.

THE HOLD OUT AND PICK UP BUILDS

This is an excellent piece of business when adroitly performed after having warmed up to the demonstration of table artifices. Secretly secure the stock onto the top of the pack and palm the stock cards in the right hand. (See "Buckley's Palm" described herein.) With the same hand push the pack across the table to be cut. As the cut is being made, drop your hand below the table and hold the cards by the bent right leg at the back of the knee, and say, "No, on second thought I will try and show you something different. Please shuffle." Casually let the hands be seen, but do not call special attention to the fact that they are empty.

When the cards are shuffled, have them cut, and during the time this procedure takes place, regain the stock cards secretly from the right knee, palming them onto the top of the pack. Spring the cards, riffle pack, cut fair, then cut (using the Erdnase triple cut), and then cut at the bridge. Square up the deck and say, "This is your deal. I have simply cut the cards after you shuffle. Right?" Deal the cards face down as you would for poker. Deal any number of hands you like—four, five, six, seven or eight." The cards are dealt, let us say to six players. It does not really matter—four or more are required, but even two or three will do as well. The idea is to get the aces later. They lie the bottom card of the first four hands because they were on the top of the pack when the deal commenced.

You say, addressing the man who dealt the cards, "Let's recall what happened. So far you shuffled, I cut and you dealt. Right? Then let us suppose that it is my deal next and I want you to be a very suspicious person and watch me very closely, and don't let me cheat you." Saying this, you casually gather up the first four hands, taking great care not to let any of the cards be exposed, and barely looking at what you are doing, but carrying on a running conversation. As six hands have been dealt, you should also deal six hands. Therefore you need to add one card to the first, second, third and fourth hands as you pick them up to lay them on the pack, but drop these hands on first, then the remaining cards which you handle with due carelessness. False shuffle, bridge, and triple cut. Then place the pack in the center of the table and cut at the bridge and say, "Isn't that absolutely fair? Now see if you can detect me 'dealing seconds', 'bottoms' or from the middle." Deal the six hands face down, and when finished dealing, lay the pack fairly in the middle of the table, and say, "Six players you designated, so I dealt six hands. Now so you won't wrongly accuse me of cheating, will you be so kind as to turn up my cards, and I think you will find either a Royal flush or four aces. Oh, it's the aces."

When three hands are dealt with the top four cards aces before the deal, the cards fall two aces the two bottom cards of number one hand, one ace on the bottom of number two hand, one ace on the bottom of number three hand. Then pick up number one hand and shift the bottom ace to the second top position of this hand, and place it on the pack. Pick up the second hand and shift the top card to the bottom, and place it on top of the pack. Pick up the third hand and shift the two top cards to the bottom, and place this hand on top of the pack. The aces are now third, ninth, twelfth and fifteenth, and will fall to the dealer when three hands are dealt.

When four hands are dealt with the aces on top of the pack, one ace will fall first card to each hand, the pick up should be made as follows: Take the top card off one hand and put it on top of another hand, and put the six cards on the top of the four cards, and place the ten cards on the top of the pack.

These are the instructions to follow when four stock cards on the top of the pack are dealt face down and in the order dealt for poker. When the four aces are on the top of the pack and are dealt for two players, the cards lie: first hand, two aces and three indifferent cards; second hand, two aces and three indifferent cards. Pick up one hand without exposing or looking at the faces of the cards, and openly shift the bottom card (an ace) to the top of this hand. The cards then read: ace, three indifferent cards and another ace. Place this hand of cards on the pack. Take up the second hand of five cards and shift the bottom ace to the second from the top of this hand of cards. Then shift the now bottom ace to the second from the bottom of this hand, and place it on the pack. Because the aces now lie from the top down, second, fourth, sixth and tenth positions, they will fall to the dealer if two hands are dealt.

Place one of the remaining hands of five cards on top of the other hand of five cards. Shift the bottom card (an ace) to second from the bottom position of these ten cards. Shift the top card to the bottom of these ten cards. Place the ten cards on top of the pack. Because the aces lie fourth, eighth, sixteenth and twentieth from the top, they will fall to the dealer when four hands of cards are dealt.

When the number of players is five, the deal is completely automatic no matter how you pick up the cards, so long as you keep each hand intact.

For six players you add a card from the fifth or sixth hand to the top of the first, second and third hands, then gather the hands in the order first, second, third and fourth, and the rest of the cards on top.

For seven players you do the same as for six, but add two cards where before you added only one card.

For eight players you add three cards, the same as you added two cards for seven players to each of the first, second and third hands from the cards in the last two hands. The procedure given here is simple to remember after a few practice trials.

DEMONSTRATION BUILD OF FOUR ACES USING THE BUCKLEY DOUBLE CUTS

This is a very mystifying effect, and if you use it to precede the cold deck, it is a knockout for poker demonstrations.

Secretly place the four aces together on the top of the pack, spring and riffle (not shuffle). This concaves the upper half of the pack slightly more than it concaves the lower half. Now undercut half the pack for the overhand shuffle, and shuffle these undercut cards onto the aces at random. If you examine the pack you will see a light bridge immediately above the four aces. Now if you can do the "Charlier" one-hand cut, you can bring the aces to the top, remove one only and drop it face up, saying, "To deal aces it is always necessary to know where they are." Spring and riffle once more, overhand shuffle and cut as before, and up shows another ace. I add to the effect by calling the suit of the ace before turning it face up. Remembering the order accounts for this. Repeat the move until all four aces lie face up on the table.

Riffle the pack a few times, and proceed with the double cut build as follows: The pack is held in the left hand, face up, and with the left thumb you spread several of the face cards to the right hand fingers and thumb, and immediately square them together again on the face of the pack. In doing this, you insert the little finger beneath five cards to maintain a break.

Now take up the Ace of Spades and place it on the face of the pack squarely. Take all the cards into the right hand, holding the pack at both ends, the second and third fingers at one end and the thumb at the other. The thumb keeps the break open about three-eighths of an inch wide.

The left hand is now brought up under the back of the pack, and cuts away half of the cards below the break and slides them in openly under the arch of the right hand onto the pack. The left hand is holding this packet of cards in the fork of the left thumb as it slides them onto the ace card. Thus the fingers of the left hand return under the back of the pack as the cut packet is slid on the ace.

The fourth finger of the left hand then engages in the opening break maintained by the right thumb, and all the cards below the break are brought up by the left hand and placed on the face of the pack. If this has been carried out as explained, the ace will now be the sixth card from the top of the pack, and if precisely the same moves as were just explained are repeated with each of the remaining three aces, they will assume the positions sixth, twelfth, eighteenth and twenty-fourth from the top, and will therefore fall to the dealer when six hands are dealt.

If you desire to deal a smaller or larger number of hands, simply resort to pushing over one card less than the players, as you did when you pushed over five cards for six players.

Now here comes the pay-off. This method of cutting the cards in no way changes their position, because after all it is only cutting, but doing it twice to accomplish what you could do in a single cut makes it illusive and difficult to follow what is happening. It also gives you a chance to place the card into position indetectably. Let us now apply this knowledge to a cold deck.

A COLD DECK WARMED UP

There are various ways explained for changing a pack of cards for another, and no doubt all magicians worthy of the title could readily accomplish the change of pack by subtle methods or simply putting away the pack after doing a trick and taking out another, though apparently the same one. These devices have their place, no doubt, but this is not one of them.

The aim here is to make the shrewd watcher say, "I know he did not switch the deck because it never left my sight!"

Having finished the deal just described where the cards received a preliminary healthy shuffling, the four aces lie face up on the table, and the packet comprised of forty-eight cards is in the left hand. The right hand spreads the aces, and the left hand goes into the left side pocket, leaves the packet of forty-eight cards and emerges with a cold set up deck of another forty-eight cards. But wait! Now the aces are cut into the pack exactly as before, and this time the dealer gets a straight flush, and another player the aces. For good measure, each of the other players is dealt a "full house."

Arrange the cold deck as follows: Lay out six packets of cards in a row, designating the six packets from your left—1, 2, 3, 4, 5, 6. These cards are all face up. The first, second, third and fourth hands are each comprised of a full house (three of a kind and a pair). The fourth hand consists of four aces and one indifferent card under the aces. The sixth hand is a straight flush, say 9, 10, J, Q, K of hearts.

Pick up the cards, one from each hand, face up, commencing with the sixth hand, the straight flush, working backwards until you have gathered them all in one at a time. As you pick up each card, turn it face down on the previous one. The last card picked up will now be the top card back up. Place this packet of thirty-six cards on the remaining sixteen cards of the pack and proceed as follows:

Hold the pack in your left hand, face towards you, and from the back push off five cards in a packet. Transfer them to the face of the pack. The bottom card, the one facing you, will be an ace. Take it off and lay it aside. Now transfer another packet from the back to the front of the pack. This time make it six, and the face card will again be an ace. Lay the ace aside and transfer another six cards as before and lay the ace facing you aside. Repeat once more and lay the ace aside.

Put the pack thus arranged in the left side pocket of your coat until you need it. Dispense altogether with the four aces from this pack.

It is now apparent that if you take the aces, one at a time, and exactly reverse your actions, you will restore the aces to their former position. That much is obvious. For clearness I shall repeat the description. Insert the little finger of the left hand under the Jack of Hearts, fifth position from the face of the pack. Place an ace on the top and double cut. The ace is now the sixth card from the top, which is of course on the palm of the left hand.

Put your little finger under the Queen of Hearts, which is now the fifth card counting from the face. Lay on another ace and double cut. You now have an ace sixth and twelfth from the top. The little finger is inserted under the King of Hearts, five down from the face. Lay on the third ace and double cut, and you now have an ace at the sixth, twelfth and eighteenth position from the top.

The last time you insert your little finger of the left hand under four cards and lay on the last ace. Double cut and deal six hands as already stated. The first, second, third and fourth hands are each a full house, the fifth hand embraces the four aces, and your own 9, 10, J, Q, K of Hearts.

THE PRACTICAL SHARPERS

This piece of deviltry requires two working together, and each must possess a unique dexterity. The man skilled in the riffle shuffle sits on the left of his confederate, who possesses unusually long thumb nails which he uses to advantage when cutting. Here is how their craftiness works.

It is the confederate's business to be able to cut off exactly twelve and exactly seventeen cards with the precision of a gauge. This is simplified because he uses his nails to gauge correctly, keeping them manicured the required length.

The other sharp is an expert at the riffle. Both players have a set course to follow. The first is to see that two cards, a high pair for example, are in the hand thrown on the top of the pack in the gather-up. Their position in the hand of cards itself is unimportant as will be seen later.

The other player arranges one or two cards on the bottom hand, preferably top and bottom. There are seldom more than six players in a poker game where stakes are worth while, so this method is described for six players.

Assuming that the cards read (owing to the help given by the two sharpers) Jack on the bottom, three indifferent cards and another Jack. On the top of the pack is another Jack, and then five indifferent cards on top of another Jack. Seldom would a better hand be sought, and this suits our description.

The sharp gives the pack one straight riffle, nothing more, and puts the cards across to his confederate to cut. The confederate, by the aid of his gauge, readily cuts off twelve cards in one heap and seventeen in the other, and drops the pack on the first cut and these on the second cut. Nothing could be fairer, or at least that is the way it seems.

What actually takes place is this. The expert finds it natural to make up the number to five cards between the bottom and the top card of the hand his ally's job was to place there. Why didn't the ally put five cards there in the first place? If you play for money you would not ask, but any move that is not consistent draws suspicion, and such gentry do go to great lengths to avoid it.

If you deal the cards after the aforesaid cut, you will find the three jacks fall, not to the dealer, but to his confederate.

KNOWING YOUR OPPONENT'S HOLE CARD

This is a clever maneuver that is practiced by the sharper who specializes in playing a single opponent stud poker because the sleight gives him a knowledge of his opponent's hole card. He learns this as he cuts the cards as follows.

As the pack is drawn across the table towards you by your right hand, you hold the cards by the sides of the pack, second and third fingers on the side furthest from you, first finger on the center of the top card, and your thumb on the side nearest you, about midway.

Without riffling, you open the pack about the middle with your right thumb and bend up the cards sufficiently to glimpse the index of the card above the break you have just made. This is done while the pack is moving towards you. Having glimpsed a card, your thumb lets it fall, and also one more card on top of it. This all takes but a fraction of a second, and in no way arouses suspicion if well performed. As soon as the cards reach you, you draw the packet below the break out endwise by the right hand, place it fairly on top of the others, and push the pack back to the dealer. You receive the top card, and your opponent's hole card is the one card you glimpsed.

THE SPREAD

This is a daring piece of business. Its extraordinary audacity gives it a certain appeal.

A sharper and his confederate understand and know each other's play. The first sharp has only a broken flush which he buys to, but is unsuccessful. He signals the suit card he is lacking, and calmly proceeds to get rid of the unwanted card back to the pack or in the discard if he is clever, on the floor if he is not. The betting goes on. Sharp number two selects a card of the desired suit from his own hand, from the discard if he has none, palms it face to palm, and waits for the betting to end. Sharp number one throws his four cards in a packet into the middle of the table and says, "All blue," or "All red." Sharp number two, who is waiting for this, lays his hand with the palmed card on the packet of four cards and says, "Well, let's take a look at them," and in spreading them out, the fifth card is added.

A STRIKE
(METHOD OF DEALING SECONDS)

The first finger of the right hand takes the second card as the thumb of the right hand pushes over the top one. The thumb draws the top card back square with the pack as the first finger and thumb of the right hand turn the second card, the Queen of Spades in the illustration, over. It's a very deceptive move when performed well.

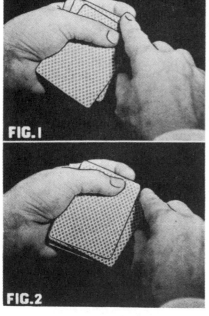

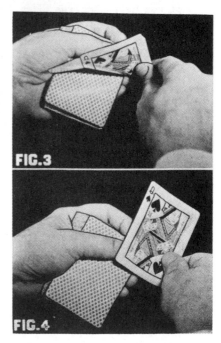

FIG.1

FIG.2

FIG.3

FIG.4

SECOND DEALING
(BLACK JACK METHOD)

The pack of cards is held in the left hand, the first finger curled up the end of the pack and the second, third and fourth fingers curled up the side of the pack. The thumb is at the side on the corner.

Thumb count two cards (see Fig. 1) and as you force your thumb in under the two cards, press down firmly on the top of the pack with all four fingers as you rotate the left hand and the pack of cards. (See Figs. 2 and 3.) You press the second top card (the two of spades in the illustration) out from under the top card (the Jack of Clubs in the illustration), and finish with the two of spades and the pack held in the position shown in Fig. 4. A beautiful sleight when it is well performed. It is used frequently by the gambling fraternity to cheat at Black Jack, but may be of excellent use to the card conjurer.

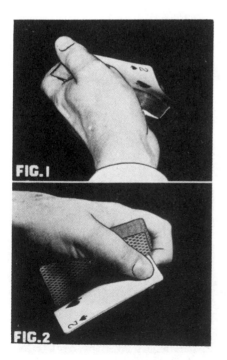

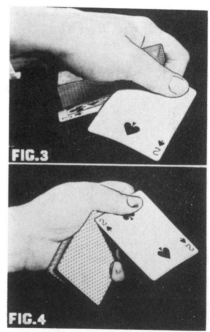

DEALING SECONDS
(DOUBLE PUSH-OFF ONE HAND)

The pack of cards is held in the left hand, first finger curled up the end and the other fingers up the side, the thumb across the top left corner.

The thumb pushes the top card out off the top about one-sixteenth of an inch. Then the side of the thumb contacts the second top card (see Fig. 1) and the two cards are pushed down and over the top of the other cards of the pack as in Fig. 2.

The left thumb moves back to the position depicted in Fig. 3, moving the top card with it. The second top card is now free as the pressure of the thumb is only on the other cards. A jerk of the left hand will cause the second top card to slide into the right hand as in Fig. 4, to be laid on the table face up or face down as desired. A very deceptive move.

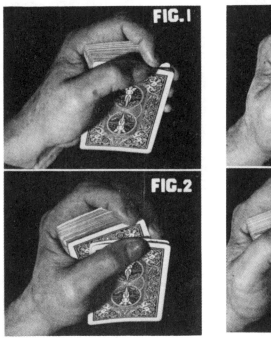

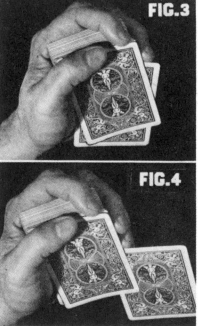

AN ORIGINAL METHOD OF RESTORING THE CUT
Fourth Method:

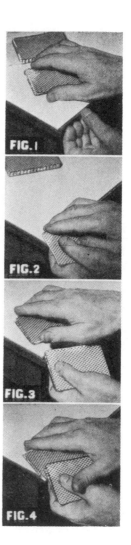

FIG. I

FIG. 2

FIG. 3

FIG. 4

The pack of cards is placed on the table before a spectator with the request, "Cut the pack." The pack has been laid so close to the spectator that he must place the part of the pack cut off nearer to you than the remainder. This is important because even if he intended to replace the bottom packet on the top packet, he is not given the opportunity to do so, for as soon as the packet is cut, you draw the top packet of cards across the table into your left hand and hold them as in Fig. 1 and 2.

You then draw the bottom half across the table in the same manner, (See Fig. 3), but instead of this packet going on top of the packet in the left hand, it passes beneath it, as depicted in Fig. 4. You cannot fully appreciate this until you try it.

Card Control

CHAPTER THREE

Manipulations

CARD MANIPULATIONS

The performance of card manipulations demands an unusual degree of skill in back hand palming of cards, grace and ease, with accurate timing of each motion, to suitable music, and special lighting effects. I shall describe these things in proper detail, first giving the necessary description and illustrations for the individual sleights involved.

I believe that T. Nelson Downs is rightfully credited with the back hand palming of coins and that an equally great artist, Howard Thurston, is likewise credited with, if not actually originating, then developing, the reverse palming of playing cards and their production singly from the back of the hand. Camille Gaultier's "Magic Without Apparatus," page 150, credits M. Harmington with originating this sleight.

I had the delightful pleasure of seeing Mr. Thurston perform these feats as a special item in his two-and-a-half-hour show. Mr. Thurston was undoubtedly far too busy to permit himself the privilege of developing these sleights with cards to anything like the possibilities they afforded. This has been left to others, and I think I may rightfully claim to have participated to some extent in this development.

It was in the year 1908 that I first learned to perform the back and front palm with cards and coins, and in 1909 I was earning a very meager livelihood in Australia with an act comprised entirely of such manipulations. In 1918 my wife and I came to America with an act that included card manipulations and telephathy. Our billing was—"Clever Hands and Startling Minds." I had originated, developed and used what is now known as the "split fans." Furthermore, I believe that I enjoyed the exclusive use of this sleight, the "split fans," for several years prior to 1922, for not until that year had I ever encountered anyone who had so much as attempted it. In 1922 at the office of Thurlow Miller, M. D., in San Francisco, California, I met a fellow card enthusiast named De Rubio. I am not sure if he is Spanish or Mexican. He was then quite accomplished at performing card manipulations, including "split fan productions," and he told me he had been using his methods for about a year and had originated the sleight quite apart from any knowledge that I had also originated a method similar in effect, though somewhat different in procedure. Today numerous card manipulators have become more or less masters of these moves.

Card manipulations have always been very dear to me, and have given me a great amount of pleasure in working out their details. Perhaps you may further explore their seemingly limitless possibilities, and add a touch here and there to develop their perfection. An outstanding artist in this branch of manipulative magic is Cardini. He has had a score of imitators, but there is only one Cardini. His work is the very poetry of motion and perfection in detail. It would be a far more simple project to build your own act and live your own character than set yourself the hopeless task of imitating so great a master, and for all your pains and efforts to be called just another poor imitator.

I saw Dick Cardini make his first metropolitan theatrical appearance at the Tivoli Theater at Sydney, Australia, and he was acclaimed a great artist then. That was a score of years ago. If you have witnessed Cardini's performance, you must have been amazed beyond description at his manipulative skill and perfect timing, his ease of manner and extraordinary precision, and, of course, his pantomime—but that's Cardini.

Had I not prefaced these sleights with a word about so marked and skillful an exponent of the back hand palming of cards, I would have felt something was lacking.

REQUIREMENTS: Two packs of playing cards.

The cards are preferably Bee Brand, and are each singly and carefully treated. My method of treating these cards was to bend each card down the middle, taking out the stiffness, but this method is definitely inferior to that used by Alec Purrell. His cards (Bee Brand) are so extraordinarly prepared that it is less of a feat to back palm a whole pack than to back palm twenty from an ordinary pack. Therefore it is essential that the cards be prepared.

They should not be allowed to touch the floor. If this does happen, they should be carefully wiped with a clean cloth or handkerchief. Dry soap is used on the cards to make them slip more effectively when fanning the cards, though I find by using Zinc Stearate toilet powder the process is satisfactory and easier to apply. Simply drop all the cards into a small cardboard box with about a teaspoonful of the Zinc Stearate, put the lid on the box and shake thoroughly for a few minutes and the Stearate will be effectively applied to each card. I do not know how Alec Purrell prepares his cards. It is his secret—someday he may tell us how he does it. Lee Paul has his own method, so does Cardini. I will give you a method I have found satisfactory although it is slow and requires care.

Take an ordinary wood lead pencil having six sides. With a brand new pack of cards proceed to wrap one card face inwards and lengthwise tightly around the pencil, then again wrap it tightly around the pencil from the opposite side and face outwards. Continue this with all the cards of the pack, square them together and place them between two blocks of wood and clamp them very tightly for twenty-four hours. This will flatten the cards. Now rub each card on both sides with a hard soap. "Cashmere Bouquet" is very good, or use the Zinc Stearate as previously instructed if you find it satisfactory. The cards are ready for use, and if handled carefully will keep in good condition for many performances.

You will find these prepared cards ideally suited for springing from hand to hand, the waterfall flourish, the ribbon drop flourish, running up the arm, the turnover, throw off the arm and catch, and excellent for palming and quite indispensable for the repeat split fans from the back palm. I am therefore assuming on giving the following instructions that you are using cards prepared in this or by some such similar method.

For the time being you are my pupil, and I advise that you forget you know how, and carefully follow these instructions, and then, if you wish, improve upon them later. In this manner you will benefit the most.

LIGHTING

Many otherwise excellent performances have been reduced to mediocrity by poor lighting.

It is most essential that ample light be concentrated on the hands and cards to enable the audience to fully interpret and appreciate the skill and mystery involved. I am presuming you are proficient and do not find it necessary to perform on a semi-darkened stage or platform to cover your deficiency in skill and timing.

If you specialize in manipulations, one or two good white spotlights will prove a worthy addition to your act—one on each side of the stage or in the footlights, or on a battan in the flies, as well as the house spot. I recommend as much concentrated white light as it is possible without discomfort when you are performing manipulations with cards or other small objects, and the only dependable way is to carry your own spotlights for this purpose and arrange them carefully, after trial, to your best advantage.

MUSIC

Music is second only in importance to lighting. It should be chosen with meticulous care. Always have a set of band parts or enough to furnish the more essential band instruments, such as piano, first and second violin, bass, drums, clarinet, cornet, trombone, etc.

Your music should be arranged with as much care as is exercised in its selection. It is best to have someone thoroughly competent do this for you. It may make or mar your performance. Do not copy the music of other acts. There is an overwhelming abundance of beautiful music available to choose from. I am partial to changing the music for each effect and selecting a musical tempo in keeping with the rhythm of the performance. It is far better for the music to be played too softly than too loudly, although fortisimo and double fortisimo are desirable on occasion, but pianisimo is the background that dresses without encroaching on the mental attentiveness of your audiences, and is definitely more pleasing to the great majority to listen to for any length of time.

A VANISH OF A CARD FROM THE TOP OF THE PACK

This is a move that is very deceptive when performed as follows.
Place the pack in the left hand, face down, and reverse the top card, face up. Push it more than half off the pack. (See Fig. 1.)

The right hand is placed fairly over the card and palms it in the right hand. (See Fig. 2.) The left hand simultaneously turns the hand and the pack over. The right hand carries the card to the right leg and rubs the hand on the card.

Repeat the move of placing the card part way off the pack, face up as before. The right hand is placed over the card, but the left thumb withdraws the card onto the pack, and the hand and pack turn over as the right hand simulates the act of having the card and rubbing it into the leg, causing it to disappear.

An excellent climax is to palm the card and produce it from the pocket.

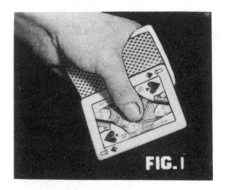
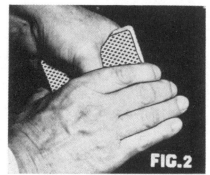

BACK PALM WITH THE OPEN FINGERS

The cards palmed in the right hand are pushed back of the left hand over the second and third fingers and pressed as far down into the forks of the fingers as possible. The fingers of the hand with the cards thus held are then opened, and the appearance is that the cards have vanished completely.

The cards are recovered in the right hand again by such moves as hereafter described for recovery of cards from the back of the left hand, when only pushed back to the knuckles. It is a difficult sleight which I use for the back palm of ten cards.

THE BENT FINGERS, BACK PALM AND RECOVERY

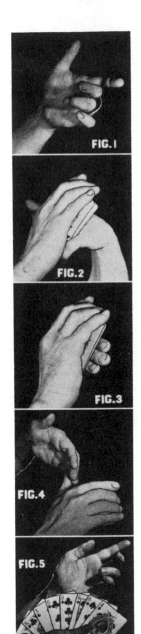

FIG. 1

FIG. 2

FIG. 3

FIG. 4

FIG. 5

Several cards, finger palmed in the right hand by the side edges, are brought up in front of the left hand. The second and third fingers of the left hand are bent forward, and the right hand slides the cards between the fingers of the left hand well back of the second joints of the left fingers, as shown in Fig. 1.

The right hand is then turned palm out for a moment and seen empty, and again turned back of hand to audience. At the same moment that the right hand turns, the left hand is partly closed to bring the cards held on the back of the fingers into position, as depicted in Fig. 2.

The left hand completes the turn. (See Fig. 3.)

The right hand, with the cards palmed, moves over and beyond the left hand, and the left hand turns over, palm to audience. (See Fig. 4.)

The right hand produces the cards in a fan at the left elbow. (See Fig. 5.)

PRODUCTION FROM THE PALM

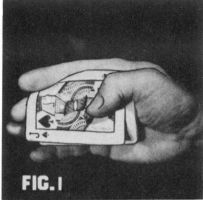

FIG. 1

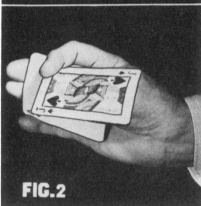

FIG.2

This is one of Howard Thurston's moves.

A number of cards, palmed in the right hand, are produced singly at the fingertips. Fig. 1 shows the thumb releasing the first card by a light upward pressure. Fig 2 shows the card supported by the first finger, while the thumb is drawn back and slipped under the card, ready to press the corner between the first finger and thumb and cause the card to spring suddenly into view as seen in Fig. 3.

FIG.3

A CARD VANISHES

Place the card, the King of Clubs, in the left hand as in Fig. 1. You will observe from the photo that the card is supported on its side edges at one end between the left thumb and second finger. The first finger is on the face of the card, while the left hand is at the other end across the edge. The right hand pushes the card, causing it to slide towards the left hand, but the outward pressure on the card by the right hand causes the card to rotate between the thumb and second finger of the left hand and come into the right hand, where it is palmed while it is seemingly pushed into the left.

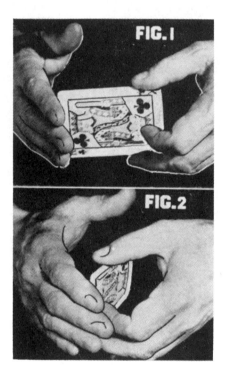

The illusion is heightened by a half left turn as the palming move is executed, and the left hand in a half closed position is raised to shoulder height with the back of the hand towards the audience. The right hand is lowered to the right knee, and as the left hand is opened and turned around, the right hand produces the card from behind the knee. The same moves may be executed with several cards.

THE PUSH DOWN VANISH

This original sleight is as effective as it is simple to do.

Place about eight or ten cards between the first finger and thumb of your left hand, face of cards up, your left thumb at the index corner on the sides of the cards and your first finger on the adjacent corner. Hold the cards at an angle of forty-five degrees with the floor, hand about chest height, and stand facing your audience.

Place the two middle fingers of your right hand at the top end, and press the cards down, causing the cards to slide between the thumb and first finger of the left hand. When the cards are all the way down between the finger and thumb, slide the right hand down the cards, half closing the fingers of the right hand, and grip them between the fingers of the right hand in back palm position. Open the right hand. Then slide the hand up above the left hand with the cards concealed.

The left hand moves slowly outwards, and your eyes follow it as it opens and is seen empty. The right hand fans the cards from the back hand position while you are watching the left hand slowly open, and then you turn your head and see the cards in your right hand.

This is a very pretty sleight and is new and different.

THE THUMB PALM MOVE
(An original piece of manipulative deception)

A fan of cards having been vanished by a toss of the right hand and the "back hand palm."

They are brought to the front palm position as the right side is brought towards the audience by a left turn of the body. (See Fig. 1.) Both hands are raised shoulder high. The fork of the right thumb presses down on a corner of the cards. The end released by the fingers is pressed against the left wrist, and the fingers are opened wide for an instant. (See Fig. 2.)

The cards are reclaimed by the fingers of the right hand, and the right thumb releases them. (See Fig. 3.) Simultaneously the left hand turns over, and the back of the hand is seen. It is then turned back to assume the position of Fig. 3 again. The non-index corner is pressed into the back of the fork of the left thumb. (See

131

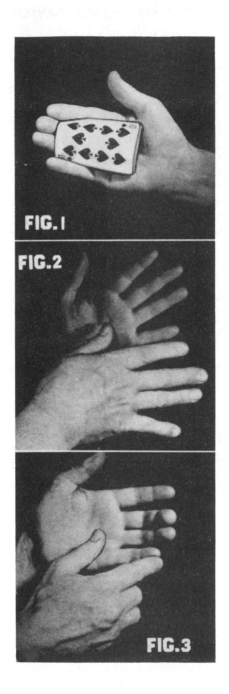

FIG. 1

FIG.2

FIG.3

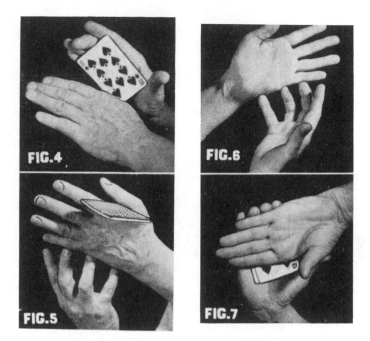

Fig. 4.) The left hand thus holds the cards loosely and assumes an angle with the floor sufficient to bring the cards parallel with it. (See Fig. 5.) The right hand offers cover. The fingers of both hands are spread apart, palms facing audience, as in Fig. 6.

The recovery is made by sliding the fingers of the right hand up the palm of the left hand and rotating the left hand to bring the cards into the right palm. (See Fig. 7.)

The move of the card coming into the right palm is completely covered by the right hand. The right hand, having palmed the cards from the left thumb fork, slides off the left hand over the fingertips and produces the cards from the right knee.

This is truly a mystifying piece of manipulation.

THE SLIDE UP VANISH

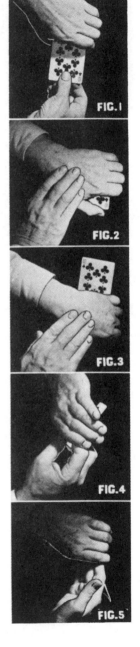

FIG.1

FIG.2

FIG.3

FIG.4

FIG.5

A card, the Ten of Clubs, is held at one end, the right thumb on the face of the card and the first and second fingers on the back of the card. The left hand is placed around the opposite end of the card. (See Fig. 1.)

The card is pushed up into the left hand. The left thumb takes a position at the end of the card, and the fingers of the right hand are placed on the back of the left hand. (See Fig. 2.)

The left thumb continues to push the card up through the hand as the right fingers rub in rotary fashion the back of the left hand. (See Fig. 3.)

The right hand takes the card at the topmost end, and the foregoing moves are repeated.

The moves are apparently repeated a third time; however, the card is actually back palmed by the right hand. (See Figs. 4 and 5.) The moves in the photos were taken from a position to reveal the moves being made for clearer understanding.

The left hand continues the illusion that the card is in it. The right hand produces the card from the left elbow as the left hand is shown empty.

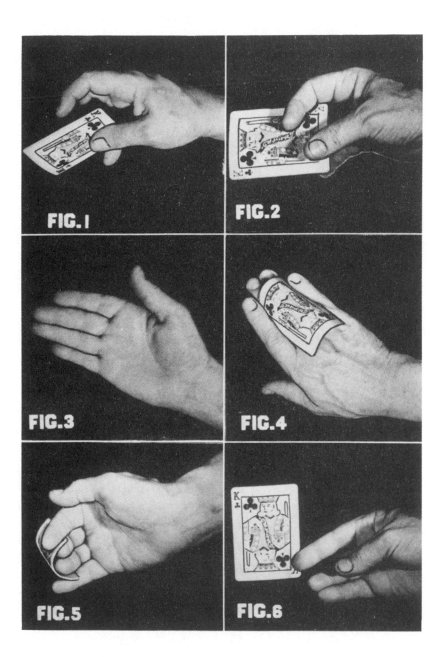

FIG. 1

FIG. 2

FIG. 3

FIG. 4

FIG. 5

FIG. 6

A CARD IS VANISHED AND REAPPEARS AT THE VERY
TIPS OF THE FIRST AND SECOND FINGERS

A card, the King of Clubs, is held at the middle of one end between the thumb and second finger of the right hand. (See Fig. 1.) Under cover of a slight toss, the card is back palmed. Fig. 2 shows the first finger in position on the face of the card. This is immediately followed by bringing the fourth finger over the adjacent corner of the card, and the hand is opened. (See Fig. 3.) The card seems to vanish into the air. Instead, it is held behind the hand as seen in Fig. 4.

The hand reaches out, and the fingers bend forward, bringing the card into the position shown in Fig. 5.

The second finger straightens, forcing the card away from the fourth finger, and the card springs to the tips of the first and second fingers as seen in Fig. 6.

REVERSE PALMING WITHOUT SWINGING THE ARM
AND ALSO WITHOUT USING THE THUMB

A lot of card manipulation is made unattractive by the performer swinging the arm to cover up for a deficiency in his manipulative ability. However, if the right moves are understood and practiced, the reversal of a card from front to back of hand and vice versa can be accomplished without detection.

The hand is turned over, front to back and back to front, and the only other movement seen by the audience is the partial closing of the hand. Besides this closing action, the hand is turned over. However, the closing and turning action are synchronized to cause the hand to move around the cards as the cards rotate as if pivoted to the same spot at their centers.

The card or cards are held in position, finger palmed, and the palm near the base of the thumb presses against the card. (See Fig. 1.) The hand is partially closed, first and fourth fingers on the face of the card, second and third fingers bent under the card as shown in Fig. 2. The hand is turned to synchronize with this action. If you stand in front of a mirror you will find the right speed to make each motion so the card passing to the back is unseen by your audience. The card is then on the back of the hand as in Fig. 3.

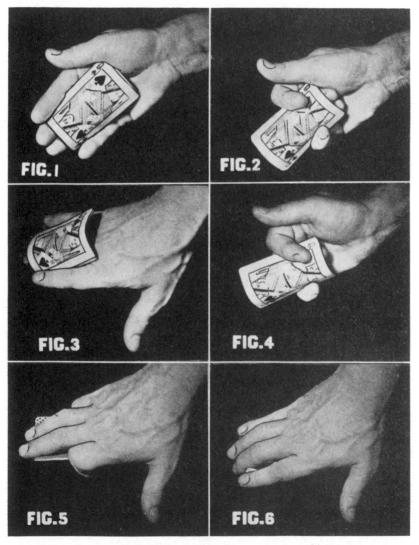

FIG. 1

FIG. 2

FIG. 3

FIG. 4

FIG. 5

FIG. 6

Bringing the card from the back to the front is a little more difficult, and requires a little more aptitude and skill than it does to pass it to the back of the hand. Fig. 4 shows the hand closed, the card on the backs of the second and third fingers, the first and fourth fingers on the card. The first and fourth fingers are straightened before the second and third fingers. (See Fig. 5.) Note how the tips of these fingers reach to the end of the card. The first and fourth fingers then straighten, as in Fig. 6, and the card is in the same position as in Fig. 1, only the hand has been reversed.

For the purpose of our explanation Figs. 1 to 4, inclusive, were taken from the rear.

THE FAN VANISH

The twenty or so cards produced in a fan from the left elbow while the balance of the pack is held in the left hand.

The fan in right hand, pack in left hand, faces towards the audience, as depicted in Fig. 1. The fan of cards is waved in front of the left hand momentarily, and in that instant the left hand turns over (see Fig. 2) and drops the packet of cards into the right hand, to be caught and held concealed between the second and third fingers of the right hand. (See Fig. 3.)

The left hand is brought into view, back of the hand towards the audience, and held as if the cards were still in it. A moment later it is turned over and seen empty. (See Fig. 4.)

The left hand is shown, back and front, and lowered behind the fan, and quickly palms the packet behind the fan from the right hand fingers. (See Fig. 5.) The body is turned so as to bring the left side towards the audience. (See Fig. 6.)

The cards in the right hand are back palmed and the packet in the left produced in a fan from the right elbow. (See Fig. 7.) Figs. 8 and 9 show the right hand closing the fan of cards and back palming them. The positions were photographed during the move.

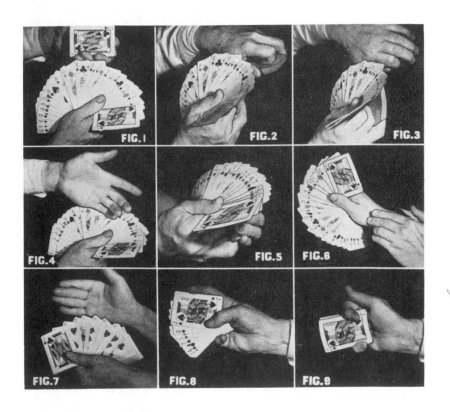

A FAN OF CARDS DISAPPEARS

A fan of several cards produced by means described are squared by the left hand, as depicted in Fig. 1. The first finger of the right hand is on the non-index corner of the squared-up cards, of which the Queen of Hearts is the face card.

The packet of cards is pushed up into the left hand, and just as the cards are leaving sight, the second and third fingers reach across to the adjacent corner. (See Fig. 2.) The second finger in front and the third finger at rear grip the packet by the corner, and instead of the cards being pressed up into the left hand, they are secretly carried away by the second and third fingers of the right hand, as depicted in Fig. 3. The photo was taken at the rear position to purposely expose the move to the camera. The hand appears to the audience as in Fig. 4.

The left hand is then turned over and shown empty. (See Fig. 5.)

The two hands are then brought together as a right turn is made. The cards held between the second and third fingers of the right hand are placed between the bent fingers of the left hand. This is accomplished as the turn is being made. The left hand, back of hand to audience, retains the cards while the right hand, palm to audience, is shown empty.

Turning face on to audience as the hands are brought around, the cards in the left hand are covered by the right hand, only a moment ago seen empty. The right hand palms the cards from the left hand in passing and continues to move to the right knee. From behind the knee the cards are brought forth in a fan.

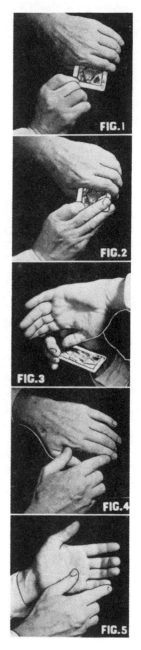

FIG.1

FIG.2

FIG.3

FIG.4

FIG.5

PAUL LE PAUL REVERSAL

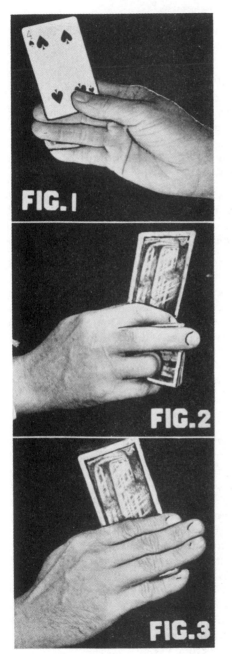

FIG. I

FIG. 2

FIG. 3

This exceptionally brilliant artiste, and one of the leading manipulators of cards on the stage today, has given me the accompanying three illustrations for their inclusion here, and writes as follows:

"A card is produced from the back palm position and is held in the hand as depicted in Fig. 1. The hand then swings across in front of the body, bringing the back of the hand into view. The remaining cards that were on the back of the hand are brought to the front by the reverse palm without the aid of the thumb. The method is clearly shown in Fig. 2. The hand and cards finally assume the position shown in Fig. 3."

Le Paul writes that he is not sure if he originated this, as it is twenty years ago since he first commenced using the move. It requires considerable dexterity to do correctly. The three illustrations are the hands of Le Paul.

COLOR CHANGE

(Instantaneous)

The pack of cards is held in the left hand between the four fingers and the thumb, facing the audience. The fingers are at the low side, thumb at the top side.

As the fingers and thumb of the right hand square the ends of the pack, they offer a cover for the preparation of the move to follow. The right thumb separates the face card from the bottom of the pack, and the third finger of the left hand is slipped behind the card so that if the left fingers are straightened out the face card will be carried to a horizontal position at right angles to the pack by the straightened fingers.

If this card is struck by a flick of the second finger of the right hand and then instantly brought to the position explained under the cover of the right hand, the effect is truly startling. The effect is that the card has suddenly vanished.

Without haste the right hand clips this card between the third and fourth fingers and the base of the thumb, and the right hand then takes the pack from the left hand, and while the transfer is made the left hand takes the single card between the fingers and thumb and returns the card to the top of the pack. Because this sleight is not illustrated in photographs don't undervalue it. I repeat, it is amazingly good.

COLOR CHANGE

(Second Method)

Lay the pack in your left hand; place the left thumb up along one side and the four fingers along the other side. Your right hand holds the pack at the ends, fingers at one end, thumb at the other end. Lift off two cards as one with your right hand in said position and replace them again on the face of the pack. But as you do so, slip the tip of the first finger of your right hand under the corner of the second card. With your left thumb hold the face card on the face of the pack, and push out the second card at the corner with the first fingertip until the tip of the fourth finger of the right hand can press down on the corner. The corner of the second card is trapped between the tips of the first finger of the left hand and the fourth finger of the right hand, and is secretly carried out of the pack under cover of the right hand and onto the face of the pack. The left first finger supports the card all the way. A very excellent sleight that has other uses.

THE CHANGE OVER

A VERY PRETTY AND DECEPTIVE PIECE OF CARD MANIPULATION

(Original)

Several cards are concealed in the right hand between the fingers, the position that precedes the back hand palm, face of cards outwards. The right side of the body is towards the audience, left hand shoulder height, palm facing audience. The right hand with the cards concealed is brought, palm to palm, cards facing the left hand. The second and third fingers of the left hand are bent forward, and the right hand passes the cards back of the left hand (see Fig. 1), where they are retained in back palm position.

The right hand turns over, bringing the fourth fingertips together, both palms facing the audience. (See Fig. 2.) The right hand is then turned around and raised above the left hand until the fourth fingertip of the right hand touches the first fingertip of the left hand. (See Fig. 3.)

With the first fingertip of the left hand touching the first fingertip of the right hand, the left hand is turned over, and the cards on the back of the left hand come naturally into the right palm. The cards are completely concealed from the spectators during the move by the cover afforded by the right hand. (See Fig. 4.)

The second and third fingers of the right hand press the cards at the end into the right palm, and the left hand, having released the cards, moves straight up until the tips of the left thumb touches the tip of the right thumb. The backs of the hands are towards the audience, thumbs touching. (See Fig 5.) The left hand is then turned over, bringing the left fourth fingertip to the right thumb tip. (See Fig. 6.)

The tips of the fingers of both hands are then brought together, and the body makes a right turn, bringing the left side towards the audience. The move brings the back of the left hand towards the audience. The right palm is hidden from view by the left hand. During the turning move the cards are transferred from the right hand to the left hand, the left hand receiving the cards between the fingers.

The right hand is raised above the left hand until the fourth fingertip touches the left first finger. The right hand is lowered behind the left hand, the right second and third fingers are bent forward and the left hand transfers the cards over the bent fingers of the right hand to the back of the right hand. The left hand is turned over, palm facing the audience, tips of fourth fingers touching.

The left hand is again turned over as the right hand reaches into the air and produces the cards fanned from the back palm position.

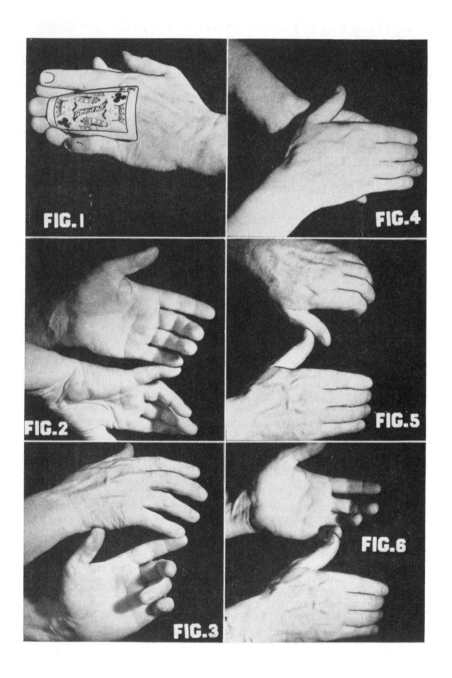

FIG. I

FIG. 2

FIG. 3

FIG. 4

FIG. 5

FIG. 6

144

THE STEAL

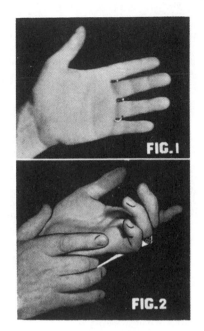

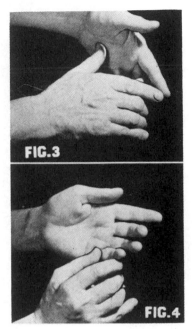

THE STEAL

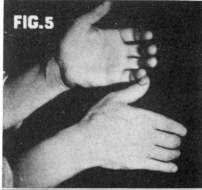

FIG.5

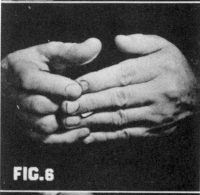

FIG.6

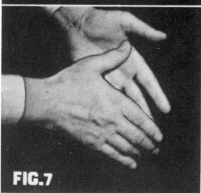

FIG.7

This is a very pretty original move that can be made with six cards almost as easily as with one. The move shown in Figs. 1 to 7 commences after the card has been vanished.

The right hand slides the front palmed card back of the left hand, pressing it far back behind the knuckles into the fork of the fingers, allowing the fingers of the left hand to be opened, although the card is retained behind it. A light pressure of the fingers and the spring of the card retains it there. (See Fig. 1.)

The right hand is brought up to the left and its palm turned face to the audience. Then the right hand assumes a position as shown in Fig. 2. The second and third fingers of the right hand grip the card between them as Fig. 2 depicts. (The photo was taken at an angle to expose the move.)

The right hand with the card moves away from the left as the body slowly turns right. The hands are brought together as in Fig. 6, and the card transferred to the middle fingers of the left hand. The right hand is seen empty. The body turns left, coming face on to the audience, and both hands are lowered to about knee level. The right hand is brought over in front of the left hand in time to prevent the card in the left hand from being seen. (See Fig. 7.) The right hand palms the card, then points to the empty left hand and produces the card from the back of the left knee. The moves of exposing the empty palms and concealing the card all blend into each other.

SPLIT FANS
BACK PALMING A PACK OF FIFTY-TWO CARDS
AND PRODUCING THEM IN A SERIES OF FANS

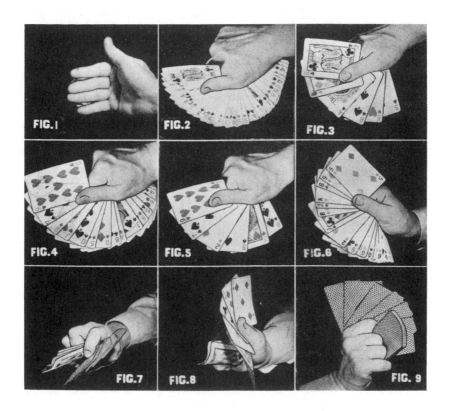

FIG.1 FIG.2 FIG.3 FIG.4 FIG.5 FIG.6 FIG.7 FIG.8 FIG. 9

This is the piece de resistance of card manipulation and formed the basis for my act called "A Gambler's Dream."

The cards are specially prepared in accordance with the instructions given at the opening of this chapter. The performer, while producing a series of cards at the fingertips of his right hand, uses the opportunity to secretly procure with his left hand from a clip under the left side of the coat the pack of prepared cards.

As the last card in the right hand is tossed away, the left hand smartly brings the pack to the right hand and places it into position behind the right hand. (See Fig. 1.) There is too much action with these movements for the cards to be observed. The right hand instantly reaches into space and produces the fifty-two cards in a fan. (See Fig. 2.)

The action stops for a moment to allow the spectators to fully observe the spectacle. Then a little toss of the hand is made, and during this minor action the fifty-two cards forming the fan are partially closed by pressure of the thumb on their faces and the second and third fingers on their backs. The first finger plays no part in this action. The fourth finger is at the lower edge of the side of the cards to steady the fan as it resumes a partly closed position. The first finger presses into the fan, separating about six or seven of the front cards from the other cards. These six cards are fanned out between the thumb and side of the first finger. (See Fig. 3.) The rest of the cards are hidden from view, but are still in the hand, gripped firmly by the first and fourth fingers on the face of the pack and the third and fourth fingers on the back of the pack. The hand is in a half-closed position, as if you were in the middle of the act of back palming the cards and stopped, for that is exactly what you do. The six cards afford you a complete cover for the cards thus held, and if you completed the back palming of the cards while holding the fan, the move would be awkward and very difficult to do with so many cards in your hand, whereas if you inspect Fig. 3 you will not see anything suspicious. These are true photos of the moves with the remaining forty-six cards held in the rear of the six cards shown. (See Fig. 3.)

These six cards are released by the thumb. At the same instant they fall to the carpet, the other cards are back palmed by the act of simply opening the hand. However, the hand with forty-six cards back palmed is not allowed to remain still, or the cards would be seen between the fingers. The hand is pushed into space and another fan of cards appears (see Fig. 4), and then a pause for a moment—another little toss of the hand—a pause, and the several cards again fall to the mat, and the cards appear as in Fig. 5. The hand reaches into the air, and another fan is seen, as in Fig. 6.

The moves described are repeated again and again. The cards appearing in Figs. 7, 8 and 9 are photographed from exposing angles.

When only five or six cards remain to be produced, the left hand procures another pack from a clip under the coat as the body makes a left turn, and the right hand reaches down and produces the fan of cards from behind the right knee.

Card Control

CHAPTER FOUR

Forty Experiments With a Pack of Cards

Experiment No. 1

Transposition

EFFECT: Two cards placed face down on the table when turned face up are seen to have changed places. (No duplicate cards used.)

REQUIREMENTS: A pack of cards.

SLEIGHTS EMPLOYED: The "double lift" and the "Mexican turnover."

Time: One minute.

THE WORKING DETAILS: Secretly place any indifferent card on top of the pack, the Jack of Spades second from the top, Two of Hearts third from the top, and Ace of Diamonds fourth from the top, and proceed.

By means of the double lift show the Jack of Spades. Place the two cards as one again on the top of the pack.

Lift off the top card, supposedly the Jack of Spades (in reality the indifferent card), and place it face down on the table on your right.

Double lift two cards, showing the Two of Hearts, placing them on the pack again. Lift off the Jack of Spades, supposedly the card just shown (the Two of Hearts), and place it at your left on the table.

Double lift again, showing the Ace of Diamonds. Place these two cards on the pack, and lift off the Two of Hearts, holding it so the face is not seen. Tap the card on your right, saying, "This is the Jack of Spades," and in the same manner indicate the card on your left as the Two of Hearts. Then make the Mexican turnover, and thus secretly exchange the Two of Hearts in your hand for the indifferent card, and with the card now in your hand, slowly turn over the Jack of Spades.

Lay the card in your hand on the pack, then double lift to allow the Ace of Diamonds to be seen. This is to be done in a nonchalant manner as if it has no purpose. Actually it allows the spectators' minds to confirm that the card used to turn the cards on the table actually was the Ace of Diamonds.

SECOND METHOD: Place any indifferent card on the top of the pack, the Ace of Spades second from the top, the Two of Spades third from the top, the Three of Spades fourth from the top and the King of Diamonds fifth from the top.

Double lift, showing the Ace of Spades. Place the two cards as one on the pack, and lay the top card, the indifferent one, on the table at your right.

Double lift, showing the Two of Spades. Place these cards as one on the top of the pack, and place the Ace of Spades about six inches to the left of the indifferent card. Repeat these moves, showing by the double lift the Three of Spades, and laying down on the table the Two of Spades.

Double lift again, showing the King of Diamonds, and with these two cards held as one, King of Diamonds showing, indicate the cards on the table from your right to left as the Ace, Two and Three of Spades.

Place the two cards held in your hand again on the pack, lift off the Three of Spades, and exchange it by using the Mexican turnover for the indifferent card. Then turn the next card, the Ace, and the end card, the Two, showing all three cards to have changed places.

Be careful not to show the card in your hand. Lay it on the pack and double lift, letting the King be seen.

Experiment No. 2

Confusion

THE EFFECT: After the pack of cards has been well shuffled, the top card is turned face up on the pack, and after being turned face down again, the card is placed in the pants pocket. The top card of the pack is again turned face up, and on being turned face down again, is placed on the table. The pack of cards is dropped face down on this card. The card is removed from the pocket and placed on the top of the pack of cards, and the spectator is requested to name the card on the bottom and the one on the top. The two cards are shown to have changed places with each other.

REQUIREMENTS: A pack of cards.

SLEIGHTS EMPLOYED: The "palm," the "turnover Change."

THE WORKING DETAILS: Commence by having the pack shuffled. When you receive the cards back, palm off the top card in your right hand by the method herein described, and with the pack of cards held in your left hand and the card secretly palmed in your right hand, turn the top card face up, using the thumb of your right hand to turn the top card over. Turn it face down, face up, face down, always in the same manner. The last time secretly drop the palmed card on top.

For clearness of explanation, let the card the audience see be the Jack of Spades, the card secretly dropped from the palm onto the Jack of Spades, the Deuce of Clubs.

Now remove the Deuce of Clubs face down, and place it in the trousers pocket, saying, "I shall place the Ace of Diamonds in here for a moment."

The right hand returns empty to the top of the pack and palms the top card, that is, the Jack of Spades. Then turn the now top card, let us say the Ten of Hearts. Repeat the move of turning the Ten of Hearts face down, face up, face down. The last time drop the Jack of Spades from the palm onto the Ten of Hearts, and then lift off the Jack of Spades, calling it the Ten of Hearts. Say, "I shall place this card here," placing it on the table face down.

The right hand palms off the Ten of Hearts from the top of the pack, and drops the pack on top of the card on the table, that is, the Jack of Spades, while you say, "I shall place the pack on top of the Ten of Hearts. Do you remember the card I placed in my pocket?" As you say this, reach into your pocket with the palmed Ten of Hearts and place it on top of the Deuce of Clubs you placed there. Bring the two cards out of your pocket as one without showing the face of the card, and place it on the top of the pack, and say, "What is the bottom card? And the top one? No, you see I confused you, for the top card is the bottom one and the bottom one the top one!" Show the cards.

SECOND METHOD: This method differs only in the manner of presentation, and demands the additional skill required to execute the "peek" and "double cutting," but if you are proficient in all these sleights the effect is greatly enhanced.

THE EFFECT: A person peeks at a card, another person calls, "Stop!" as the cards are riffled, and you obey instantly. The person who requested you to stop withdraws a card from the pack at that position. The card is replaced, and after a few simple cuts of the pack, the person who peeked at a card is requested to name his card. You turn the top card of the pack face up, showing it to be the card named. You openly take the card off the pack and place it in your pocket.

You ask the second person to name his card, and you turn the top card over, showing it to be his card. You turn this card face down and lay it on his palm, which he is told to cover with his other palm. Then you request the first person again to name his card, and on hearing the name you appear slightly bewildered, and you say, "It seems I am a little confused. I thought that was *your* card," addressing the latter part of your remark to the person who is holding this card between his palms.

He is almost sure to say, "No, my card is ———," and you say, "Would you mind taking another look." And the card turns out to be the one named! Still with the serious manner you say, "I thought I was right. You see, the card you thought was yours is the one I placed in my pocket," and suiting the action to the words, you draw the card this person selected from your pocket.

THE WORKING DETAILS: It is assumed you are already familiar with the workings of the first method, and that all that is now necessary is to acquaint you with the procedure of how you make the top card an indifferent one, the second top card the card the first person peeked at, and the third top card the card the second person withdrew from the pack at the position that you stopped when he told you while you were riffling the cards. From there on the workings are sufficiently similar to require no additional explanation.

You had a card peeked at, and retained the position with your little finger in accordance with the explanation herein.

You then cut about half of the cards below the peeked-at card to the top of the pack, and then the remainder of the cards below the peeked-at card to the top. The peeked-at card is then the bottom card.

Then cut about one-third of the pack from the bottom to the top, but keep a break with the little finger below the peeked-at card, which is now about the seventeenth card from the top of the pack.

Riffle (not shuffle) the cards at the ends, asking a spectator to say, "Stop!" If he doesn't say, "Stop!" before you reach the break held by the little finger, commence again. Stop when told, and have a card withdrawn. After the person has seen the card and remembered it, have it replaced, but open the pack at the break so the card will be replaced next to and below the peeked-at card.

Now by sliding the upper packet over the tips of the fingers of the left hand, the peeked-at card and the one above it can be easily and inconspicuously transferred to the under packet, and a break maintained above this indifferent card by the little finger of the left hand.

Cut half the cards below this break to the top of the pack. Then cut the remainder of the cards below the break to the top of the pack. The top card is now an indifferent card, the second top the peeked-at card, and the third top the one the second spectator withdrew from the pack. The working from here you will follow from the first method if you are not already acquainted with same.

Note: The "double lift" may be used to replace the "turnover change" in both of these effects. Either sleight is optional.

Experiment No. 3
Do You See Red?

THE EFFECT: Four black cards are held in the left hand, and the cards are dealt face up, showing them to be all black cards. Again the cards are taken up and dealt face up, but the last card is now red. The cards are dealt again, and they are now all black.

REQUIREMENTS: Four black cards and one red card on top of the four black cards.

SLEIGHT: The "glide."

WORKING DETAILS: Hold the five cards between the fingers and thumb of the left hand in position for the glide. Take the bottom black card and deal it face up, saying, "A black card." Do the same with the next card, repeating, "Black." Then execute the glide, drawing the bottom card back. Take the two top cards as one and toss them on the first two black cards, saying, "Black." Flick the card in the left hand, show it and say, "Also black." Throw it face up on the others.

Pick up the cards together, turn them over in position for the glide, and repeat all the moves as before. The last card left in your left hand this time will be red. Pick up the four black cards and lay them on the red card held in your left hand so the red card will be at the top. Repeat the procedure as first explained, and all the cards are seen to be black. This is a very pretty interlude if you do the sleight well.

Experiment No. 4
Matching Pairs

THE EFFECT: The cards are shuffled and cut. The spectator takes half the pack, and you the other half. Both the packets are held face down so that the faces of the cards are not shown.

You place a card from your packet face down on the table and tell the spectator to take any one of his cards and place it face down without looking at it, and you will make your card match his card. You flip over both cards, and they are seen to be the Four of Clubs and the Four of Hearts. Both match in numerical designation. This is repeated five or six times in fairly rapid succession.

REQUIREMENTS: A pack of cards with six pairs arranged on top of the pack, and preferably a baize top table.

SLEIGHTS: The "Mexican turnover," the "false shuffle," the "bridge" and the "Erdnase triple cut."

THE WORKING DETAILS: Having secretly arranged the twelve top cards of the pack in pairs, proceed to give them a false shuffle, bridge and cut. Then false triple cut and place the cards on the table. The twelve arranged pairs are now on the top of the under packet that is below the bridge. Cut fair, handing the top packet which you cut off at the bridge to the spectator, saying, "Shuffle these, please, and I'll shuffle these." You false shuffle your cards to keep the pairs on top. Request the spectator to lay one card from his packet on the table face down, without seeing it. You place one from the top of your packet face down also, and take the next card in your right hand and flip over his card with it, executing the Mexican turnover, and saying, "A six," or whatever his card is. "And here we have another six." Say this as you flip the card over with the card in your hand. The move is fair, but do it the same as you did to flip the first card, only so slowly that it is obviously fair. Pick up all three cards and place them on the bottom of your packet, and repeat the procedure as before.

A beautiful, snappy interlude if well performed. Be sure to have a table with a covering suitable for the execution of the Mexican turnover.

154

Experiment No. 5

The Lost Aces

EFFECT: Four aces are inserted half-way into the pack at different positions, then pushed into the pack together. The pack is cut and fanned. No aces are visible. The four bottom cards are openly placed into the fanned-out pack, the pack is closed and the four indifferent cards are visibly withdrawn. The pack is then placed on them face up. The pack is turned face down, and the four cards dealt face down. The pack of cards is spread, and the aces are gone. The four indifferent cards are turned face up, and these prove to be the aces.

SLEIGHTS: Dai Vernon's "multiple card shift," the "thumb riffle" and the "pressure fan."

THE WORKING: With the four aces fanned out in the right hand, and the pack held in the left hand face up, insert the aces in different parts of the pack as you release the cards with the left thumb riffle. Then execute the Vernon multiple card shift, bringing the four aces to the top of the pack. Fan the cards by a pressure fan, being careful not to disclose the aces. Take four cards, one at a time, off the bottom of the pack and insert them in the fanned-out pack at different positions. Close up the fanned cards, leaving the four indifferent cards protruding.

Hold the pack in the left hand, face up, left thumb at the index corner, first finger at the end of the protruding four indifferent cards, second and third fingers at the corner opposite the thumb. The second finger of the right hand is at the other index corner, first finger on the face of the card, thumb at the side corner. The thumb of the right hand, by pressure, releases the four aces. It does not matter if several other cards besides the aces are also released.

The thumb and first fingers easily carry away the released packet of cards, that is, the aces, etc., sliding up the sides of the protruding indifferent cards. The packet comprising the aces is brought up square with and behind the protruding indifferent cards, and the packet held between the thumb and second finger of the right hand is drawn away and dropped fairly on the faces of the indifferent cards in the left hand. The aces are now on the top of the pack. The pack is turned face down, and the aces dealt, one at a time, face down, either in a row or a heap as fancy dictates. The pack is spread face up, and the aces turned over. Smartly executed, the effect is worthy of the most expert of card performers.

155

Experiment No. 6

The Convexed Aces

Credit for the conception of this ingenious sleight of convexing and pushing together cards belongs to Joe Berg. The daring procedure makes it an amazing effect. With permission and due credit it was published in 1942 by Sam Berland in his "Blue Ribbon Card Tricks." However, due to a misunderstanding, it was not at that time correctly explained.

THE SLEIGHT: Take four aces and bend them lengthwise so that if you place each ace on the table face down there will be an arch about one-inch high at the middle, tapering off to the sides; that is, the sides rest on the table and the ends are off the table.

Take three cards together from the top of the pack, and place them face down on one ace, but do this by spreading the three cards so that the back of the ace is completely covered; that is, the top and the bottom card of the three cards overlap the sides of the ace. In the same manner cover the remaining three aces, each with three indifferent cards.

Now you place the fingers of your left hand on the left end packet so that the three cards raise slightly over the arched back of the ace, and at the same time place the fingers of the right hand on the next packet in a manner to cause the indifferent cards to also tilt slightly up at the edge nearest the first packet. If you then slide the two packets together, you will find that while the indifferent cards of each of the two packets are dovetailed together, the aces, because of their convexed condition, come together.

Repeat this move with the remaining two packets, and then, in a similar fashion, push the two packets, each comprised of two aces and six indifferent cards, together, and if you have followed the instructions as given, you will have all four aces together on the bottom of the packet. Even you will not believe it until you look, so the effect so far is that the aces are carelessly mixed in with the indifferent cards in the most haphazard manner.

Take up approximately half of the remaining thirty-six cards and drop them on the packet containing the aces. Pick up this packet and drop it on the other packet, and square up the pack of cards in your left hand. Do these moves in a very nonchalant manner. You can't lose the aces—the bridge formed by the arch in the aces will take care of that.

Execute the Erdnase triple blind cut. Drop the pack on the table and cut fairly, or rather most unfairly, because you cut at the bridge, thus transferring the aces to the bottom of the pack again. Square the cards very thoroughly, taking the convexity out of the aces. Openly transfer the lower half of the pack to the top of the pack, but secretly keep a break with the fourth finger under the aces.

Slide off two aces from the top packet onto the bottom packet, and insert the fourth finger again. Two aces are on top of the under packet, and the other two aces are on the bottom of the top packet. Cut the cards, preferably using the double undercut, thus bringing two of the aces to the top and two of the aces to the bottom of the pack.

Transfer the pack to the right hand, second and third fingers on the face of the bottom ace, and thumb on the back of the top ace.

Say to the spectator, "How long do you imagine it would take me to find all four aces if I did not look through the pack?" No matter what the answer is, you say, "No," and at the same time throw the pack suddenly sideways into your left hand, and smartly back into your right hand, and table the four aces, two held in each hand. This is a very old sleight taken from the "Lady's Looking Glass," but the cards must be in good shape or you will fumble.

The right hand, in position on the top and bottom aces, retains them as the pack slips out between the top and bottom aces. When the cards are thrown from the left hand in similar fashion, the top and bottom aces are also thus retained, the pack being caught in the right hand between the back of the first finger and the second, third and fourth fingers, the first finger and thumb being occupied holding the two aces.

Experiment No. 7

Charlier Location and Speller

There have been a lot of opinions volunteered as to the impracticability of performing the Charlier pass in an indetectable manner. I would venture the opinion that this can be accomplished at a gambling table if the cards are held in the left hand ready for executing the Charlier pass, and a gesture, made natural by a request, permits the right arm to pass momentarily in front of the pack the instant the pass is executed. I say this in defense of a beautiful sleight that will live on to a very, very old age, not because it has the requisite qualities of indetectability, but is an excellent device for locating. Perhaps it should have been named the Charlier "one-hand cut" rather than a "pass." It is in that category that it is here related.

Did you know that if you have someone cut the pack of cards, look at the bottom card of the packet cut off, the packet then returned as before, and the pack fairly squared on all sides, that with the Charlier one-hand method of cutting you can cut the card thus looked at to the bottom of the pack? The reason for this is that an air pocket is formed at the place cut at by the spectator. Of course the cards must be in good condition. No crimps, breaks or bridges, or those imperfections in the squared pack will predominate over the air pocket, and the pack will open at such a place more readily than with the tiny air pocket. I mention this in order that you may perceive how small a bridge is required for you to cut at when using the Charlier cut.

For many years I enjoyed the almost exclusive use of this sleight used in conjunction with the spring-made bridge described herein for locating. Here is an example.

Spring the cards from hand to hand, waterfall fashion. The pack is face up. Place the pack, now slightly bowed from the springing action, in the left hand, and ask a spectator to peek at a card (see the peek described herein), remarking, "About the middle, please." When the card has been noted in this fashion and you have retained the location with your fourth finger, cut off the packet above the break, raise it a few inches and spring these cards onto the other cards. Then immediately spring all the cards, waterfall fashion. No, you won't lose the card, but it certainly seems that way. What happens is this: The cards being sprung face up at the beginning bowed the pack one way. When you sprung the top half of the cards, of which the peeked-at card was the bottom card, you bowed this packet in the opposite direction, making a very wholesome bridge below the peeked-at card. This you reduced to practical working limits by springing the pack in fair waterfall fashion. It is a simple matter to bring the peeked-at card to the bottom by the Charlier cut.

Then if you wish, shuffle by using the overhand shuffle as follows: Suppose the peeked-at card is the Jack of Spades. Holding the top and bottom card (the Jack of Spades) draw them into the left hand together, saying to yourself, "You took the Jack of Spades." This is done as you shuffle the cards from the pack, one by one, onto the two cards in your left hand, repeating a letter of the sentence for each card. Then cut the pack, keeping a break, double undercut to the break, place the deck on the table, and say, "What card did you peek at?" Then proceed to lift the cards off as you say, "You took the Jack of Spades," turning the card up at the last word.

Experiment No. 8
The Card Through Case

With my permission this original effect was published in "Blue Ribbon Card Effects" by Samuel Berland (1934). It has some unusually clean-cut manipulation, and has a very surprising climax.

It is by no means easy to do well, and will miss fire frequently unless careful attention is given to the details, and it should not be performed for the same person or for the same group more than once because the surprise is the climax.

THE EFFECT: A spectator peeks at a card, and without any shuffles or cuts, the pack is placed into its case and the flap closed. The cards in their case are then handed to a spectator to hold. The name of the card he peeked at is requested, and when the card is named, the box is struck smartly down out of his hand, and he is left holding his card face up between fingers and thumb of his hand.

SLEIGHTS: The "peek," the "single card shift," and the "longitudinal glide."

THE WORKING DETAILS: The card case is laid on the table with the flap side down and away from you (this is important). A card having been peeked at by a spectator is secretly transferred to the bottom of the pack by the "single card shift." The right hand then holds the pack face down between the fingers and the thumb, fingers at one end, thumb at the end near the index corner. In this position the fourth finger executes the "glide," and the peeked-at card on the bottom of the pack is thus freed from the thumb at its index corner. This happens while the left hand picks up the case. The left hand is placed face down on the case, and the left hand and case turned over. During this action the right hand with the cards is brought up against the case, and the fingers of the left hand procure the peeked-at card and hold it against the case. The left hand with the case and the card is turned again into position to bring the flap side of the case on an even keel with the floor. In this position the right hand slides the cards into the case, turns in the flap and hands the case to a spectator, saying as you offer the case, "Will you please hold the case like this between your fingers and thumb, thumb on top. That's right."

"What card did you think of?" Slap the pack smartly as the spectator says the name of the card, and the card will remain in between his fingers and thumb. It takes considerable judgment to know how hard or light a blow to deliver. In the case of a lady who may be nervous, the tap should be light, while for the boilermaker you may need considerable force. Your success or failure with this trick lies right here.

Experiment No. 9

The Unexpected Ending

THE EFFECT: A spectator peeks at a card and is requested to remember it. The pack is riffle shuffled.

A second spectator is requested to say, "Stop!" while you are releasing the cards by the riffle, and you withdraw the card only half way from the pack at the position stopped at. The spectator is told to remember the card.

The cards are then riffle shuffled several times, cut and squared up. The person who peeked at a card is requested to name the card. The cards are spread ribbon fashion on the table, and this card is seen face up. The second spectator is asked to name his card, and you say, "This card," pointing to the first card, "indicates the position of your card." Counting from the face-up card to the number indicated, you turn over the card and show it is the card named.

THE SLEIGHTS: The "peek", "double cut", "reverse", "crimp" (new method), "riffle stock shuffle".

THE WORKING: The first spectator is asked to peek at a card by lifting up the index corner while you hold the pack. Retain the position with the fourth finger, and undercut twice to bring the peeked-at card to the bottom of the pack. Then in the act of riffle shuffling, reverse the bottom card. (See the "reverse".) Then riffle shuffle once more to place any card beneath the faced card.

Approach the second spectator and request him to say, "Stop!" while you riffle (not shuffle) the cards. When he calls, "Stop!", you stop and pull the under card of the top packet out about half way only, and in doing so you turn it slightly to the left. This causes the corner of this card to protrude about three-sixteenths of an inch at the third finger, which applies a downward pressure and "crimps" the card. The card is pulled out half way, and the hand is raised with the pack so the card is readily seen. It is now pushed into the pack ever so fairly, and the cards sprung. Be careful not to show the reversed card.

Turning the pack edgewise, you may see the "crimp" clearly. Separate the bottom packet from the top, taking the crimped card in the packet in the right hand, and riffle the two packets together, being careful to maintain the several cards of the right hand packet on the bottom and top of the left hand packet so the reversed card lies second from the bottom and the crimped card is on the top of the pack.

Take the pack in the right hand and draw off, as you would during an overhand shuffle, one card less than the numerical value of the reversed card. Throw the remainder of the pack in the right hand onto the cards in the left hand. Place the pack on the table, and cut about the middle. Square the pack, and ask the first spectator to name the card peeked at. Ribbon spread the cards across the table, and the card shows up reversed. Ask the second spectator to name the other card, and say, "The spots on this card indicate the position of that card." Count to that number and turn it over.

Experiment No. 10

Birds of a Feather

EFFECT: The cards are thoroughly shuffled, and while riffling, someone is requested to say, "Stop!" You cut the pack and lift off the card stopped at, showing it to the spectators. While you still hold the card exposed in your right hand, you riffle the corner of the pack under the left thumb, and again request someone to say, "Stop!" At the place stopped, you insert the card held in your right hand into the opening in the pack, placing it in face down until only about half the card is left protruding. The cards above this protruding card are cut off, and the protruding card lifted off. Then the three cards below it are taken off, one at a time, face down, and all four cards are turned over together as you say, "Birds of a feather." All four cards are seen to be the same denomination.

SLEIGHTS: The "strip", the "quadruple lift", the "slide" and the "stock shuffle".

THE WORKING: Run through the pack face up, and strip four cards of the same denomination to the top. (See the "strip" sleight.) Shuffle the cards, using top stop riffle shuffle, cut the stock to the center, keeping the break with the fourth finger on the stock cards, riffle the end of the pack, and ask someone to say, "Stop!" Cut at the break to bring the stock to the top of the pack. If this is done correctly, not even the closest observer will detect that you did not cut at the selected place.

Slide the top cards over so you can count four, insert the fourth finger of the left hand under the four cards and lift them off the pack as one card. This is not difficult to do.

Hold the four cards in the right hand as one, and ask someone to say, "Stop!" as you riffle the corner of the pack with your left thumb. This is fair, so make the most of it. Place the four cards into the break made by the thumb, and execute the slide.

Cut off the cards above the protruding card, and slowly lift off the protruding card, but don't show it. Then lift off the next three, one at a time, and say, "I suppose you know that birds of a feather —?" Show the four cards to be the same denomination.

Experiment No. 11

Simplicity

This is a classic. It is simple, smooth and completely indetectable, even when executed in slow motion. You may just want to do it as a color change. I prefer it as follows:

THE EFFECT: A spectator takes a "peek" at a card. You shuffle the pack, and then, calling attention to the front card of the pack held in your left hand, you inquire, "Is that your card, sir? Then please name it." You pass your hand over the pack, and the card named is seen to have taken the place of the other card. Of course you can do this, but wait—read how perfectly these moves blend to make this a piece of real magic!

THE SLEIGHTS: The "peek", "double cutting", "shuffle and hold", "palm-off of several cards", and "replacement". These sleights have all been explained herein, so I shall assume you are fully conversant with them.

THE WORKING: After the peek, you use the flesh grip and transfer the peeked-at card to the bottom of the pack. Turn slightly sideways so the backs of the cards are towards the audience while you give the pack an overhand shuffle, holding the bottom card (the peeked-at card) with the fingers in a manner that lets the top and bottom cards come off the pack together, with the rest of the cards shuffled onto these two cards.

You may riffle shuffle if you wish—just keep the bottom card from being seen, and keep it on the bottom.

Turn the pack face up in the left hand, but at the same time see that the right hand covers the face of the pack.

Palm off several cards, and hold the pack between the first finger and thumb of the right hand in which the cards are secretly palmed. Show the left hand.

Place the pack in the left hand, the left thumb fairly across the face of the card showing.

Bow the cards in the right hand ready for the replacement. Slip the left thumb into this arch, and move the right hand away as if it carried the card off the pack. (Don't overdo it.) Show the right hand empty. The peeked-at card is on the face of the pack. Simplicity in itself, but it's a beauty!

Experiment No. 12
Next to Yours!

This effect is a little off the beaten path as card effects go. You riffle the pack, and while doing so, a spectator, who has been requested to do so, says, "Stop!" You have a card withdrawn from this position, noted and replaced in the fairest sort of manner—no crimps or bridges. Then you take the top card and insert it into the pack just where you think the selected card is. Again you take another card from the top and insert it where you think the selected card is, each time asking someone to remember the card as you insert it. Place the pack on the table, and remark, "When I am really in practice it is not impossible for me to guess so accurately the position of a card in the pack that I am able to place a card immediately below the selected card and another next to and above it. Do you people remember the cards I inserted? Then name the selected card, please?"

The cards are spread ribbon fashion, face up, on the table, and the selected card is seen to be embraced on either side by the two other cards.

THE SLEIGHTS: The "top stock riffle shuffle", the "break", and "springing" or waterfall flourish".

THE WORKING: Give the pack a true riffle shuffle, and follow this up with a top stock riffle shuffle. As you do this, remember the names of the two cards in the left hand packet that fall on the top of the right hand packet. As you square up and squeeze the left hand packet into the right hand packet, the fourth finger of the left hand enters the pack to keep the top stock under it as is the requirement of this top stock riffle. However, we are concerned with the two cards immediately above the fourth finger (not the top stock). The right thumb releases the bottom one of these two remembered (by you) cards, and the fourth finger shifts its position between them. You hold this position, and with the thumb of the right hand at the inside end of the pack and the fingers of the right hand at the other end, you bend the cards, and release them from the fingers, one by one, at a slow, even pace, requesting someone to say, "Stop!" You do this riffle very deliberately so that it can be clearly seen. All is quite fair and aboveboard (but strictly and secretly below the fourth finger). At the place you are told to stop, a card is removed and noted.

When the card is withdrawn, you say, "Put it back in the same place, please." Quite innocently you take advantage of this minor digression to ease the packet above the fourth finger forward about three-sixteenths of an inch over the under packet. In this position the fingers of the right hand can open the pack as if it were really the place from which the card was just removed.

Of course, the selected card is thus inserted between two cards that you have secret knowledge of.

You spring the cards, waterfall fashion, several inches (as you are not showing how dexterous you are, but merely displaying that the cards are free). Lift the top card off casually, but be careful not to let it be seen, and as you put it into the middle of the pack, christen it with one of the names of the two cards next to the selected one. Call the second card by its right name, and say, "No, I don't like that card," and toss it face up on the table. Take the next one and christen it with the name of the other card next to the selected one. No one will dream you are not playing fair because they cannot have any knowledge that such a ruse would aid you because how could you know the cards next to the selected one?

Spread the cards face up after the spectators have renamed all three cards. The effect is really very good when these simple sleights are well performed.

Experiment No. 13

Four Chances—A Novel Card Location

This is an effective sleight that requires considerable exactitude in secretly estimating the number of cards in a packet cut off or remaining in the pack, but because this is practical to do after a reasonable amount of practice, it meets the required standard set to warrant its inclusion.

THE EFFECT: A spectator in front of whom you place the pack on the table is told to cut the pack any place and memorize the bottom card of the packet he removed. Then replace the card and meticulously square the pack on all sides.

You cut the pack a few times, riffle shuffle, and square the pack, and ask the person to name his card. You cut the pack at the card named.

THE METHOD: This is no effect for a bungler, but there is nothing exceptionally difficult that practice won't straighten out. You must be capable of estimating the number of cards cut, plus or minus two. When you can do this every time, you may proceed. Also, you will be required to do a shuffle which I originated several years ago and gave permission for publication in Berland's "Blue Ribbon Card Effects". For your reference this shuffle is described herein. It has the property of maintaining several cards in the center of the pack in an undisturbed order and without change as to their numerical location with reference to the other cards of the pack.

A spectator cuts the pack, lifting off twenty-three cards. You secretly estimate the number is between twenty and twenty-five cards, that is, the card is either the twenty-first, twenty-second, twenty-third or twenty-fourth card. This is not too difficult as a trial or two will prove.

You reclaim the pack, and with your right hand draw out of the center of the pack about twenty-six cards, leaving an opening from the place these cards were taken, and there should be about the same number of cards above and below the opening, that is, about thirteen cards.

Riffle the packet in the right hand into the packets in the left hand as follows: Riffle about ten cards in the right hand packet into the lower packet in the left hand, and then let about ten cards or so from the right hand packet fall onto the top card of the lower, left hand packet. Then continue riffling both right and left hand packets, square up the pack and you will find the selected card is the same number of cards from the top as it was before the shuffle. If, however, a spectator cut less than twenty cards, you undercut to make the card selected about center of the pack before you riffle shuffle as just explained.

Now cut the pack at the position you think the card is to be found, and secretly glance at the two bottom and the two top cards as you square up the pack. The selected card should be one of them. When the card is named, either turn over the pack to show the card, or use the glide to take the second bottom one, or show the top card or the second top one by means of a double lift.

Experiment No. 14
Naming the Top Card

THE EFFECT: You place a pack of cards, which you have thoroughly shuffled and cut, on the outstretched fingers of your hand.

You ask a spectator to cut the pack and place the packet cut on your palm, face down.

You pick up the packet with your right hand which the spectator just laid on your left hand, and openly look at the bottom card of this right hand packet. Then with your left thumb you push off the top card of the left hand packet and let it drop unexposed, face down, on the table, saying, "This card," looking at the bottom card of the right hand packet, "informs me the card on the table is the Jack of Clubs," (or whatever the card really is).

THE METHOD: This effect improves with repetition and may be successfully performed, if well done, several times in succession. The secret lies in glimpsing the top card of the packet you hold in your right hand while you openly look at the card on the bottom of this packet.

THE SLEIGHT: As in the foregoing effect, ask your magician friend to shuffle the cards and place the pack face down on your outstretched left palm. Square the pack meticulously and shift it onto your fingers, saying, "I am going to ask you to cut the pack in two packets about equal, like this." At this point you place your right hand in the following position on the pack. This position is very important. Your first finger of your right hand is placed at the index corner on the side of the pack, and the other three fingers are lined up alongside the first. The left thumb is at the opposite corner of the same, and in this manner you pick up about half the pack.

The right hand holds its packet for a moment almost at three-quarters arm's length a few inches above the pack, and in a vertical position. If this position is correctly followed by you, you will just be able to see the face card index enough to read it. (See "Methods of Glimpsing" herein.)

At this moment you press lightly with the tip of the fourth finger of your right hand on the back edge of the card. The amount of movement of this little finger is imperceptible, though sufficient to cause the index corner of the top card to open back and reveal the index to you. Don't open the break more than is necessary, and only long enough for you to learn the top card.

Place this packet back on the top of the packet in the hand, and say, "Will you do that, please?" in your most disarming manner.

The spectator cuts the pack. You then say, "Place it on my palm, face down." Continue talking as you take up the packet on your fingers, saying, "Do you know that a knowledge of the bottom card of this packet informs me the name of the top card of the packet in my left hand? It's really quite simple. This six tells me this is a four—the four of hearts to be correct."

You have been afforded ample time and opportunity to again secretly observe the top card of the packet by the sleight described.

You slide the top card of the left hand packet, the four of hearts in the description, onto the table and drop the right hand packet on the left hand packet. As you do so you name the card dropped on the table.

You are set to repeat the effect as you will continue to be after each declaration is made of the card on the table.

Experiment No. 15

A Gambler's Aid

Here is another of those clever gambler's subtleties for which we magicians and card conjurers should be thankful. Carmen Domico showed it to me, and I have his permission to include it herein in the following effect.

A spectator thoroughly shuffles a pack of cards and places them on the table face down. You ask the spectator to name a number between six and twelve. He does so, say for example the number named is nine. You proceed to pick up off the pack with your right hand a card at a time until you have taken five cards in this manner. Then you say, "Oh, nine is your number," and you drop the five cards on top of the pack again. This does not make sense, but it all seems fair enough because nine is the number. At this point you say, "Would you mind counting off the cards face down and look at the ninth card. Place it on the bottom of the pack face down. If I held the pack for even a moment you might suspect me of doing some sleight of hand—that quicker than the eye business—so let's play fair. You concentrate on your card and I'll try to name it for you. Will that be fair? You are thinking of the two of spades!"

The effect has no explanation so far as sleight of hand known to the conjuring fraternity goes because, as I said before, the sleight has remained a well kept secret of the gambling fraternity.

THE SLEIGHT: The pack of cards, having been fairly shuffled and squared up, is on the table. You have no knowledge of the position of a single card thus far. A number is named—eight, nine, ten—it makes no difference. Say nine is called.

You reach for the top card of the pack with your right hand and lift it off the pack between the second finger and thumb of your right hand, and place it face down in your left hand, secretly glancing at its face as you do so. Now that is what you seem to do. Actually you lift off two cards instead of one, just as explained. It is a move I find myself unable to clearly explain. I have the pack before me as I write, and I can easily lift two cards off as one. I let go with the second finger, and the card snaps around with a click to be caught between the first finger and thumb and placed in the left hand. The next two are taken in the same way, and when you have counted off four in this fashion, you have really taken eight unbeknown to anyone. The number being nine, you lift a single card and drop it on the eight cards in your left hand. Then say, "Your number is nine." Drop the packet of nine, which everyone thinks it five, back on the pack. You know now what the ninth card is.

The spectator counts off nine, looks at the one you know, and you apparently read his mind.

I repeat, the sleight is a classic. It takes a little practice. Try it according to the foregoing instructions.

Experiment No. 16

A Card Gets Out of Hand

Having shown the spectator his card by means of a double lift, you place the two cards as one on the pack face down, so that the two cards overlap the outside edge of the pack by two-thirds their width, and are firmly held by the left hand between the thumb on top and the fingers underneath which encircle and hold the pack.

The right hand takes hold of the pack, first finger at index corner, thumb at opposite end, hand completely covering the overlapping two cards. The left thumb plainly and visibly draws the top card onto the pack. The unsuspected card covered by the right hand is secretly palmed. The pack is turned face up by the left hand, and then held by the right hand.

The left hand draws away about half the pack from underneath, and places the cards on the face of the pack.

The card palmed in the right hand may now be secretly returned on the pack in a reversed position. For the proper return of the card to the pack, see the "Replacement" sleight.

The left hand turns over with the pack. The cards are cut and ribbon spread on the table. The spectator's card is seen reversed in the middle of the pack.

Should you prefer it, the palmed card, instead of being replaced on the pack and produced as just explained, is produced in a new and very startling manner. The pack is held in the right hand by the first fingers and thumb at the ends near the outside corners. The left hand cuts the cards by bringing the under half up and placing them on the face up card.

A spectator is asked to lend you his left hand for a moment. Say, "Just extend it palm down, please, and place it on the cards in my left hand." You place the pack in the left hand as you say this.

You now place your right hand on the back of his hand, with the palmed card between the back of his hand and your right palm.

You turn his hand, your hand and the cards over, and as you do so, you withdraw your right hand, leaving the selected card behind his hand. The card is held in place by your left thumb and second finger, which encircle his hand and hold the card by its sides. You place his hand on the table, palm up with the cards, and ask the name of his card. Tap the pack, turn the pack face up and look as if you expected to find the card on the pack, saying, "I must have tapped too hard." Turn the spectator's hand over, and the card is found under his hand. The card is not felt by the spectator. Try it.

Experiment No. 17
A Difficult Routine

THE EFFECT: You riffle the cards until a spectator says, "Stop!" You place the card stopped at face down on the table before him. Repeat this procedure three more times until four cards lie on the table before as many spectators.

Before you take up the four cards, ask each spectator to remember the card before him.

Put the cards on the pack and proceed to lose them in the pack by shuffling and cutting.

Then say, "It is my intention to show you people how your cards can be controlled. I will try to bring each, one by one, to the top of the pack again, but in order that you may not make me nervous, I want you to refrain from making any remarks you may be prompted to make because of my seeming dumbness."

You take off the top card and show it, and lay it face up on the table, not in front of anyone in particular. Shuffle and cut, and lift off another card and lay it alongside the first. Repeat the foregoing procedure twice more until four cards are lying faces up in a row on the table.

You now turn the cards face down and proceed to shuffle the pack and place it face down on the table. At this point you remark, "I am amazed at the silence which greeted the conclusion of this trick. Don't you think it extraordinary that I found all your cards?" As you say this you turn over the four cards which have changed from four queens to four aces, the cards the spectators originally had looked at.

At this point in the effect someone usually remarks, "What happened to the queens?" and you say, "Oh yes, the queens. Contrary little ladies. Here they are." And you spread the pack with one hand, showing them reversed in the middle of the pack.

ARRANGEMENT: Four queens and four aces on top of the pack.

SLEIGHTS REQUIRED: "Double cut", "riffle shuffle", "double lift", the "reverse", an improved Down's change, "overhand false in jog shuffle", "Hindu shuffle".

THE WORKING: With the four aces on the four queens secretly on top of the pack, riffle, keeping top stock intact. Overhand shuffle and double cut to give the impression the cards are very completely shuffled. Hindu shuffle, keeping the break above the stock. Toss the cards above the break from the pack in the left hand to the right hand, and then toss the remaining packet on top of the packet in the right hand. This is quite an effective action, and creates an illusion that the cards are carelessly handled without thought or care as to their location.

Take off the top card, an ace, and show it to one spectator only, or if a group sees a card, be sure they only see one. Lay the ace on the table face down.

Hindu shuffle again, keeping the break as before. Toss the packet above the break to the right hand, and then the remainder in the left hand toss on top of the packet in the right hand. Lift off the top card, the second ace, and show it to the second spectator. Lay it alongside the first ace, also face down.

Repeat all the aforesaid moves, show the ace to the third person and place the third ace face down alongside the second one. Repeat all the moves again and show the fourth ace to the fourth person and lay the ace on the table.

At this point spread the three top cards, that is, the queens, in a manner that the sides are even but they are secretly stepped, each about a quarter of an inch more than the one beneath it, from the top down.

Take up the four aces without letting their faces be seen, and insert them every second card, with the last one on top. This is easy because of the steps. It looks, or should look, as if you place them on the top. A slight irregularity of this procedure will not matter very much.

Proceed to false shuffle, riffle shuffle, keeping top stock, and on the whole see how convincing your action can be that the sole purpose you have is to thoroughly mix the pack. Don't say so—let your actions do the convincing, but finish with the eight cards secretly arranged on top as they were before you began the shuffling and cutting procedures. There is plenty of information herein to help you.

Double lift and show a queen, and place it face up on the table. Bend the cards lengthwise so they will stay together more readily.

Do this same move three more times, and you will have four queens face up and an ace secretly under each queen.

Because each set of two cards, queens lying face up on the table bent with their edges up, the next sleight is the turnover change.

Hold the pack in your left hand, face to palm, pressed well into the fork of the thumb by the first finger, thumb easily able to touch the fingertips.

The fingers slide under the first queen and ace, thumb tip at near side edge. Thus the cards are turned over. The thumb draws the queen secretly on the back of the pack and tosses the ace face down. The act looks as if you simply turned over the queen. The same move is repeated without any undue delay. All cards are thus changed, and the four queens lie on the top of the pack reversed.

Without letting the queens be seen, the pack is cut to bring the reversed four queens to the center. The pack is then placed on the table.

The climax is in showing the four cards to really be the spectators' cards, all aces, and the queens reversed in the pack.

Experiment No. 18
Lost and Found

THE EFFECT: After a spectator has well shuffled a pack of cards and placed them on the table, you ask him to cut the pack at about the center into two packs and to secretly look at the top card of the under packet.

You cut off about half the cards of the other packet and place them on top of the spectator's card, and then drop the remainder of the cards on top of that packet. Square the pack, cut it once more on the table and proceed to pick off one card at a time from the top of the pack, counting aloud as you place them face up in your left hand. Ask the spectator to tell you when you pick up his card. However, you count all the cards without his card turning up, and there are only fifty-one. The spectator's card has vanished.

You gather up the cards and hold them face down in your left hand, and commence dealing the cards off the pack, face down, on the table, saying to the spectator, "You just say 'stop' any time, please."

When the word to stop is given by the spectator, you turn over the card in your hand, and it is seen to be the spectator's card.

SLEIGHTS REQUIRED: "Sighting while cutting", "Domico's Count", "Thompson's Stop", "second deal", "stock shuffle".

THE WORKING: When the spectator has shuffled and squared the pack face down on the table, you ask him to cut the cards into two packs, about equal.

Tell him to look at the top card, the card cut at, and to put it back in the same place on the top of the packet.

You say, "Please don't forget the card you just looked at." As you say this, pick up half the top packet and place these cards on top of his card. In doing this, sight the bottom card (see "sighting while cutting"), and then take the remainder of this packet and place them on the pack, and cut the pack. Be sure when doing so to take off a few less than the spectator did. This is so his card will be about five or so from the top.

Because you looked at the card you placed on his card, you will be warned when the spectator's card is on top of the pack. So with the pack squared up, you pick off the top card, flip it by bending the card between its ends while holding it between your second finger and thumb and letting go the second finger and catching it between your first finger and thumb.

You place each card face up in your left hand after you pick it off the pack.

When you reach the card you sighted, you know the spectator's card is on the top of the pack and will be the next one for you to pick up. So you do the Domico double pick-up, which is, when done well, not discernable from the act of picking up a single card. The two cards are flipped as the single cards that preceded it, and the spectator's card is not exposed as the cards are placed face up in your left hand.

You continue picking up the other cards smartly, one by one, counting aloud. The sleight is pretty, and if the same rhythm is maintained throughout, the long count is not tiresome as a trial will prove.

The card not seen and the count of fifty-one completed, the conclusion is that it has vanished.

Square up the pack face down. Cut the pack to bring the card a few from the top, and deal off the cards from the pack, turning them face up until you reach your key card which informs you that the next one is the spectator's card. Say to the spectator as though the idea just occurred to you, "Will you say 'stop' any time while I am dealing these cards face down."

You now deal seconds, but watch the spectator's mouth. It is a fact which you can prove by experiment that the spectator will unintentionally warn you he is going to say "stop" a split second before he does so by the movement of his lips. When you are thus warned, take the card from the top, his card. Until then you deal seconds. The big punch is that when he says, "Stop!", you have the card in your right hand just about to place it on the table.

James Kater Thompson has informed me the finesse of this principle of watching the spectator's mouth and synchronizing the action of the deal are of his own origination. It is worthy of the required practice. It is included in this effect with his permission.

Experiment No. 19
The Mysterious Marker

This is a favorite of mine. It is a streamlined puzzling effect in the first rank of such brevities.

THE EFFECT: You spread the pack ribbonwise face down on the table. Have a spectator select a card freely by removing any card from the pack.

You gather the cards, taking care to avoid seeing any of their faces. Pressure fan the cards in your left hand. Replace the spectator's card in the middle of the pack. Do this very deliberately, clearly free from any possible trickery, all the way in even with the other cards.

Close the fan and cut the pack several times. Then take the top card, exposing it to view before you partly insert the card in the middle of the pack as a marker, saying, "I judge the card you selected is about here!"

Place the pack on the table, marker card protruding. Ask the spectator to name the selected card. As the card is named, withdraw the marker slowly and turn it over. It is the selected card.

SLEIGHTS REQUIRED: "Pressure fan location", "slide", "double lift".

THE WORKING: The whole procedure is tied in with a smooth sequence of the ribbon spread of the cards and having any one card selected.

Then gather up the cards, placing them in your left hand face down. Pressure fan the cards in your left hand so the spectators see their faces. Take the selected card and insert it in the middle right in front of him so that he may appreciate the fairness of everything you do. (Let your actions do the talking. Silence here is golden, and any verbal stress on your fairness may arouse suspicions.)

Close the fan and turn the pack over endwise, face up, in your left hand. If you put the card into the pack fair and square, emphasis on the *square*, then having squared the ends of the cards after turning the pack as this sleight, the pressure fan location, requires it to be done, the selected card is left slightly protruding at the inside end.

Double undercut to this location while the pack is face up in your left hand. This makes the top card of the pack the selected card.

Turn the pack face down in the left hand, and double lift the two top cards, exposing the face of the under card, secretly concealing the selected card.

Riffle the left non-index corner of the pack with the left thumb, saying to the spectator to call, "Stop!"

When told to stop, you maintain the opening at the corner of the pack by pressure on the cards not thus released.

Insert the two cards as one into the break, and with the fingers of the left hand straight and the pack held by the fork of the left thumb, the inserted cards are rotated to the side, and the fingertips of the left hand secretly press the under card into the pack, leaving only the selected card protruding at the side of the pack. Lay the pack down and ask the spectator to name the selected card.

Withdraw the protruding card, and show it to be the one selected.

Experiment No. 20

Blackjacks

This a very snappy effect that may better be presented in an impromptu manner. It is sufficiently different to encourage its adoption by the advanced and more skillful card handlers.

THE EFFECT: A spectator's card is revealed between the Jack of Spades and the Jack of Clubs, which a moment before had been disposed of in widely separated parts of the pack.

THE SLEIGHTS: "Riffle shuffle for top stock", "two-handed fan", "Buckley's method of side steal", the "bridge".

THE WORKING: The pack is held face down in your left hand. You take off the top card and show it to be the Jack of Spades, and then push it half-way into the end of the pack about ten cards from the bottom of the pack.

You take the now top card, show it to be the Jack of Clubs, and insert it half-way into the end of the pack about ten cards from the top of the pack, saying. "I once knew a fellow that did a cute trick with a 'blackjack'. He is serving five years now, so let's hope this one does not end quite so disastrously. Please observe, I have placed one jack near the top, the other black jack near the bottom of the pack, so as to have them at widely separated points."

While you are thus pattering away, turn the pack face up in your left hand so the two protruding jacks are seen again, and then push them home. Cut the pack, using the Vernon shift for this move to bring the two jacks together at the top of the pack, face up. The right hand takes away about twenty cards, and the two packets are riffle shuffled together, face down, just sufficient care being exercised to insure the two jacks being kept at the top of the pack when the shuffling is completed. Riffle shuffling twice is enough to indicate a thorough mixing of the cards.

Pressure fan the pack in the left hand and extend the fan face down before a spectator, saying, "Would you please select any one card. Don't take it out of its position in the fan. Just allow it to protrude from the other cards about halfway. Thank you."

You raise the fan so the selector and others may see the protruding card.

"Please remember the protruding card. Now watch me very closely to insure that there is no monkey business on my part, because I would not care to have anyone say I deceived them by trickery, or perhaps slipped the card up my sleeve."

While you patter away, close up the fan, and then push home the selected card. Use the Buckley side steal, and with the selected card thus secured in your right palm, push the corner of the top jack off the pack over the fourth fingertip with your left thumb. Maneuver this protruding corner in between the palmed card and your palm. The fingers of the left hand then extend outward and draw the palmed card onto the pack under the top jack and onto the second top jack. The moves are quite indetectable executed under the excellent cover of the top card and the act of squaring the ends of the pack with the fingers and thumb of the right hand and the sides of the pack with the fingers and fork of the thumb of the left hand.

Downspring and up riffle the pack to precondition it for the bridge.

Then by a series of cuts, Hindu shuffle fashion, draw off a packet of about fifteen cards from the top of the pack into the left hand, and then several other packets in succession, each dropping on the preceding packet in the left hand. Place the pack on the table and cut at the bridge which is formed at about fifteen cards from the bottom of the pack. Square the pack carefully and say, "If the experiment has worked out correctly your card will be found between the two black jacks."

Lift off the top card and lay it face up, saying, "One jack." Lift off the next card and say, "Your card." Lift off the third card and say, "Old faithful, the Jack of Spades."

Experiment No. 21

The Ladies and the Deuces

THE EFFECT: Spectator selects a card which is placed down on the table without the performer seeing its face.

Performer ventures to find the other cards of the different suits but the same denomination as the selected card, and proceeds to cut and shuffle the cards several times, stopping occasionally to expose a card at the top of the pack and lay it on the spectator's card, face down.

After three trials it is quite obvious to the spectators that the cards placed on the selected card are all incorrect ones. However, on turning them over they have changed, and now match the spectator's card. The cards first shown were queens, and it is now a problem for the spectators to guess what happened to the queens! The performer obligingly proceeds to find them in different pockets, and one actually in his wallet.

SLEIGHTS: "Hindu shuffle", "double lift", "top palm of several cards".

ARRANGEMENT: Top stock, reading from top of pack down —two twos, two queens, a two, a queen and a two.

PROCEDURE: Hindu shuffle the bottom half of the pack onto the top half, keeping the break with the fourth finger of the left hand above the stock.

Thumb riffle until stopped, and cut to the break.

Spectator is shown top card, a two, which is placed face down on the table.

Hindu shuffle the bottom half of the pack onto the top half, keeping the break with the fourth finger of the left hand on the stock.

Cut to break, double lift, show a queen, replace on the pack and take off the top card, a two. Without exposing the two, place it on the other "two" on the table.

Shuffle off five cards from the top of the pack, one at a time, and replace them on the top of the pack again.

Hindu shuffle the bottom half of the pack onto the top, keeping break as before.

Cut to break, double lift, showing a queen, replace and deal the top card, a two, face down on the other twos.

Shuffle off three cards, one at a time. Replace them on top of the pack, shuffle off two cards, one at a time, and replace them on the top of the pack.

Hindu shuffle the bottom half of the pack onto the top of the pack (keeping break as before with the little finger of the left hand).

Cut to break, double lift, replace and deal off the top card, a two, face down on the other twos.

Palm off the three queens from the top of the pack, and at the first opportunity dispose of them in your pockets or in some place where it will be a surprise to your audience to find them. The one queen which you did not require for the effect is disposed of in an impossible place for you to reach after the trick is begun. Inside your wallet is a good place.

If no one remarks about the queens, you say, "Is no one curious to know what happened to the queens?", and proceed to unearth them from their hiding places, producing them one at a time, palming them from one pocket to another, and finally recovering the one in your wallet.

Experiment No. 22

Transition

THE EFFECT: Four aces are dealt face down on the table in one packet, and four kings are similarly dealt in another packet. A moment later both packets are turned face up, and the cards are seen to have changed places with each other.

THE SLEIGHTS: "Culling", "palming off the top of the pack four cards", the "Mexican turnover".

THE WORKING: Using system of culling described herein, run through the cards face up, sliding them one at a time from the left hand over the face of the following cards into the right hand until you come to an ace or a king. If an ace, drop it face up on the table. If a king, cull it, that is, place it in back of the cards in the right hand packet and lower the packet with the king at the back of it half way down the following card. Continue as before, discarding the aces face up on the table and collecting the kings at the low level packet. After the fourth king is thus made to protrude down, cull in the same manner four indifferent cards.

The position of the cards is now as follows: several indifferent cards in the low packet, a king or kings, then indifferent cards; in the upper packet a king or kings protruding down half way out of the top packet, more cards in the top packet, perhaps another king, and four indifferent cards protruding down from the top packet, and more cards in the top packet.

Draw out all the cards in the lower packet with the right hand and place them on the face of the upper packet, placing your fourth finger down on the face card of the upper packet to maintain a break between the two packets.

Double under cut to bring the top packet to the bottom and the bottom packet to the top.

The position of the cards from the top of the pack is four indifferent cards and then the four kings. The four aces are lying face up on the table.

Hold the pack in your left hand with the tip of the fourth finger keeping a break below the four top indifferent cards, and palm them off the pack into your right hand. (See description entitled "To Palm From Off the Top of the Pack An Exact Number of Cards Up to Ten".)

As soon as the four indifferent cards are palmed in your right hand, turn the pack face up on the four aces lying face up on the table. Pick up the pack with the aces, and secretly add the palmed cards onto the aces as you square the cards.

Deal the supposed aces one at a time off the top of the pack face down. Actually they are the four indifferent cards.

With your left thumb count eight cards and slip your fourth finger under them to maintain a break. The right hand may be over the pack supporting the ends to, aid in these moves.

With your left thumb spread the four top cards (the aces). Do this openly so the onlookers may plainly observe this action. Push them back on the four kings under which you have your left fourth finger.

Turn over the packet of eight cards above the break, and spread the four kings, indices exposed, but be careful not to show the aces under them. The second and third fingers of your left hand pressing on the side edges of the several cards as you are spreading them act as a safety measure to prevent the aces from becoming exposed.

Place your second and third fingers of your right hand into the break below the aces and your right thumb on the inside end at the non-index corner of the face king, and lift the eight cards with the four kings still spread. Turn the packet of eight over face down on the pack, but insert the tip of the fourth finger again to maintain a break under the kings.

The aces are now on top. Deal them off one at a time face down on the table, saying, "The four kings I shall deal here!"

With the inside non-index corner you can easily lift the four kings as one card because of the break you are holding with your left fourth finger.

The following moves are to be carried out very deliberately and without undue haste or jerkiness.

Lift off the four kings as you would a single card, and immediately turn over the supposed packet of four aces (actually the indifferent cards), but with the kings that you turn them over with, execute the Mexican turnover. The move is no more difficult than if you changed a single card.

Immediately bring the four indifferent cards now in your right hand to the top of the pack, and leave three of the cards on the pack, moving away with a single card you used to turn over the four aces. Toss the single indifferent card carelessly on the table.

The whole series of moves herein related are practical and quite indetectable under the most keen observation. Follow the instructions closely.

Experiment No. 23

The Ambitious Card

This is a title by which the fraternity has been made familiar with an effect wherein a spectator is made highly suspicious that the pack of cards you are using is composed of fifty-two cards of one suit and denomination, and it is not my desire to rechristen the effect, though I hope to add in a slight measure to the fundamentals of the illusion.

THE SLEIGHTS: "Hindu shuffle", "double undercut", "double lift", "top change", "throw down change", "side steal", "force", "shift", "riffle shuffle" and "palm".

THE WORKING: Secretly place the seven of hearts on top of the pack, and the eight of hearts under the seven.

With the pack now held face down in your left hand, undercut half the pack with your right hand and execute the Hindu shuffle, placing the fourth finger of the left hand on the seven of hearts to maintain a break.

Thumb riffle the pack, asking someone to say, "Stop!" Stop when told, but cut at the break, passing the top packet under the packet on which you held the break.

The seven of hearts will now be on the top again, but the spectator who called, "Stop!" while you thumb riffled will think he selected the place.

Double lift, showing the eight of hearts. Replace the eight face down and push off the top card, the seven. Catch it at the index corner by the first finger and thumb of your right hand, and without showing the card push it endwise exactly half-way into the middle of the pack.

At this point the bottom card of the pack should be completely covered by the left hand.

Turn the left hand over with the pack and still hold the index corner of the seven concealed. It is thus mistaken for the eight as you push it completely into the pack. However, as you do so maneuver the fourth fingertip under the seven to hold a tiny break below it.

Tap the top of the pack and throw the eight face up on the table. Double undercut to the break, thus bringing the seven of hearts to the bottom.

Turn the eight of hearts face down and drop the pack on top of it.

Hindu shuffle, place the fourth finger on top of the second last packet taken by the Hindu shuffle to keep the break under the eight of hearts.

Double undercut to the break, bringing the eight of hearts to the bottom of the pack again.

Riffle shuffle and double undercut, again returning the eight and seven of hearts to the bottom. Be careful while shuffling so that none of the faces of the cards are exposed to the spectators.

Say, "I'll let you people in on a secret—all these cards are the same."

As you make this statement, proceed with the Hindu shuffle. Each time pull off the pack held in the right hand a packet of eight or ten cards, and swing the right hand over each time, thus showing the bottom card, the eight of hearts.

If this action is performed smartly, no one will recognize the fact that you show the self-same eight of hearts every time.

As you drop the last packet, the fourth finger again keeps a break.

Slide these cards over, and shift the break to the top of the seven of hearts from under the eight of hearts.

Double undercut and bring the seven of hearts to the top and the eight of hearts second from the top.

Double lift, showing the eight. Again place the top card, the seven of hearts, into the middle, but cover the index. Allow it to be mistaken for the eight. Palm it from the middle, replacing it second from the top.

Turn the eight face up on the top of the pack and double lift, placing the two cards over the left fingertips where you hold them with your left thumb.

The right hand partly covers the pack as the left thumb now draws the face-up eight onto the pack. The face-down seven of hearts is palmed in your right hand.

The eight of hearts is flipped over face down with your right thumb, and the palmed seven of hearts is dropped secretly on top of the eight. (See Merlin's Book "A Pack of Cards".)

Double lift and show the eight of hearts.

Replace and take off the seven of hearts. Place it on the bottom of the pack. Let the first finger of your left hand lie over the index as you turn over your hand to let the supposed eight of hearts be seen on the bottom. Don't call it the eight—just let it be seen as such. Momentarily tap the pack on the top and turn over the eight of hearts face up. Lift it off and, if you are good at the move, make the top change.

Put the indifferent card in the middle and say, "If you want it on the bottom, it's on the bottom." Covering the index of the seven, flash the bottom card by simply turning the left hand with the pack momentarily, saying, "And if you want it on the top, it's on the top." As you say this, flip over the top card, showing it is the eight of hearts.

Palm the seven off the bottom, side steal into the right palm and replace it on the top.

Hindu shuffle and double cut to return the eight and seven to the top again.

Double lift and place the seven as the eight once again in the pack. Palm off the eight, and with it an indifferent card, and as you ribbon spread the pack face up, place the eight of hearts and the indifferent card into your right side pants pocket.

Say, "I was beginning to believe these cards were all alike— eight of hearts—until I remembered I had placed the eight of hearts in my pocket."

So saying, take the two cards as one from your pocket, showing the eight, and seemingly toss it on the table. By means of the throw change, throw the indifferent one.

Place the eight of hearts secretly on the pack, Hindu shuffle it to the center and say, "Will you please take a card?" Force the eight of hearts and show the card on the table is an indifferent one.

Experiment No. 24

The Mix-Up

THE EFFECT: The spectator is given a riffle peek at a card; performer cuts and riffle shuffles the pack. Half the pack is reversed and the two halves are shuffled into each other, cut several times and spread ribbonwise face down on the table. The spectator's card is seen in the middle of the pack face up. All the other cards are face down.

SLEIGHTS: "Riffle peek", "flesh break", "double cut", "finger reverse", "ribbon spread" and "Buckley's red and black false riffle shuffle".

THE WORKING: A spectator is asked to say "Stop!" as you riffle the index corners of the cards near the middle of the pack, and to remember the card thus stopped at as described in the "peek riffle". The location is secretly maintained by the fourth finger of the left hand. You then double undercut to bring the peeked-at card to the bottom. Immediately riffle shuffle the pack, keeping the peeked-at card on the bottom.

Cut off about twenty-six cards with your right hand and fan them face up, saying, "If you see your card here, don't help me." (They won't, because the card is on the bottom of the packet in your left hand.)

Place the fan of cards face up on the packet, backs up, in your left hand, and remember the face-up card now on the top of the pack. This is to be the indicator to tell you where the peeked-at card is at any time. Let us assume that the indicator is the ace of clubs. Riffle shuffle the twenty-six cards from the middle of the pack into the top and bottom sections of the pack held in your left hand. This does not mix the face-up cards with the face-down cards. Cut off about thirteen cards from the top and place them on the bottom, thus bringing the ace of clubs next to the peeked-at card.

Show that some cards are face up, others face down. As you do this, don't spread the cards, lift up packets of them carelessly, dropping them on the pack. It makes them appear to be well mixed when actually about thirteen reds are at the top face up and thirteen or so red ones are at the bottom face up. The others are in the middle, face down.

Cut the pack about the middle and repeat the cutting and dropping action for a moment or two. This gives a perfect illusion that the cards are well mixed, face up and face down.

While you are showing the cards are mixed in reversed order, locate the ace of clubs, your indicator. This card is about thirteen from the top of the pack, and because it is face up, its location is elementary.

Insert the fourth finger of the left hand above the peeked-at card (the one above the ace of clubs), and double cut the pack to bring the peeked-at card to the top. Let the cards at the middle of the pack be seen.

You now have about twenty-six cards face up on top of the pack, a similar number under them face down, and the peeked-at card on top face down.

As you again carelessly let the cards be seen in this more or less mixed fashion, slip the third finger of the left hand in between the top face up packet and the bottom face down packet.

The right hand holds the top packet, second and third fingers of the right hand at one end of this top packet, and the thumb of the right hand at the other end of the top packet. In this manner, turn-over the bottom packet. With the hold you have with the third and fourth fingers, the move is simple, and the top packet affords you excellent cover for the move to be indetectably executed.

The top card (the peeked-at card) is now face down, and all the other cards are face up.

Cut the cards in the middle, bringing the center card to the top. It is face up, but that adds to the illusion of the card still to be reversed and mixed.

With your left hand place the pack on the table, and ask the person to name the card he is thinking about. Spread the pack, and the card is seen in the middle reversed, face up.

Experiment No. 25

Wishful Thinking

This is another little originality which it pleases me to pass on to those interested in presenting these snappy, puzzling disclosures of a card which is seemingly only thought of.

THE EFFECT: A card is peeked at by one of the spectators. The performer does not cut, shuffle or apparently disturb the pack except to openly place the top and the bottom cards into the middle of the pack and show that the then bottom card is not the peeked-at card. He then turns over the top card (no double lift here), showing it is not the peeked-at card. Performer then places the pack face down on the table and asks the spectator to place his finger on the top of the pack and to wish for his card. After a moment of silence for the wishing period, the spectator is asked to tell the performer the card he wished for. On naming the card, he is asked to turn over the card under his wishing finger, the top card, and see if he got his wish. It is his card.

THE SLEIGHTS: The "riffle peek", a "side steal and shift" peculiar to this effect which I shall describe with the working, "top palm and replacement".

THE WORKING: The pack is held in your left hand facing the palm, the four fingers up the sides pressing the opposite side of the cards into the crotch of the thumb which lies across the middle of the back of the pack.

With the first finger of your right hand on the index corner, the thumb at the back of the same index corner, riffle the corners by pulling the cards back with the first finger and letting them go again. Do this once or twice, holding the pack so it is not possible for your spectator to see the indices of the cards.

Ask him to tell you to stop, confining your riffle to about the center of the pack. Riffle fairly slowly. Stop when told, and permit him to see the index of the card at the position stopped at.

At the moment the spectator notes the card, open the break sufficient to insert your left fourth fingertip below the card noted.

Take the pack in between the thumb and fingers of your right hand, holding it face down, your thumb at one end of the pack, your fingers at the other end. By light pressure of the thumb and fingers, the break is readily maintained, and the left hand is removed, leaving the pack thus held in the right hand.

You now address the spectator, saying, "You have the card clearly impressed on your mind and you promise not to forget it? Thank you. Then I want you to observe that everything is fair and above board, if you know exactly what I mean. You do? That's fine, because you now know that I intend to take every mean little advantage of you that I can, so we both understand the situation quite clearly. "

While you have been pattering away, your left hand has been brought up and the pack placed into it, the little fingertip entering the break, and the spectator's card is pushed out the side of the pack about an inch. This is not detected because of the cover afforded by the right hand holding the pack at the ends between the fingers and thumb. When the spectator's card is protruding an inch from the side of the pack, the index corner of this card should be at the first joint of the fourth finger of the right hand.

Without disturbing the pack, the top card is pushed over the side of the pack about half an inch by the left thumb.

The left thumb is then shifted to the back of the exposed corner of the second top card and exerts a holding pressure on the pack, while the right hand fingers and thumb by light pressure on the ends of the two protruding cards carry them to the right of the pack.

This act to an observer is nothing more than seeing you carry to the right off the top of the pack one card, the top one, but secretly you have been able to withdraw the spectator's card also by the cover this act and the top card afforded you.

The replacement is quite as important, and is accomplished as follows.

With the two cards drawn just clear of the edge of the second top card, this second top card is pushed to the right about a quarter of an inch, and the two cards in the right hand are now carried back by your right hand onto the pack. The spectator's card now passes easily and indetectably under the second top protruding card as the top card is carried back into place on the top of the pack.

The pack is squared, and the top card is withdrawn again exactly as before, except this time it is alone. It is then flipped over and inserted face down into the middle of the pack as you say, "The top card I shall place in here."

Take off the bottom card, show it and place it also in the middle of the pack, saying, "The bottom card I shall place here also."

Turn the top card face up on the pack, saying, "This, of course, is not your card. It could not be because your card is closer to the middle if my memory did not deceive me."

As you are pattering away, you slide the face up top card and the face up second top card half way over the side of the pack. The left thumb and fingers help hold the cards together as one card only.

The right hand is placed palm down over the face up top card and covers it for a second only, moving off the card to the right and carrying the spectator's card in the right palm from under the face up card. At the moment the right hand is clear of the face up card, the right thumb tips the face up card face down on the pack (Jack Merlin, "A Pack of Cards"), and the right hand moves over the pack and secretly drops the palmed spectator's card on the pack.

The pack is placed on the table, and the unsuspecting spectator is told to place his finger on the top card and wish for his card. After the right amount of byplay, the wished for card is revealed at the top of the pack under his finger.

Experiment No. 26
Color Memory

This is another of those original surprises that are over almost as soon as they begin, but leave the onlookers amazed and mystified.

THE EFFECT: A card is turned over face up on the top of the pack, and is seen to be a black ace. It is then laid face down on the table, a little to your right. A second card is turned face up on the top of the pack and is seen to be a red ace. This card is laid face down on your left. A third card is turned face up on the top of the pack, is seen to be a black ace and is then laid face down on the first black ace. A fourth card is turned face up on the pack and is seen to be the other red ace. This card is dealt face down on the first red ace. After suitably questioning the memory of the spectators, the aces on the right are seen to be red instead of black, and the red aces placed on your left are turned face up and are black.

SLEIGHTS: "Double lift", "Mexican turnover".

THE WORKING: Secretly place the four aces on the top of the pack, alternating red and black. On top of the four aces place any indifferent card.

Double lift the two top cards, showing the first ace. Place the two cards face down on the top of the pack, and deal off the indifferent card.

Double lift two aces, replace them on the pack and deal off the top ace to the left of the first card dealt.

Double lift the next two aces and replace them on the top of the pack. Deal the top ace on the first card dealt.

Double lift and replace the two aces. Deal the top ace on the ace on your left.

Openly take the ace off the top, exercising just sufficient care not to let its face be seen, and execute the Mexican turnover to change the indifferent card just dealt on the table for the ace in your hand.

Use the indifferent card to nonchalantly flip over the other aces in proper order to show they have changed their positions.

A nice climax to this effect is to have someone peek at a card, and then secretly pass this card to the top of the four aces and proceed as before. Then you are left holding the spectator's card, but no one has any reason to suspect it.

Replace the spectator's card on the pack without referring to it or letting it be seen.

Pick up the aces, place them on the pack in a spread-out packet, and as you square them, secretly maneuver the spectator's card to the second top position.

Immediately deal the four top cards face down about six inches apart in a row on the table so that the peeked-at card lies in the position which would be most readily selected by the spectator who peeked at the card in the beginning. Say, "Put your finger on one of these aces."

Carelessly gather the other three cards, letting them be seen without special attention being called to them, and say, "What card did you think of at the beginning of this experiment?"

After the proper delay, ask him to turn over the ace he selected, and he will find it changed into the card of his thoughts.

If you desire a more sure fire means of forcing the card, say, "Name a number between one and four." Two or three is all the choice given, but this is seldom noticed. If two is the number, count from the left to the card. If three, count from the right to the card.

Experiment No. 27
Think of a Number

THE EFFECT: A spectator is requested to think of a number between one and twenty, shuffle the cards and carefully note the name of the card at the number he thought of without disarranging the order of the cards, and then give you the pack. Your head is turned away to insure that you do not glance at the number of cards or the name of the card looked at. Upon receiving the pack, you shuffle and cut it and hand it back to the spectator.

Request that he remove from the top of the pack to the bottom of the pack as many cards as the number he thought of, and place the pack squared up on the table. You cut the pack and turn over his card.

SLEIGHTS: "False shuffle", "double cut", "gauge cut".

WORKING: The principle itself is a very elementary one in simple arithmetic. The spectator looks at a card; for example, say it is five from the top (the number does not really matter, so long as he remembers it and remembers the card at that number down from the top of the pack).

On receiving the pack, you undercut about half the pack and shuffle on ten cards to the top of the pack, jog and shuffle the rest. Place the pack on the table and cut to the jog. Ask the spectator whether he left the cards on top or placed them on the bottom (you know very well what he did, but it adds a little confusion). Say, "Oh, no! It makes no difference at all. But will you please count off silently so I do not know your number and place them on the bottom of the pack, and then square the cards up face down here on the table." Turn your head away again while the cards are counted off by the spectator.

Turn around and cut off nine cards. The top card is the one the spectator looked at.

You may make the cut any number to suit your fingernail, because that is your gauge for cutting the same number, and of course you shuffle on one card more than you cut off. The rest works automatically.

The card may be produced in any one of several different ways, depending on your ability with the various sleights. If you are proficient at second dealing, you may take up the pack and deal off the nine cards and then say, "Will you please tell me when to stop dealing?"

From now on you deal seconds and turn up the selected card when told to stop. Or you may double lift after shuffling off to the selected card, and execute the throw down change.

Or if the sleight is in your repertoire, you may shuffle the selected card to the bottom of the pack and execute the Greek shift. Allow the spectator to find the card by inserting another card into the middle of the pack.

Or the selected card may be found reversed.

Or perhaps you may prefer to palm it, and produce it from your own or the spectator's pocket.

Or you may prefer to glimpse the card and spell it out or make it eleven down and spell it out without the necessity of even glimpsing the card.

However, you should have many different methods in your repertoire—then seldom indeed are you compelled to repeat the same effects for the same groups of people, and you are never embarrassed by a mishap, either on your own part or that of the spectator getting confused about his card or number.

Experiment No. 28

A Brilliant Climax

(My Pet Effect)

THE EFFECT: Four cards are freely selected by as many different spectators and returned, one at a time, in different parts of the pack, which is then shuffled by the performer in a manner that disperses any suspicion of false moves. Each card may be initialed on the face by the spectators who chose it. Performer shows his inside coat pocket to be quite empty, places the pack, after it is shuffled by the spectators, into this empty pocket.

As each spectator names his card, the performer reaches into his pocket and unhesitatingly shows the card he withdraws to be the card named and bearing the spectator's initials on its face for further identification.

After the four selected cards are thus shown, they are carelessly dropped face down on the table. The performer remarks, "Gentlemen, I have a confession to make. These are not your cards at all. In fact, they are the four aces." Performer turns the aces face up to prove the truth of his words, and then drops them again on the table face down. Pattering away while shuffling the pack, he says, "These are your cards," and he deals four cards off the top of the pack face down on the table. He then turns them face up, but to the performer's own apparent surprise they are the aces. He hurriedly turns over the first packet of four which a moment ago was composed of the four aces. They are now the four initialed spectators' cards.

I want to say a word or two of encouragement to you. This whole effect is based on proper timing. If you can do the sleights, to be enumerated, well, you will find it a not too difficult task to perfect your timing to blend the moves in an evenly paced, beautiful illusion that will leave your audience spellbound at the dazzling climax.

THE SLEIGHTS: The "Hindu shuffle shift", the "riffle shuffle", the "double cut", "palming off the bottom of the pack", the "top change with four cards", the "throw down change".

THE WORKING: On the bottom of the pack, unknown to your audience, are the four aces. As you approach the first spectator, rapidly perform the Hindu shuffle, that is, undercut about twenty-six cards off the pack and draw them off on the packet in your left hand, several at a time, until you have only the aces and several other cards remaining in your right hand. Drop these on the packet in the left hand, keeping a break below the aces with your left hand fourth finger.

Immediately double cut to bring the aces to the bottom of the pack again; that is, cut half the cards below the break, place them on top of the pack, and then cut to the break and place them on top of the pack. (This is done while the cards are in the hands, not on the table.)

Extend your left hand with the pack face down, and thumb riffle the corners. Say, "Would you please say 'Stop' as I riffle these cards so you will have a free choice of the position." You stop when told, and cut the pack slowly and fairly at the position, placing the upper packet under the other cards. In doing so, insert the tip of the fourth finger of your left hand to secretly maintain a break below the aces.

Allow the spectator to lift off the top card from the pack, and request him to initial the face of the card with a pencil. (Provide a number of pencils for this purpose.) When he has initialed the face of the card, request him to lay it on the top of the pack face down, but before you permit him to do so, you draw away the packet below the break and Hindu shuffle them onto the top of the pack, thus bringing the aces to the bottom of the pack.

When the initialed card is replaced on the top of the pack, undercut half the pack and drop this packet on the top packet. In doing so, insert the fourth finger of the left hand on top of the initialed card, that is, between the four aces on the bottom of one packet and the initialed card on top of the other packet.

Now again draw off the packet below the break, but this time apply just sufficient pressure with the fourth finger of the left hand on the back of the initialed card to retain it as the packet is drawn from under it, thus bringing the initialed card to the bottom of the packet in the left hand, with the four aces immediately above it. Draw off small packets of cards from the right hand packet onto the left hand packet till the packet is exhausted, Hindu shuffle fashion.

You approach the second spectator. As you do so, undercut two-thirds of the pack, draw off and drop small packets on the one-third packet, keeping a break with your left fourth fingertip as you drop the final packet embracing the initialed card and the aces.

Double cut to bring the initialed card and aces to the bottom of the pack again.

Thumb riffle the corners of the cards as you did for the first spectator, and have him say 'Stop'.

Cut the cards inserting the left fingertip between the packets, and have the top card removed and initialed.

While waiting for the card to be replaced on the top, double undercut, bringing the initialed card and the four aces to the bottom of the pack. Riffle shuffle, maintaining the stock cards on the bottom, Hindu shuffle and double cut.

Extend the left hand, and have the second initialed card replaced on top of the pack.

Undercut half the pack, thus bringing the two initialed cards together in the center of the pack. As the packets come together, insert the little finger of the left hand between the two initialed cards. Draw away the bottom packet, exerting a light pressure on the back of the second initialed card, thus retaining it with the first initialed card and the aces on the bottom of the packet in the left hand.

Hindu shuffle the right hand packet onto the left hand packet, and riffle shuffle the pack, maintaining the stock cards, that is, the second initialed card at the bottom, the first initialed card second bottom and the four aces next in order.

The foregoing moves are repeated as you have two more cards selected and initialed and similarly returned to the pack.

Then follows a move not heretofore described.

Hold the pack in your left hand, faces away from palm and towards the table in position for riffling.

Riffle about half the pack; that is, release them one at a time rapidly from the left thumb.

Take these released cards in your right hand in the same position as those cards in your left hand, and riffle exactly four cards, that is, release them from the right thumb. These are the four initialed cards. Let them fall from the one corner away from the left thumb, and slide the right hand packet over them, thus transferring under the left hand packet for riffle shuffling the two packets together. All this takes only a second, and passes quite unsuspected of guile or trickery.

You now have the four aces on the bottom of the right hand packet, and the four initialed cards on the bottom of the left hand packet.

Riffle the packets together so that the aces fall second, fourth, sixth and eighth cards from the bottom of the pack. This is the most difficult sleight of all to do well, but it is important to the effect, so practice it often.

After this placement riffle, give the pack a Hindu shuffle and double cut. Sliding the bottom cards over each other a little ways, count eight cards. Slip the fourth finger of the left hand above the eight cards.

Take away about two-thirds of the bottom cards of the pack with the right hand, keeping the break by side pressure on the cards with the fingers and thumb of your right hand only. Hindu shuffle these cards onto the left hand packet, thus transferring the stock cards to the top of the pack. But as this packet of eight cards is placed on the top of the pack at the termination of the Hindu shuffle, the fourth finger of the left hand is inserted to maintain a break below them.

Attention is drawn to the inside coat pocket. A spectator is requested to place his hand inside to assure everyone that it is really empty.

At this moment, hand the pack to a spectator to shuffle, saying, "You look like a man to be trusted. Will you shuffle this pack?"

Palm off the eight cards kept at the fourth finger break. When you receive the shuffled pack again, replace the eight cards on top. (See "replacement".) Hand the cards back to the person and say, "I wonder if you would oblige me by dropping the pack into my empty pocket."

You now have an ace on top of the pack and an ace third, fifth and seventh cards down. The first initialed card is the second top card. The other initialed cards are in the order selected, and lie fourth, sixth and eighth cards from the top.

Place your right hand into your left inside coat pocket and secure the two top cards in the proper position for the throw down change. Ask the first spectator to name his card.

Withdraw the two cards thus held in your right hand as one card, and call attention to the initials.

Execute throw change, secretly dropping the ace face down. Return the hand into the pocket and replace the initialed card on the bottom of the pack.

Have the second, third and fourth cards named in proper order, each time showing the initialed card and throw changing it for an ace.

Remove the pack from the pocket, and as you patter, Hindu shuffle the initialed cards from the bottom of the pack to the top of the pack, finally leaving them protrude inward about half their length over the ends of the other cards.

Say, "Gentlemen, you have been deceived. These cards I showed you are not your initialed cards, but aces." Turn them faces up.

Now without haste, but in tune with the surprise created, pick up the aces, and not giving the spectators time to completely recover their composure, exchange the four aces for the protruding initialed cards, letting them fall face down on the table.

Then casually remark, "I'll let you in on a secret." As you say this, Hindu shuffle briskly and double cut, thus returning the initialed cards to the top of the pack again.

Deal these four cards one by one face down, saying, "These are the four initialed cards." Turn them over together and affect surprise because they are the aces.

Turn over the cards that a moment ago were shown to be the aces, and they are now the four chosen cards bearing the initials of the spectators.

Experiment No. 29

An Ace Introduction

THE EFFECT: A pack of cards is thoroughly shuffled, and the cards are cut to the top, one at a time, and dropped on the table face up.

After each ace is produced at the top of the pack, it is again well shuffled and cut, but the aces nevertheless appear on top of the deck until all four aces lie face up on the table.

SLEIGHTS: "Charlier pass", "bottom stock riffle shuffle", "Hindu shuffle", "double cut".

THE WORKING: The four aces are second, third and fourth and fifth from the bottom of the pack and are placed in your pocket. You remove the pack and proceed to riffle shuffle, retaining the position of the five bottom cards. These five cards are then brought to the top. Hindu shuffle and double cut. Then riffle for bridging and cut proper. Aces are now together about the center of the deck and locatable by the bridge. Make the Charlier pass with your left hand. The aces are thus brought to the top. Lift off the ace from the top and drop it face down so that it strikes the fingers of the left hand and falls face up on the table.

Take away less than half the bottom of the pack and overhand shuffle these cards onto the three aces. The bridge will still be maintained. False cut and Erdnase triple cut. Then execute the Charlier pass at the bridge to bring the three aces to the top. Lift off the top ace and drop turnover again so the ace falls face up. Repeat the foregoing moves until you have all four aces lying face up on the table.

It is my opinion that this effect creates a very desirable impression on your audience, whether they be magicians or the less card wise public. It reveals you in their eyes a master of the deck of cards. You have established yourself, and will have a very attentive audience for your effects to follow.

Pick up the four aces and insert them into different parts of the pack for the Dai Vernon shift. Execute same, secretly passing the four aces to the bottom of the pack. Shift two of the aces to the top of the pack, using the Hindu shuffle to bring the four aces to the middle. Insert the left fourth finger between the aces, two above and two below the finger, and double cut to bring two aces to the top of the pack and two aces to the bottom of the pack.

Riffle shuffle, keeping the aces in their places at the top and bottom of the pack.

Hold the pack in your right hand, fingers on the face of the bottom ace and thumb on the back of the top ace. Throw the pack with a sudden short side jerk to the left hand, and retain the top and bottom aces with your fingers and thumb.

Do exactly the same move again, throwing the pack from the left hand to the right hand, and this time retain the top and bottom aces in between the thumb and fingers of the left hand. Catch the pack in the right hand, the first two aces being held by the first finger and the tips of the second, third and fourth fingers. Then drop the pack and lay the four aces face up. This is a brilliant piece of business.

Experiment No. 30

The Aces and the Chosen Card

This effect should preferably follow one of the effects in which you have used the four aces.

THE EFFECT: The aces held in the right hand are placed into different sections of the pack, which is held face up in the left hand, and the pack is afterwards cut and riffle shuffled.

A spectator is asked to say, "Stop!" as you riffle the cards, and then to note the index of the card you expose at the place stopped during the riffle.

The pack is immediately riffle shuffled, then overhand shuffled, and then Hindu shuffled. The peeked-at card is turned up on the top of the pack.

The peeked-at card is then pushed into the middle of the pack about half-way, and is then withdrawn and thrown face up on the table. It is an ace.

The pack is cut again and the card on top is shown to be the peeked-at card. It is inserted as before in the middle of the pack, and withdrawn, and thus changes to another ace. Twice more the same procedure is followed of cutting and showing the top card each time to be the peeked-at card, inserting it half-way into the pack, withdrawing it and showing that it has changed to the ace. Once more the pack is cut and the top card turned over. This time it is an indifferent card. It is thrown face down on the table. A moment later it is turned face up, and it is seen to be the peeked-at card. There is some really beautiful card manipulation in this effect.

SLEIGHTS: The "Vernon four card shift", the "riffle peek", the "riffle shuffle top and bottom stock", "milk build shuffle", "Erdnase in jog shuffle", "Hindu shuffle transfer", "double lift", the "slide", the "break" and "double cut".

THE WORKING: With your right hand place the aces into the middle section of the pack, several cards apart, as you thumb riffle the pack face up in your left hand.

Execute the Vernon shift and thus bring the aces secretly to the top of the pack.

Riffle shuffle, keeping the aces on top.

Finger riffle the index corner for a stop peek, allowing the index of the card to be seen by the spectator when you are told to stop.

Secretly cut the cards at the peeked-at card so that the right hand packet has the four aces on top and the peeked-at card on the bottom.

Riffle shuffle the left hand packet into the right hand packet so that at the top of the pack you have the four aces and at the bottom of the pack the peeked-at card.

Without any change in pace, place the pack face down in between the fingers and thumb of your left hand for the overhand shuffle.

Shuffle off, one at a time, three cards from the top of the pack. As you draw off the first top card with your left thumb, also throw off the peeked-at card from the bottom with your left fingers. This is the milk build. In jog the next card as you draw it off the top of the pack onto the four aces and the peeked-at card now in your left hand.

Continue the overhand shuffle in small packets, falling on and over the jogged card.

Square up the pack with the fingers of the right hand at one end of the pack and the right thumb at the other, but in doing so, lift up a little with your thumb on the jogged card to form a break below the jogged card and the ace packet.

Transfer the grip on the pack to the fingers and thumb of the left hand which hold the pack by its sides, the fourth finger maintaining the break during the transfer.

The right hand takes away the pack by the sides near the inside end corners, thus maintaining the break.

The second finger and thumb of the left hand draw off small packets from the top of the pack held in the right hand into the left hand. Hindu shuffle, finally dropping the packet of four aces and the peeked-at card on top of the pack. As this is happening, the fourth finger of the left hand slips in under the peeked-at card to maintain a break beneath it.

The right thumb is placed on top of the non-index inside end corner, and the first finger enters the break below the peeked-at card, and, thus gripping the packet of five cards, turns them over as one card.

A single trial, following the description carefully, will prove the indetectable simplicity of this move, although it sounds difficult.

The fourth finger is kept in place to maintain a break even after the packet of five cards is turned face up.

With the packet of five cards face up on top of the pack, the fourth finger of the left hand maintaining the break, the thumb and second and third fingers pressing lightly on the sides holding them together, the right thumb tip is now placed into the break at the inside end, and the packet of five is turned over endwise face down.

The left thumb riffles open a break at the end, and the packet of five cards is inserted into the pack at the break, being forced in about two-thirds of their length. Then the first finger of the left hand extends over the end of the four cards concealed from view by the top ace of the packet and pushes the four cards into the pack as the right hand thumb and finger withdraw the ace and drop it face up on the table.

As the finger of the left hand presses home the four cards into the pack, it keeps up sufficient pressure to cause the tip of the pad of the finger to maintain a small break above the four cards.

After the ace is thrown face up on the table, the right hand covers the pack, and the break is transferred to the fourth finger of the left hand.

A double undercut to the break brings the three aces and the peeked-at card to the top of the pack.

The left thumb pushes several cards over the top, and by visual count, the fourth finger of the left hand is readily inserted under the peeked-at card, fourth one down this time.

Then the same moves are repeated—turning over the four cards as one card, turning the packet over endwise and inserting it into the pack, the first finger of the left hand pressing the under three cards into the pack, and the withdrawal of the ace and dropping it face up on the table.

The same procedure is followed twice more, until the four aces are face up on the table and the top card of the pack is the peeked-at card.

Then double lift and execute the throw down change as you apparently throw down an indifferent card instead of the one the spectator peeked at. Finally turn it face up and show it to be the correct one.

This effect reads and is repetitious, but from experience I know it to be very entertaining to the magicians and also to the general public. That is the real and only test any effect should have.

Experiment No. 31

Quintuplets

This is an effective and original method of finding five selected cards which has not heretofore been revealed.

THE EFFECT: Five spectators are each asked, one after another, to note a card in the pack (by the riffle peek method). Each time a card is noted, performer shuffles the pack. After the fifth card is noted and the pack shuffled, performer places the pack on the table and asks a spectator to cut it. On second thought, performer has the spectator shuffle it first and cut it and deal five cards, from the shuffled pack onto the table, faces down.

The performer squares these five cards in his hand and spreads them apart on the table before the five spectators who peeked at the cards in the beginning.

A spectator is asked to place his finger on the back of any one of the spread-out five cards. Another spectator is asked to name the card he is thinking of. The card is turned over and seen to be the card named.

The four cards are pushed from place to place, and another spectator is asked to choose one of the four. He is asked to name his card—it is the one he chose from the four.

Another spectator is asked to make a choice of one card, and another spectator names the card aloud.

The two last spectators are each told to take one of the two remaining cards, but not to look at them. Then each is told to name the card the other is holding.

SLEIGHTS: The "peek riffle", "bottom stock riffle shuffle", "Hindu shuffle", "double cut", "Hindu shift", "top stock palm", the "exchange", "table replacement", "Cardini's spring".

THE WORKING: As you approach the first spectator on your left front, riffle shuffle the pack, give it a Hindu shuffle and double cut. (This is for the purpose of letting the spectators see that the cards are mixed.) You say to the first spectator, "I am going to have several cards remembered, and I want you to remember one that you see in the pack. So we are sure to play fair, I am asking that you say 'Stop!' as I riffle the cards in this manner." Riffle the cards quickly; then commence over again slowly. Hold the pack face down so the spectators cannot see any cards until you stop. Then hold the pack up before him with the top packet pulled back so the index of the card is plainly visible to the spectator.

Close this opening and secretly maintain a break with your left fourth finger. Then execute the Cardini spring with your little finger in the break. As you approach the second spectator, double undercut to the break, secretly bringing the peeked card to the bottom of the pack. Then riffle stock shuffle, keeping the peeked-at card on the bottom.

Finger riffle the index corners, and have the second spectator say "Stop!", letting him see the index of the card at the position stopped.

Maintain the break with the fourth fingertip of the left hand. Then shift the card to the bottom under the first peeked-at card. To do this, use the Buckley single card shift. Riffle shuffle, keeping the cards peeked-at on the bottom of the pack. Use the bottom stock riffle shuffle.

Have three more spectators each peek at a card, following the procedure just related for the second card. You thus bring all five cards in their selected order on the bottom of the pack.

Put your left hand fourth finger into the pack to make a break above the five peeked-at cards.

Transfer the pack to the right hand, taking it on the sides near the inside end between fingers and thumb, thus maintaining the break.

Execute the Hindu shuffle to bring the packet of five peeked-at cards to the top of the pack.

Insert the fourth finger of the left hand under the packet of five as they are dropped on the pack.

Execute the top palm of the packet of five, and place the pack on the table.

Ask a spectator to cut the pack. Then say, "You had better shuffle it, please." When he has shuffled the pack, say, "Please deal five cards in a heap on the table—any five. Thank you. You may lay the pack here." Indicate a place at your right convenient for you to reach with your right hand when the time arrives.

Now comes the exchange—a very effective sleight. You should practice it carefully and follow the instructions to the letter to do it indetectably. That is the only way any sleight should be performed.

After the exchange, spread the five peeked-at cards with your left hand. Pick up the pack with your right hand and say, "We won't need these." Put them into their case as you say this, and lay them aside. Remember that the five cards spread out face down are the spectators' cards and lie as follows: First card peeked at is at your right; second, third, fourth and fifth lie in the order of their selection from your right to left.

Ask any one of the spectators to draw any one of the cards towards him without lifting it from the table. After the card has been selected, ask the person who you know peeked at that card to name the card he is thinking of. When the spectator turns it over, it is, of course, right.

Move the cards about as if you don't care what happens to them. However, each move must be a very carefully rehearsed one, and when the pushing around is finished, you have simply moved them into position Number Two, which is one, two, three, four and five from left to right instead of right to left, with one of the five missing.

Ask another spectator to choose a card, and if you have placed his card in a position of least resistance, he will probably take his own card. Ask him to name his card, and casually say, "Just turn it over." If he takes someone else's card, you then ask that person to name his card, and it is turned over. You can't lose so long as you have kept track of the cards and the spectators, which is a relatively easy thing to do under the circumstances.

The whole effect must be thoroughly rehearsed and carefully timed.

Experiment No. 32
The Slop Over Card Location

THE EFFECT: A spectator peeks at a card. The pack is slop shuffled and spread ribbonwise, face down on the table. The peeked-at card makes its appearance face up in the ribbon spread pack.

The only thing new about this is the manner in which the effect is produced. If you follow the moves exactly as hereinafter described, you will acquire a very pretty, smooth effect that has a mystifying climax, mainly because of its very simplicity.

THE SLEIGHTS: The "peek", the "double cut", the "slop over shuffle", the "spread".

THE WORKING: Because of the relatively simple working of this effect, you are likely to rush ahead of the description. I am requesting you not to do so or you may miss the true beauty of the procedure, which resides in its very simplicity, but the details are important.

Commence with the pack face down in your left hand, and while riffling the index corner of the card with the first or second finger of the right hand, ask a spectator to say, "Stop!"

Upon being told to stop, you raise the pack to his eye level and open the break at the position at which you stopped the riffle, and have him remember the card.

Double cut, bringing the peeked-at card secretly to the bottom of the pack.

Riffle shuffle once, keeping the card there without exposing it on the bottom of the pack. (This is optional.)

Overhand shuffle, secretly holding the peeked-at card with the left fingers as you do so.

Now perform the slop over shuffle as follows:

The pack lies in the fork of the left thumb, face down, left thumb across the middle of the top card, first, second and third fingers curled up the side, fourth finger at the end. The right hand is palm up, and the back of the fourth finger of the right hand rests across the back of the pack at the end near the fourth finger of the left hand.

The left thumb now pushes off the pack about six or seven cards onto the fingers of the right hand, the right thumb retaining them on the fingers of the right hand. The right hand, with this packet of six or seven cards, is turned over, bringing the six cards face up and laying them, still held in the right hand, half-way over the side of the back of the top card of the pack.

The left thumb pushes off of the top of the pack in the left hand another six or seven cards. These cards pass above the right thumb, but under the right fourth finger.

The right hand turns over with the two packets comprised of six or seven cards each, and separated at one end by the right fourth finger.

The left thumb pushes off six or seven more cards. These cards pass under the bottom cards in the right hand, passing above the right hand fingers, that is, they are added to the bottom of the first packet of six or seven cards pushed off the pack into the right hand.

The right hand is again turned over with the cards it holds, and several more cards are pushed off the pack to be added to the bottom of the face down packet in the right hand.

The moves of turning over the right hand with the accumulating two packets of back-to-back cards it holds are repeated until only a single card remains face down in the left hand. This is, as you know, the peeked-at card. Here follows a simple, but nevertheless very important, move.

You have just pushed the last few cards but one under the right hand packet above the right thumb. Now turn the right hand over with the cards and slide the single card remaining in the left hand under the fingers of the right hand, that is, face to face on the card next to the right fingers.

You should now have all the cards in the right hand as follows: Under your right thumb is the peeked-at card, face down, on about twenty-six cards, all face up, which are separated by the fourth finger of the right hand from a similar number of cards which are all face down.

The right hand continues its turning action without change of pace, first leaving the packet of cards which is below the right fourth finger in the left hand, then turning the face up packet, with its face down card, over on the left hand packet.

All the cards but one, the peeked-at card, are face down, and a ribbon spread reveals the peeked-at card face up in the middle of the pack.

Experiment No. 33

Card and Pocket Mystery

THE EFFECT: Performer, having shuffled a pack of cards, riffles them and has a spectator say "Stop!"

Performer cuts the pack, turns the top card face up and offers the pack in this manner to the spectator. He then hands him a pencil with the request that he initial the card for later identification.

On receiving the cards from the spectator, the performer merely turns the initialed card face down on the pack, lifts it off and places it in his pants pocket, but he makes a point of showing the card at the last second before it enters the pocket.

Performer again shuffles the cards and asks anyone to take the pack, name a number less than fifteen and deal that number of cards face down on the table. He is then to look at the next card on the pack, remember it and take up the cards dealt on the table and place them back on the card looked at. Then cut the cards and square up the pack.

Performer says to spectator, "I am going to try to locate your card. Would you mind helping me by calling 'Stop!' while I riffle them. I believe in the adage—'Two heads are better than a stitch saves nine.' Or is it—'Glass houses never gather moss?' "

Performer cuts the pack after the spectator says "Stop!", and shows the spectator the card by turning it over on the pack after the cards are cut.

Performer turns it face down on the pack, then lifts it off and drops it face down on the floor, saying, "Step on it, please."

Turning to the spectator, performer asks, "Do you know what card you selected?" On receiving an affirmative answer, the performer says, "That's right—this one," and pulls it out of the pants pocket for a moment, allowing the card to be seen. Performer now says, "I am going to try to accomplish an effect that I have never before succeeded in doing satisfactorily, but I figure it this way—

if I don't keep on trying, how can I possibly expect to succeed? So I know you won't mind me running through a little rehearsal."

Addressing the first spectator, performer says, "What did you say your card is? That's what I thought you said." Turning to the spectator standing on the card, performer says, "Would you mind getting off this gentleman's card? Thank you. Do you recognize your initials? They are yours? Good!"

"Now comes the part that makes me nervous. Your card, sir? What is its name, please? Would you mind taking it from my pants pocket? It is your card. Thank you. You can't imagine what a great help you have both been."

Before describing the working of this effect, I want to say a few words in defense of using a duplicate card. I believe there are times when such a procedure is warranted, and I consider this one of them, although the indiscriminate use of duplicates and fake cards is to be avoided. It usually proclaims a lack of manipulative skill.

SLEIGHTS: The "thumb riffle force", "double lift", "crimp", "finger location", "top card palm", "replacement" and "Hindu shuffle".

THE WORKING: On top of the pack are duplicate sixes of hearts. Their index corners are lightly crimped to make it possible to locate them later.

Undercut about half the pack and Hindu shuffle them on the top of the pack, inserting the fourth finger of the left hand on the top six of hearts to maintain a break.

Thumb riffle the corners and have someone say "Stop!" Cut to the break, bringing the two sixes of hearts on the top again.

Double lift and turn the two sixes face up on the top as one card.

Hand a pencil to a spectator and ask him to initial the card. It is not necessary to let the cards out of your hands if you are afraid to do so.

Turn the two cards face down as one card. Take off the top six of hearts and place it in your pocket. Let the card be seen as you put it in your pocket. The initials will not be missed in the flash given of the card entering the pocket.

Shuffle the cards, keeping the initialed six of hearts on the top of the pack.

Hand the pack to a spectator and request him to think of a number between three and fifteen.

Ask him to deal that many cards off the pack face down on the table; then tell him to remember the top card on the remaining packet.

Have the packet of cards dealt off the pack replaced on top, and the pack cut several times.

Take the pack and locate the initialed six of hearts by the crimped corner, and cut it to about the middle of the pack.

Insert the fourth finger of the left hand on the initialed card.

Thumb riffle force, asking the spectator to help you find his card by calling "Stop!"

Cut to the break, bringing the initialed card to the top of the pack. Double lift and show the spectator his card, turning it face up on the pack and keeping the break with your little finger. Turn the two cards face down again on the top of the pack.

Slide off the top card, the initialed card, letting it fall face down on the floor. Do this very deliberately so the spectator will assume quite positively that it is his card which you just a moment ago showed him face up on the pack.

Have him stand on the card while you palm the top card. Place your hand in your pocket with the palmed card and withdraw the six of hearts, saying to the person who initialed the six of hearts, "Do you recall your card?" On receiving an answer, say, "That's right—the six of hearts." Show it briefly and push it in your pocket. Then palm it out of your pocket onto the pack.

Turn to the spectator standing on the initialed card and say, "Would you mind stepping off this gentleman's card?" Let him pick it up, and have the initials identified. Then say, "Would you mind taking your card from my pocket?"

The removal of the card from your pocket by the spectator shows the pocket empty.

Experiment No. 34

Your Favorite Ace

THE EFFECT: After the performer has thoroughly shuffled the pack of cards, he requests a spectator to name his favorite ace, and another to name a number. Performer immediately deals that number of cards, and the ace named by the spectator is shown to have been at that very position.

Another spectator is asked to name one of the three remaining aces, and also a number. The ace named is found at that number.

A third and fourth spectator names the other aces, and these are found at the desired places, but the third ace turns up again in place of the fourth ace, and the fourth ace is found on the table where a moment ago the third ace was seen to be.

SLEIGHTS: "Second dealing", "overhand in jog shuffle", "double cut", "Hindu shuffffle".

THE WORKING: Unknown to anyone you have the four aces on the top of the pack, reading from top down: H, D, C, S.

Thoroughly shuffle, keeping the aces on top of the pack. Ask a lady among the spectators to tell you her favorite ace. Suppose it is clubs, the third ace down. Ask her to name aloud a number less than a dozen. Suppose it is eight. Deal face down two cards from the top, and second deal the third, fourth, fifth, sixth and seventh. Deal the ace of club face up at the eighth place.

Pick up the cards dealt face down, but leave the ace of clubs on the table, face up. Place these cards on the pack.

Shuffle off the number placed on top, one at a time, thus reversing their order, and drop them on top. Undercut for overhand shuffle, in jog, shuffle on, undercut to in jog and throw on top. You now have the three aces on top—Hearts, Diamonds and Spades.

Hindu shuffle and double cut, keeping the aces on top. All this shuffling that takes so much time to tell is executed in a few seconds.

Ask the spectator what her second favorite ace is. Suppose it is diamonds, the second ace from the top.

Ask her to name a number less than twelve. Suppose it is four. Deal the first card from the top. Then deal three seconds, turning the fourth card, the ace of diamonds, face up on the table. Pick up the cards dealt face down and place them on top of the pack.

Lift off the top card, show it casually and place it in the middle of the pack. The next card is the ace of spades. If the number of cards dealt had been eleven or any less number, simply push off all the cards corresponding to the number, show them to be indifferent cards and put them right way up in the middle.

With the ace of spades on top and the ace of hearts second from the top, you lift three cards off the top as one card, and lay them as one card face up on the pack, but slightly separated from the pack by the flesh of the fourth finger.

Call attention to the face up card, saying, "The numerical value of this card tells me the position in the pack of the next ace you are going to name. Now let's see if you can out-guess the prediction of this card. We have yet to find the ace of hearts and the ace of spades—make your choice. You choose the ace of spades? And the face up card is a seven. That should make the seventh card from the top the ace of spades."

Turn the three cards face down on the pack, thus bringing the ace of spades on top. Second deal one less than the number of the face up card. The number is seven in this instance; therefore, second deal six cards and turn the ace of spades face up on the pack.

As you say to the spectator, "You really did have a perfectly free choice," you pick up the packet of cards dealt face down on the table and slide the ace of hearts, the bottom card of this packet, under the ace of spades face up on the pack. Then casually slide the rest of the packet into the middle of the packet. This must be done apparently without purpose or special intent.

Now lift the two top cards as one, the ace of spades face up, the ace of hearts under it face down. Place them between the fingers and thumb of the left hand circling the pack. They are thus lying half-way over the side of the pack.

As your right hand is placed over the pack to take the pack between the right fingers and thumb at opposite ends, the left thumb draws the face up ace of spades back on the pack, and the left fingers push the ace of hearts up into the right palm. The right thumb tips the ace of spades over face down on the pack, and the palmed ace of hearts is secretly replaced on top of the ace of spades.

You immediately double lift the two cards as one, showing the ace of spades as you rotate it on the pack, and then apparently dropping it face down on the table. You actually secretly drop the ace of hearts on the table in its stead.

Note the bottom card of the pack—suppose it is a queen.

Overhand shuffle, drawing off the top ace and the bottom queen into the left hand as you commence the shuffle. Slide these two cards onto the top of the pack. Then undercut for the overhand shuffle from the top of the undercut packet ten cards, that is, two less than the numerical value of the card sighted on the bottom (the queen).

In jog the twelfth card shuffle the remainder on the in jogged card, undercut to the in jog and throw the undercut packet on top of the pack.

You now have a queen the eleventh card, and the ace of spades the twelfth card from the top of the pack.

Shuffle off eleven cards into the left hand, one at a time, and drop the packet of eleven cards back on the pack. The top card is now a queen and indicates the position of the ace of spades, which card the spectator believes lies on the table face down.

Give the pack the Hindu shuffle, and double cut to bring the pack to its original set-up position.

Turn over the queen and say, "You know a queen is priceless, but someone with a distorted sense of values said a jack is eleven, a queen twelve and a king thirteen. So her ladyship tells us the other ace is the twelfth card from the top. Let's see, perhaps you won't mind counting." Hand spectator the pack and let him count to eleven.

"Then the next card is the ace of hearts, I believe?" On turning the twelfth card it is seen to be the ace of spades again. Register mild surprise as though this unexpected happening is not of your doing, and say, "I could have sworn that this card was the ace of spades." Turn it over, and it is seen to be the ace of hearts.

A few words may not go amiss. This is a difficult effect to master. If you cannot do all the sleights correctly and moderately well, do not try this effect publicly or you will hurt rather than enhance your reputation.

The example I have given will guide you only, but the rest will come easy with a little patience and practice. If you master this effect, a dozen others will come easy to you.

Experiment No. 35

The Double Surprise

This beautiful effect calls for considerable skill in handling the cards, but it is worth the effort required. The moves have been described herein, so it is to be assumed you are already familiar with them. I shall proceed with the description with that assumption.

Preliminary moves: The performer has a spectator peek at a card. After the peek this card is transferred to the bottom of the pack by my method of double cutting.

Another spectator is asked to peek at a card. The break, held by the tip of the fourth finger of the left hand, is now transferred to the left flesh palm grip, as explained for "Greek Shift".

The right hand now covers the squared pack, still held in the left hand. The fourth finger of the left hand is inserted above the bottom card of the pack. The right hand takes the pack away from the left hand, maintaining an opening with the right thumb pressure against one end of the pack, and first finger at opposite ends of the pack above the first peeked-at card, the bottom card of the pack, and below the last peeked-at card in the middle of the pack.

Now execute the reverse by Buckley's method, drawing off the top packet with the left thumb and reversing the first peeked-at card, on the bottom of the right hand packet, onto the second peeked-at card on the bottom of the left hand packet, and follow up with the riffle shuffle, riffling one card, any card, on the bottom to cover up the back of the reversed card.

The foregoing moves are to be executed smoothly and unhurriedly, with an even, unchanged pace. This is the preliminary to the double change which I shall now describe.

THE SLEIGHT: The cards are an indifferent card on the bottom, the first spectator's card second bottom, face about, facing the second spectator's card, the third card from the bottom.

Cut the pack about even, drawing off about half the pack with the right hand from the bottom of the pack and turn over the packet in the left hand. Place the two packets face to face. Turn the pack over with the right hand and back again to the left hand, calling attention to the exposed face cards.

Then with the right thumb secretly riffle to open a break between the two faced cards (these are the spectator's cards), and place the fourth finger of the left hand into position at the end of the back-to-back two cards, ready at the correct moment to push up on the two cards to cover the exposed card. The right hand momentarily covers the card exposed and shields the act of the fourth finger pushing up the two cards. The right hand is moved away, and both the face cards are now shown to be the cards the two spectators peeked at. A really beautiful effect!

Experiment No. 36

The Chivalrous Kings and The Four Ladies

THE EFFECT: Four queens, after having been shown, are placed in the card box furnished with the pack of cards.

Four cards are placed on the table face down, but preceding each act of placing a card on the table, the pack is cut several times. The four cards are turned over, and they are four kings.

The four kings are each pushed, face up, into a different place in the pack, which is held face down. The pack is placed on the table.

The attention of the audience is called to what has taken place. In the pack are four face-about kings, and in the card box are four imprisoned ladies, the queens. Such a condition cannot be long tolerated by such gallant gentlemen as kings.

The pack is quickly spread from end to end, and in the middle of the pack are seen four face-about queens, and from the box are taken the four kings.

REQUIREMENTS: A duplicate set of four kings, and a pack of cards in their case.

ARRANGEMENT: In the card box place four kings, on top of the pack place the other four queens, and under the four queens place four kings. Dispose of four cards of the pack anywhere in your pockets so the pack fits into the box.

Place the pack in the card box with the extra four kings. The flap side of the card box should open up, and all the cards should be face down. The pack of forty-eight cards should protrude a little out of the box over the kings therein.

THE WORKING: The card box containing the pack is taken up and laid on the left hand. The second finger of the left hand is on the end of the four kings. With the second finger and thumb of the right hand, remove the packet of forty-eight cards while the second finger of the left hand retains the kings in the box.

The box is placed on the table, apparently empty. Trickery is never suspected because of the disarming manner in which the pack is removed from the box.

Hold the pack in your left hand, take about twenty-six of the bottom cards with your right hand and place them on the top of the pack, secretly placing your little finger on the pack to keep the two packets separate. Hold the pack in your right hand, thumb at one end of the pack and fingers at the other end. Remove the left hand. The break is maintained by pressure on the ends of the pack between fingers and thumb of the right hand.

With your left hand take away about a dozen of the bottom cards and place them on the top of the pack. Then take away with the left hand the remainder of the cards below the break and place them on top of the pack.

Place the top card of the pack on the table, face down. (It is a queen if you have followed instructions.) Repeat all the cutting moves as described, and deal the top card, the second queen. Repeat the same moves for the third and the fourth queens.

Pick up the four cards and show that they are four queens. See that the pack is in front of you on the table, one side of the pack towards you.

Pick up the card box with your left hand, first finger and thumb of the left hand just near the flap. Open the flap back with your right hand, and then, holding the four queens face down, slide the queens seemingly into the card box. I said seemingly, because actually they slide underneath the box between the first finger and thumb holding the box.

Lift the flap back and draw out the face-down kings about an inch. As you do so, lower the box onto the pack and secretly leave the queens on the pack. Push home the four kings into the box

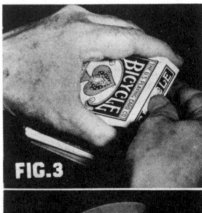

FIG.1

FIG.2

FIG.3

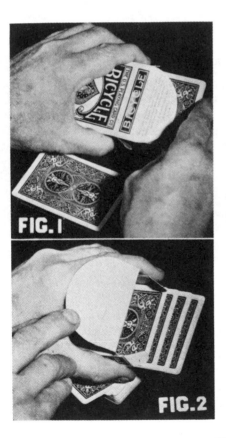

FIG.4

and close the flap and place the box aside, one side of the box facing you to facilitate this.

On the top of the pack are now four queens. Under the queens are four kings. Cut the pack, but place the little finger below the queens and cut half the cards below the break to the top of the pack, and then the remainder of the cards below the break to the top of the pack. The four queens are on the bottom and the four kings on the top.

Hold the pack in your left hand, and with your right hand draw away a packet of about twenty of the bottom cards and place these cards on the top of the pack. Drop your little finger on top of the pack as you do so to keep a break between the queens and kings. Transfer the pack to your right hand and keep the break by pressure on the two ends of the pack.

With your left hand take away half the cards below the break and place them on top of the pack. Then take the remainder of the cards below the break and place them on top of the pack. Lift off the top card, a king, and place it face up on the table.

Repeat all the cutting moves just described and place the second king on the first face up. Repeat twice more all the cutting moves until you have placed all four kings on the table, face up. Secretly reverse the four queens on the bottom of the pack.

Pick up the four kings and insert them, one by one, face up into the pack. (See a description of the Dai Vernon "shift".) The kings are pushed into the pack, but secretly transferred to the bottom by cutting the pack once only. This move also shifts the face-about queens on the bottom of the pack, secretly, to the middle.

The pack is placed on the table and spread. The queens a moment ago placed into the box are now face up in the middle of the pack, while from the box are taken the four kings.

The duplicate kings are palmed away at the first opportunity.

I wish to add that this is a composite effect made up from sleights by Dai Vernon, Karrell Fox and myself. The method of apparently placing a card in the box evolved from the brain of Karrell Fox of Detroit.

The effect is worthy of the practice it requires to do well, and once these sleights are mastered, a whole field of magic with cards is revealed to you.

The accompanying illustrations show the manner of placing the cards into the box.

Experiment No. 37

A Quickie

EFFECT: A card is peeked at near the middle of the pack. Half the cards of the pack are turned over face up on the other half. A moment later when the cards are spread face down on the table, the peeked-at card is seen in the middle face up, while all the other cards are face down.

SLEIGHTS: "Riffle peek", secretly turning over the under half of the pack under cover of the top half of the pack, the "spread".

THE WORKING: With the pack held face down in your left hand, riffle the index corner of the pack. Have someone say, "Stop!" and have him note the card stopped at.

Insert the fourth finger of the left hand above the peeked-at card.

Turn over face up on the peeked-at card all the cards above the peeked-at card. Add the peeked-at card to the face up cards. Secretly turn over all the cards below the peeked-at card and spread the pack face down. The peeked-at card appears face up in the middle of the spread cards.

A simple way of secretly turning over the under cards of the pack is to place the first and fourth fingers of the left hand bent under the pack, and the second and third fingers of the left hand pressed into the pack above the break. While the fingers and thumb at opposite ends of the top packet press the top packet sideways into the fork of the left thumb, the left fingers straighten out, and in doing so rotate the under half of the pack under cover of the top half of the pack.

Experiment No. 38

Four Aces Par Excellence

First take out the four aces, secretly bend them down at the ends, and bend the rest of the pack up so as to form a sizeable "bridge". Place the aces into the end of the pack held in the left hand face up, and execute the "Vernon Multiple Shift", causing the aces to pass to the top of the pack.

Place the pack face down on the table with your left hand. The aces are the top four cards. Cut the pack with your right hand at the middle, making two heaps. Pick up the bottom heap, turn it face up and place it on the other heap, and carefully square the pack.

Cut at the bridge. The four aces are now face down on the bottom of the face up right hand packet.

Execute the push through, "blind riffle shuffle", riffling cards first and last from the right hand packet. This facilitates the push through. During this shuffle the two packets change hands, and the right hand packet is placed on the left hand packet. (This shuffle is described herein.) The cards are squared. Cut off about fifty cards, saying, "Some face down". Replace cut and cut about forty, saying "Some face up". Replace cut and cut about ten cards, saying, "And some face down".

Then cut at the point where the top packet is face to face with the bottom packet. Execute the "blind push through riffle shuffle" again, the packets changing hands as the shuffle is executed. The "face up" packet finishing in the right hand has the aces "face down" on the bottom, and is brought face down under the left hand packet without exposing the face up aces. The pack is squared, placed on the table with the left hand and quickly spread, revealing the four aces face up together in the middle of the pack and the other cards all face down.

Experiment No. 39

The Obtrusive Queens

EFFECT: The queen of clubs and the queen of spades are shown held slightly spread between the finger and thumb of the right hand. The pack is held face to palm in the left hand.

The two queens are placed on the top of the pack, and the first one is inserted into the middle of the pack. The second one is shown and placed on top of the pack and then placed into the middle of the pack again. The two top cards are lifted off and partly spread between the thumb and finger, and they are the obtrusive queens. The effect is repeated several times without a clue to the mechanics.

THE WORKING: On the top of the pack are two indifferent cards. The third and fourth cards are the black queens.

Left "thumb count" four cards, take them off together and hold them in the right hand as illustrated. The four cards are slightly bent, which aids in keeping them together. The thumb and first finger may move the front queen to expose the second queen, but the extra two cards remain behind the other queen. It takes a little practice to do this. See illustration.

The cards are placed face down on the pack. One of the indifferent ones is lifted off as you say, "One Queen in here," inserting it into the pack. "Double lift" and replace them on top of the pack. Then take the indifferent card only off the pack and insert it also into the pack, declaring it to be the queen. Proceed to lift the two queens off the top to the observers' amazement. Lift the two cards as you did the first time when you had four cards.

Now secretly count two with your thumb, letting them move away from the left thumb. Behind this opening insert the two queens, turning the left hand over with the pack to conceal this maneuver. The four top cards are rotated, bringing the queens face up on the pack. Spread the queens as you did the first time, keeping the two indifferent cards again hidden behind the second queen. Repeat the moves as before.

Experiment No. 40

The Illusive Transfer

THE EFFECT: A card near the middle of the pack is noted by a spectator, and although the spectator does not remove his eyes from the pack while it is in the performer's hands, the card nevertheless is shown on the top of the pack. No passes—no duplicates.

THE SLIGHTS: The cards are held face down in the left hand, the left thumb in counting position. With the left thumb the cards are riffled while the performer instructs one of the spectators to say, "Stop!"

When told to do so, performer stops riffling the cards, and with the right hand the packet is cut off unmistakably at the break stopped at. This packet, supported by the fingers at one end and the thumb at the other end, is moved forward on the lower packet about an inch.

The left thumb bends the inside end of the packet up and allows the inside end of the bottom card of the packet it is supporting to fall on the top of the lower packet. The little finger of the right hand is moved onto the back of this card to hold a break.

The left hand holds the pack so that the card at which the riffling was stopped may be observed. The right hand is withdrawn for a moment.

When the card on the bottom of the overlapping packet has been observed by the spectator, the right hand squares the two packets together, but the fourth fingertip secretly keeps the break. The cards may be casually riffled and sprung from hand to hand, without altering the position of the fourth finger maintaining the break.

Now, because of this break, the packet above the noted card may be secretly moved over the rest of the pack about one-eighth of an inch by the left thumb, which remains at the edge of the cards to completely conceal this slight irregularity. The right hand is now brought to the pack, fingers at one end, thumb at the other, the side of the fourth finger of the right hand at the side of the overlapping top packet near the index corner.

A slight pressure of the fourth finger of the right hand against the overlapping top packet forces the cards against the ball of the left thumb, and the packet of cards is caused to pivot to the right palm. The first finger and the thumb of the right hand with the palmed top packet is now slid along the ends of the pack to the outer corners.

The right thumb pushes the spectator's card, which is the top card of the packet in the left hand, slightly off the pack, about three-sixteenths of an inch, or far enough for the index corner to be engaged above the packet of cards palmed in the right hand. The right hand moves back over the pack, bringing the selected card to the top of the pack as the palmed card slides onto the pack.

The move is hidden by the top card. The fingers of the left hand aid in squaring the pack. When these moves are executed with the correct degree of skill and proper timing, the card appearance is magic to an observer rather than skill in sleight of hand, because it seems incredible that the position of the card could have been thus changed when the pack remained in sight at all times except at the instant of the palming action, which even to a magician would not suffice for the change.

The illusion is completed by extending the pack in your left hand and performing the Domico double lift, showing the card not to be the spectator's card, saying, "Of course this is not your card?", and placing the two cards face down on the pack as you remark, "Would you please tell me the name of your card?" The lady may express her disappointment by remarking, "Must I tell you?", and you answer in a coaxing tone, "Please."

The card named is turned over between the left thumb and first finger without aid from the right hand. The move is the same as in the Domico double lift, but made with one card.

Card in Pocket Book

(An old plot with a new and simplified method)

THE EFFECT: A spectator removes any card from the pack spread fanwise, face down, in the performer's hands.

THE ESSENTIALS: A pack of cards, a conjurer's card reel to which has been affixed a safety pin, and a small hook of the hook and eye variety.

SLEIGHTS: The "crimp". (See Hugard's "Expert Card Technique", page 90.)

THE ARRANGEMENT: Sew the hook onto the top center seam of the back of your pants. Pin the conjurer's card reel inside the top of your inside left breast coat pocket. Draw the celophane disc, to which the thread of the conjurer's card reel is attached, from the reel down to the hook, and pass the end of the thread under the hook—don't fasten it. The celophane disc won't pass through the hook, and will therefore be kept in place by the tension placed on the thread by the reel. Of course you have a little conjurer's wax or diachlyon on the aforesaid celophane disc.

The pocket book is of the usual billfold variety as shown in t' picture. The bands are placed around only one side of the billf and this side is hung in the pocket. If you can perform the "c' for locating the chosen card, then you are ready to practice wife or sister or the baby.

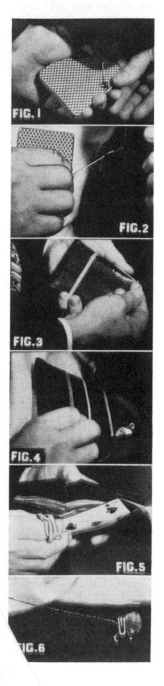

FIG. I

FIG. 2

FIG. 3

FIG. 4

FIG. 5

FIG. 6

The spectator writes his name on the face of the chosen card and returns it to the pack, which he is permitted to take from the performer's hands and immediately shuffle.

When the spectator is satisfied the chosen card is lost in the shuffle, he hands the pack to the performer, who places the pack for a moment only behind his back and proceeds to quickly find the chosen card. Now note this—both of the performer's hands are brought forward with the pack of cards, and the spectator is requested to hold his own hands palm up.

The performer places the pack of cards, face down, on the spectator's left hand and lifts off the top card. He lays it face down on the spectator's right hand, and, glowing with pleased expectancy, says, "Name your card, please." The card is turned over, and lo! the performer is taken aback. Acting quite perplexed, he says, "There can't be any mistake because you wrote your name on the card."

Performer rubs his hands together and recovers his composure.

"Well, we will see what we can do about it." The rubbing of the hands together is to cause the spectators to see that both of the performer's hands are unmistakably empty.

The left hand holds his coat lapel; the right hand is thrust into his inside left breast pocket and takes out his pocket book, calling attention to the pocket book, he says, "You can't be too careful these days with all these magicians running around. That's why I keep it closed with these rubber bands." The several rubber bands are removed by the performer while he says this, and opening the pocket billfold, he registers pleasure when he looks inside. Addressing the spectator, he says, "What was your card? Then here it is. Will you take it out of the billfold? Just the card, please. You identify the signature? Good."

The Working: Have a card selected, signed and returned to the pack. Crimp it secretly when the card is replaced, and permit the pack to be shuffled. When you receive the pack, turn it on its side, and without telegraphing what you are about, sight the crimp and slip the little finger of your left hand into the pack above the crimped card. Don't cut—leave the pack in the position you received it from the spectator. Place the pack behind your back. Now cut the pack, bringing the chosen crimped card to the top. The left hand holds the pack, and the second finger and thumb of the empty right hand procure the waxed celephone disc and press it firmly onto the back of the chosen card, near the side. (See Fig. 1.)

The top card is then released. The pull, arranged as described, will cause the card to be drawn secretly up to the packet. The pack of cards is placed on the spectator's hands, and the procedure of taking off the top card and feigning failure is gone through. Finally the performer reaches up to remove his pocket wallet, being very sure the spectators know his hands are empty. (Don't *say* they are empty.)

As the chosen card will be waiting at the pocket for you, (see Fig. 2), press the celophane disc off the card with your right thumb and quickly, but unhurriedly, insert it into the waiting pocket book which you remove from your pocket, (see Figs. 3 and 4), and proceed to take off the rubber bands which the audience will believe completely encircle the pocket book. Let the spectator remove the card from the pocket book. Fig. 5 shows the spectator's card, the five of spades, in the pocket book and Fig. 6 shows the hook holding the celophane disc and wax.

It's a real dandy, and will baffle any magician not familiar with this subtle use of the conjurer's card reel.

ART IS IN THE DOING

Nomenclature

The pack—A complete set of cards comprised of fifty-two different cards, made up of four suits, namely, hearts, diamonds, clubs and spades, and designated ace, 2, 3, 4, 5, 6, 7, 8, 9, 10, jack, queen and king.

The top of the pack—The back of the last card of a pack of 52 cards.

The top of the packet—The back of the last card of several cards or less than 52.

The bottom of the pack—The face of the last card of a pack of 52 cards.

The bottom of the packet—The face of the last card of any number of cards more than one and less than 52.

Shuffle—Mix the cards together.

Riffle—Bend the cards at their edges and allow them to spring back into normal position as the applied bending tension is relaxed.

Thumb riffle—To accomplish the riffle by the thumb action on the edges of the cards.

Finger riffle—To riffle the edges of the cards with the finger or fingers.

One hand thumb riffle—To hold the pack in either hand and use the thumb of that hand holding the cards to riffle them. (See "riffle".)

Riffle shuffle—To riffle both halves of the pack, one half in each hand, and cause the cards in one packet to interleave in between the cards of the other packet.

A perfect riffle shuffle—To interlace in alternate fashion every card of one riffled packet on every card of the other riffled packet.

Overhand shuffle—To take all or part of the pack of cards into one hand and draw them off singly, or drop them off in packets, into the other hand in a manner that causes them to fall on top of the cards preceding them, so that the original order of the pack is disarranged.

The Hindu shuffle—Disarranging the order of a pack or packet of cards by drawing off packets of cards with the fingers and thumb on the side edges of the cards from the top of one packet, held by its side edges in one hand, onto the packet as it thus accumulates in the other hand.

The milk shuffle—Shuffling the cards by the overhand method, thus drawing off cards from the packet in one hand onto the packet in the other hand, and drawing a card secretly from the bottom as one is drawn from the top. The two cards taken together in this manner pass unsuspectedly as only one taken from the top.

The cut—To openly remove a packet of cards from the top or bottom of the pack and transfer them in one packet to either hand or onto the table.

False shuffle—Any shuffle that appears to fairly mix the cards, but permits their predetermined order to remain unchanged.

The build—A shuffle that changes the order of cards into a predetermined order.

The reverse—Any sleight that secretly permits a card or cards to be turned face up in relation to the other cards of the pack.

Buckley's single card shift—A sleight that permits a card to be secretly extracted from the pack and transferred to the bottom without palming the card.

Buckley's double peek and recovery—A series of sleights blended together that permits two cards to be peeked at in different parts of the pack, and by a series of breaks, cuts and shuffles they are arranged on the bottom for palming.

Springing—The act of bending the cards in a manner that causes them to fly singly in rapid succession from one hand to the other hand.

The force—Any sleight by which the spectator's choice of a card is directly or indirectly influenced or restricted.

Pick up build—Any procedure that aids in arranging the cards in a predetermined order while apparently only collecting the cards in a haphazard manner.

The gambler's spread—The act of secretly adding a card or cards to the middle or bottom of the packet you are spreading.

Fanning—This is a fancy sleight as it is performed without any intention of deceiving anyone. It is very useful and requires considerable dexterity to perform effectively. By a single arcing of the hand or hands, the cards are arranged in uniform steps in a perfect semi-circle held in one hand.

Pressure fans—The pressure fans are made by holding the cards to be fanned in one hand, with pressure of the fingers and thumb causing them to bend in a concave manner, whereupon they are released into the palm and thumb of the other hand as the hand turns in an arc while springing the cards.

Location—The term which designates the exact position of a card or cards in relationship to the other cards of the pack either by a crimp, step, insertion, break, bridge, mark, number or faked card.

The Sight—See Glimpse.

Sighting—See Glimpsing.

Dealing from the center—Secretly taking a card from out of the center instead of off the top while dealing.

The Greek shift—A sleight that permits a card placed in the pack at one place to be indetectably shifted to another predetermined position to locate a spectator's card.

Cold deck—A prearranged pack of cards, usually one exchanged secretly for one that has been in use previous to the exchange.

Fancy sleight—A sleight not intended to deceive, but one that is confined to an artistic and proficient display of skillful handling.

Thumb count (one hand)—The act of secretly and silently riffling the cards with the thumb of the hand holding the pack, and mentally counting the number released by this method of riffling. Any number of cards designated may be accumulated on top in this manner above the thumb break on top of the pack.

Thumb count (two hands)—Whereas the cards are counted by the thumb at the side near the corner when using only one hand, and therefore when released are the topmost cards on the pack, the two-handed thumb count is used for the purpose of accumulating a desired number of cards on the bottom of the pack below a break. One hand holds the pack face down on the palm, and the other holds it at the ends, permitting the thumb to riffle the bottom cards, and you may count them while releasing them.

The spread—This is a fancy sleight. It is the simple act of neatly and effectively spreading the pack or packet of cards evenly in a line or semi-circle on the table. It is accomplished by springing the cards as the hand moves in a suitable arc, or else by the more simple though just as effective act of laying the hand on the pack and sweeping the cards under the requisite pressure.

A completed cut—To cut the cards and restore the cards to the opposite top or bottom from which they were cut.

Center cut—(or Scotch poke) Pushing a packet of cards out of the middle of the pack and placing it on the top of the pack.

Undercut—Taking away a packet of cards from underneath the pack and transferring it to the top of the pack.

A break—An opening or division maintained by inserting a finger-tip or part of the flesh of the hand in between two cards of the pack.

Flesh grip—A break into which a small portion of the flesh of a finger or the palm is inserted.

Mechanic's grip—A commonly accepted method by which a pack of cards is held in the hand when the dealer intends to deal seconds or bottoms. It is presumed that the grip is unorthodox.

Seconds—To secretly deal the second top card while supposedly dealing the top card off the pack.

Bottoms—To secretly deal a card or cards from the bottom of the pack while supposedly dealing them from off the top of the pack.

Shift—The accepted term for secretly transferring a card from one position in the pack to another.

The palm—That part of either hand extending from the first joint of the fingers and thumb to approximately less than an inch from the wrist.

To palm a card—To secretly conceal a card in the grip of the palm.

To palm off the top—To secretly procure a card or cards from off the top of the pack and retain the card or cards concealed in the hand.

To palm off the bottom—The act of secretly procuring a card or cards from the bottom of the pack and retaining the card or cards concealed in the hand.

Side steal—The act of secretly shifting a card from within the pack and palming the card.

The peek—Allowing a spectator to see only the index of a card in the pack.

The glimpse—Secretly looking at the index of a card anywhere in the pack.

The dealer's glimpse—Secretly looking at the top card, or a card close to the top of the pack, while dealing the cards or in between the intervals of dealing.

The glimpse while cutting—Secretly looking at the index of the bottom card while cutting the pack or restoring the cut.

The bottom glimpse—Secretly looking at the index of the bottom card while holding the pack in both hands, face down.

The shuffle glimpse—Secretly looking at the top card while commencing the overhand shuffle.

The jog—To jog a card in the act of shuffling to cause it to protrude somewhat from among the other cards of the pack.

The jog glimpse—To secretly glimpse the index corner of a card that is "jogged".

Out jog—To cause the jogged card to extend in a direction away from the body of the pack.

In jog—To cause a card to extend from the pack towards your body.

The step—To allow a packet of cards to overlap another packet of cards, thus forming a step.

The bridge—To arc two packets of cards in a manner that causes a secret opening between them which may be freely cut to.

The side bridge—When the bridge opening between the packets is in the middle of the cards' length.

The end bridge—When the bridge is in the middle of the cards' width.

The crimp—Any small part of the side, the end or the corner of a card secretly pressed or bent out of conformity with the rest of the cards in order to make it locatable by a cut after it has been returned anywhere in the pack.

To cull—The act of removing any number of cards and transferring them to the top or the bottom of the pack, while seemingly only looking through the pack and then cutting it.

Stock—Any number of cards arranged on the top or the bottom of the pack.

Shuffle on—In executing an overhand shuffle to shuffle onto the top of the top packet any predetermined number of cards from the other packet.

Shuffle off—To shuffle off any predetermined number of cards from the top of the top packet into the hand and throw the rest of the pack onto the cards shuffled off.

Shuffle reverse—To shuffle off a number of cards, one at a time, onto one hand from the pack held in the other hand, and then replace the packet consisting of the singly reversed cards on the top of the pack.

Buckley's double undercut—A method that confuses the closest observation of the uninitiated into believing the cards are haphazardly cut twice while actually they are being transferred to a predetermined position by the simple expedient of retaining a location by the crimp, bridge, jog, step, flesh grip, finger or thumb, or by memory, and undercutting twice to reach the desired location, placing the first packet cut on the pack, and then the second packet cut on top of the first packet cut.

Top change—To secretly exchange a card or cards in the hand for a card or cards on the top of the pack.

Bottom change—To secretly exchange a card or cards in the hand for a card or cards on the bottom of the pack.

The throw change—A method of holding two cards in the hand as though they are one, and throwing the unexposed card face down while seemingly throwing face down the card shown.

The slide change—A method of holding a card so it secretly hides another card behind it, then partly inserting the two cards into the pack as one. The card, the face of which was previously exposed to view, secretly slides into the pack under cover of the other card, which, upon being withdrawn, appears to have changed.

The lift—When a card is lifted off the pack and conceals another card or cards secretly lifted off with it.

The glide—This is a form of second dealing. With the pack or packet of cards face down, the bottom card is secretly moved back by the fingers of the hand aiding in holding the pack, and the other hand drawing off from the bottom of the pack the second card from the bottom.

The pass—The sleight that is intended to secretly transpose the upper and lower two packets of cards held in the hand or hands.

The Charlier pass—A sleight that transfers the lower packet from the bottom to the top of the pack by the first finger of the one hand rotating the outside edge of the bottom packet under and over the inside edge of the top packet supported between the fingers and the thumb.

The Vernon multiple shift—An indetectable method of transferring several cards, simultaneously pushed into different parts of the pack, to the top or bottom of the pack by what appears to be nothing more than a simple cut.

The diagonal insert—A method of inserting a card or cards into the pack diagonally at one end, and thus causing their corners to partly emerge at the other end and side of the pack.

The double diagonal insert—A method of inserting a card or cards into the pack diagonally at one end and causing their corners to emerge at the ends and sides of the pack, whereupon they are shifted by the fourth finger to a diagonally opposite position to facilitate their secret withdrawal into the palm preceding the act of cutting the pack.

The exchange—A sleight that permits the secret exchange of a number of cards palmed in one hand for a similar number of cards in a packet on the table.

The Mexican turnover—A method of secretly exchanging a card on the table for one used for the purpose of tipping it over.

The slap shift—A method of secretly palming a card from the bottom of a packet in one hand and conveying it to the top of the packet in the act of slapping the hand on the packet to emphasize the count.

Replacement—A method of secretly replacing cards that are palmed on or in the pack.

False count—Any sleight that permits the cards being counted to appear as a number different to that which the cards comprise.

A CATALOG OF SELECTED
DOVER BOOKS
IN ALL FIELDS OF INTEREST

A CATALOG OF SELECTED DOVER
BOOKS IN ALL FIELDS OF INTEREST

CONCERNING THE SPIRITUAL IN ART, Wassily Kandinsky. Pioneering work by father of abstract art. Thoughts on color theory, nature of art. Analysis of earlier masters. 12 illustrations. 80pp. of text. 5⅜ x 8½. 23411-8

ANIMALS: 1,419 Copyright-Free Illustrations of Mammals, Birds, Fish, Insects, etc., Jim Harter (ed.). Clear wood engravings present, in extremely lifelike poses, over 1,000 species of animals. One of the most extensive pictorial sourcebooks of its kind. Captions. Index. 284pp. 9 x 12. 23766-4

CELTIC ART: The Methods of Construction, George Bain. Simple geometric techniques for making Celtic interlacements, spirals, Kells-type initials, animals, humans, etc. Over 500 illustrations. 160pp. 9 x 12. (Available in U.S. only.) 22923-8

AN ATLAS OF ANATOMY FOR ARTISTS, Fritz Schider. Most thorough reference work on art anatomy in the world. Hundreds of illustrations, including selections from works by Vesalius, Leonardo, Goya, Ingres, Michelangelo, others. 593 illustrations. 192pp. 7⅛ x 10¼. 20241-0

CELTIC HAND STROKE-BY-STROKE (Irish Half-Uncial from "The Book of Kells"): An Arthur Baker Calligraphy Manual, Arthur Baker. Complete guide to creating each letter of the alphabet in distinctive Celtic manner. Covers hand position, strokes, pens, inks, paper, more. Illustrated. 48pp. 8¼ x 11. 24336-2

EASY ORIGAMI, John Montroll. Charming collection of 32 projects (hat, cup, pelican, piano, swan, many more) specially designed for the novice origami hobbyist. Clearly illustrated easy-to-follow instructions insure that even beginning papercrafters will achieve successful results. 48pp. 8¼ x 11. 27298-2

THE COMPLETE BOOK OF BIRDHOUSE CONSTRUCTION FOR WOODWORKERS, Scott D. Campbell. Detailed instructions, illustrations, tables. Also data on bird habitat and instinct patterns. Bibliography. 3 tables. 63 illustrations in 15 figures. 48pp. 5¼ x 8½. 24407-5

BLOOMINGDALE'S ILLUSTRATED 1886 CATALOG: Fashions, Dry Goods and Housewares, Bloomingdale Brothers. Famed merchants' extremely rare catalog depicting about 1,700 products: clothing, housewares, firearms, dry goods, jewelry, more. Invaluable for dating, identifying vintage items. Also, copyright-free graphics for artists, designers. Co-published with Henry Ford Museum & Greenfield Village. 160pp. 8¼ x 11. 25780-0

HISTORIC COSTUME IN PICTURES, Braun & Schneider. Over 1,450 costumed figures in clearly detailed engravings—from dawn of civilization to end of 19th century. Captions. Many folk costumes. 256pp. 8⅜ x 11¾. 23150-X

CATALOG OF DOVER BOOKS

THE STORY OF THE TITANIC AS TOLD BY ITS SURVIVORS, Jack Winocour (ed.). What it was really like. Panic, despair, shocking inefficiency, and a little heroism. More thrilling than any fictional account. 26 illustrations. 320pp. 5⅜ x 8½.
20610-6

FAIRY AND FOLK TALES OF THE IRISH PEASANTRY, William Butler Yeats (ed.). Treasury of 64 tales from the twilight world of Celtic myth and legend: "The Soul Cages," "The Kildare Pooka," "King O'Toole and his Goose," many more. Introduction and Notes by W. B. Yeats. 352pp. 5⅜ x 8½.
26941-8

BUDDHIST MAHAYANA TEXTS, E. B. Cowell and others (eds.). Superb, accurate translations of basic documents in Mahayana Buddhism, highly important in history of religions. The Buddha-karita of Asvaghosha, Larger Sukhavativyuha, more. 448pp. 5⅜ x 8½.
25552-2

ONE TWO THREE . . . INFINITY: Facts and Speculations of Science, George Gamow. Great physicist's fascinating, readable overview of contemporary science: number theory, relativity, fourth dimension, entropy, genes, atomic structure, much more. 128 illustrations. Index. 352pp. 5⅜ x 8½.
25664-2

EXPERIMENTATION AND MEASUREMENT, W. J. Youden. Introductory manual explains laws of measurement in simple terms and offers tips for achieving accuracy and minimizing errors. Mathematics of measurement, use of instruments, experimenting with machines. 1994 edition. Foreword. Preface. Introduction. Epilogue. Selected Readings. Glossary. Index. Tables and figures. 128pp. 5⅜ x 8½.   40451-X

DALÍ ON MODERN ART: The Cuckolds of Antiquated Modern Art, Salvador Dalí. Influential painter skewers modern art and its practitioners. Outrageous evaluations of Picasso, Cézanne, Turner, more. 15 renderings of paintings discussed. 44 calligraphic decorations by Dalí. 96pp. 5⅜ x 8½. (Available in U.S. only.)
29220-7

ANTIQUE PLAYING CARDS: A Pictorial History, Henry René D'Allemagne. Over 900 elaborate, decorative images from rare playing cards (14th–20th centuries): Bacchus, death, dancing dogs, hunting scenes, royal coats of arms, players cheating, much more. 96pp. 9¼ x 12¼.
29265-7

MAKING FURNITURE MASTERPIECES: 30 Projects with Measured Drawings, Franklin H. Gottshall. Step-by-step instructions, illustrations for constructing handsome, useful pieces, among them a Sheraton desk, Chippendale chair, Spanish desk, Queen Anne table and a William and Mary dressing mirror. 224pp. 8⅛ x 11¼.
29338-6

THE FOSSIL BOOK: A Record of Prehistoric Life, Patricia V. Rich et al. Profusely illustrated definitive guide covers everything from single-celled organisms and dinosaurs to birds and mammals and the interplay between climate and man. Over 1,500 illustrations. 760pp. 7½ x 10⅛.
29371-8